Women of the New Right

In the series

Women in the Political Economy,

edited by Ronnie J. Steinberg

Women
of the
New Right

REBECCA E. KLATCH

Temple University Press ☆ *Philadelphia*

Temple University Press, Philadelphia 19122

Copyright © 1987 by Temple University

Published 1987

Printed in the United States of America

The paper used in this publication meets the
requirements of American National Standard for Information
Sciences—Permanence of Paper for Printed Library Materials,
ANSI Z39.48-1984

Library of Congress Cataloging-in-Publication Data

Klatch, Rebecca E.

  Women of the new right.

  (Women in the political economy)
  Includes index.
  1. Women in politics.   2. Women in politics—
United States.   3. Right and left (Political
science) I. Title. II. Series.
HQ1390.K53   1987   320'.088042   86-23089
ISBN 0-87722-470-6 (alk. paper)

FOR ALIDA,

Whose Wit and Friendship

Continually Renew Me

Acknowledgments

While research and writing are solitary acts, there are always people contributing their ideas and support "behind the scenes." I would like to thank Lee Rainwater, Nathan Glazer, and Gosta Esping-Andersen, who acted as knowledgeable guides throughout the research for this book. I am also grateful to David Karen, Steve Cornell, and Michael Shifter, all of whom offered the necessary balance of criticism and encouragement along the way. Murray Wax, Roger Cobb, and Carole Joffe aided greatly in rethinking the framework of the manuscript. As a teacher, researcher, and friend, Krista Luker has been an inspiration to me for many years; I am indebted to her for her continual support and wisdom. In addition, the invaluable advice of Jane Isay carried me through many difficult transitions. Special thanks to Michael Mills for his donation of primary source materials and to Radcliffe College and the Woodrow Wilson National Fellowship Foundation for providing funding. Susan Banes, Adele Tuchler, and Dan Blain worked wonders in the final months of researching, word processing, and proofreading the manuscript. The book could not have been completed without the superb editing and perception of Ronnie Steinberg, Mike Ames, and Doris Braendel; to each, my warmest thanks. And endless thanks to the women of this study for the time, energy, and trust involved in sharing their lives with me. In particular, I would like to thank Betsy Barber Bancroft for her interest in my work and for her insights about the aims and motivation of women's participation. Finally, there is one person whose integrity and intelligence have deepened my understanding of scholarship, bringing new meaning to the word "teacher." To David Riesman, my deepest gratitude and respect.

Contents

ONE
Introduction   3

TWO
Two World Views   20

THREE
Communism   55

FOUR
Big Government   84

FIVE
Feminism   119

SIX
Portraits of Two Women   154

SEVEN
The Future of the New Right   195

Epilogue   215

Notes   217

Index   243

Women of the New Right

CHAPTER ONE

Introduction

Even the most abstract ideology, the most utopian scheme, has an empirical content that must be squared with the small world of experience of the individual confronted with the problem of finding meaning in his world.[1]

Although the first wave of feminism in America granted women the vote, it was not until the second wave of feminism during the late 1960s and 1970s that women were integrated into the mainstream of political life. The past two decades in American politics have been marked by an extraordinary degree of activism by women. Such pathbreaking events as the appointment of the first female Supreme Court justice and the first national campaign by a woman for vice president, as well as a burst in the number of women elected to local and state offices, signify a turning point in women's political participation.[2] Further, notable differences in the voting patterns of men and women point to a "gender gap" in political attitudes.[3] Women's greater degree of support for issues of peace, welfare measures, and gun control has caught the attention of both the Democratic and Republican parties.

Yet, if one of the achievements of the feminist movement is this escalation of female participation, paradoxically this very success has also meant the increased involvement by women opposed to the goals and values at the core of feminism. Thus, during the same time in which thousands of women mobilized to place feminist issues on the political agenda and to secure women's place within the public realm, groups of women on the right joined together to promote a return to traditional ways, endorsing women's role within the family. Similarly, contrary to the "gender gap," a constituency of women on the right is actively organized *against* the nuclear freeze, *against* increased welfare, and *for* the reassertion of American military might. In fact, one of the distinguishing characteristics of the new conservative movement is the leadership and prominence of women. How are we to understand this discernible force of female activists? How do women of the New Right look at the world? What motivates their political involvement? How do they see themselves as women and political actors?

Typically, when people hear "right-wing women" they think of Phyllis Schlafly or conjure up images of angry housewives venturing into the political arena. In fact, the New Right as a whole is often assumed to be synonymous with Schlafly, anti-feminism, and social issues. Yet this is only part of the picture. Right-wing women are *not* a monolithic group nor is the New Right a cohesive movement that shares a single set of beliefs and values. While one part of the New Right *is* concerned, above all, with social issues and *does* consider feminism a fundamental threat, there is a whole other constituency within the New Right that actually shares part of the feminist vision and that is primarily concerned with issues related to the economy and defense.

This book is about this fundamental division among women of the New Right. I characterize these two constituencies as the "social conservative" and the "laissez-faire conservative" world views. While social conservativism is rooted in religious belief, laissez-faire conservatism is rooted in the classical liberalism of the nineteenth century. Thus, religious values color all perceptions within the social conservative world; laissez-faire conservatives, on the other hand, measure the world in terms of the political and economic liberty of the individual. Further, while social conservatives consider the family to be the sacred unit of society, laissez-faire conservatives believe the primary element of society is the rational, self-interested individual.

Given these different vantage points, social and laissez-faire conservatives evaluate contemporary America in different terms. While both decry the current state of the country, believing America has moved away from her founding principles, each assesses America's problems in essentially different ways. One laments the fact that America has departed from her religious traditions; the other deplores America's departure from the principles of laissez-faire. One envisions contemporary America in terms of moral decay; the other views the nation in terms of threats to the individual's economic and political freedom. Accordingly, while social conservatives believe it is the social issues—ERA, abortion, homosexuality, busing, school prayer—that are of utmost importance to solving America's problems, laissez-faire conservatives believe protection of the free market and property rights, through, for example, tax reductions and welfare cutbacks, and the restoration of America's role as leader of the free world through increased defense are the issues that must top the political agenda of the nation.

Although social and laissez-faire conservatives analyze America in these different ways, common symbolism sustains the unity of the New Right. Thus, it is through the *naming* of the sources of America's problems that the two worlds converge. In locating the forces responsible for present conditions, social and laissez-faire conservatives share a common hostility toward two particular symbols: Communism and Big Government.

Like the Old Right that preceded them, the New Right is unified in its virulent opposition to the symbol of Communism. For both constituencies Communism evokes images of the feared society, the inversion of those beliefs most cherished by each world view. Thus, although there is a shared emotional response to Communism, in reality there is little agreement on its substantive meaning. Essentially, for social conservatives Communism represents atheism and an attack on the family, while for laissez-faire conservatives Communism poses a threat to the economic and political liberty of the individual. In short, while both groups join together in resisting Communism, they do so for fundamentally different reasons.[4]

Similarly, Big Government is a potent unifying symbol of the New Right that mobilizes people of varying interests and backgrounds. "Get government off our backs" is a rallying cry of the new conservative movement. Yet again, beneath the surface of this common symbol rest substantively distinct meanings. While both groups consider Big Government a symbol of America on the road of decline, for social conservatives Big Government signifies the promotion of immorality, the endorsement of Secular Humanism, and the usurpation of traditional authority. Laissez-faire conservatives, on the other hand, view Big Government as an impediment to the individual's economic liberty and as an intrusion on the individual's political liberty.

Understanding the various meanings of Communism and Big Government not only reveals the diversity of belief among women of the New Right but also points to areas of potential conflict between the two worlds. For example, social and laissez-faire conservatives actually hold adverse views regarding the role of the state in the private realm. While social conservatives believe there is no such thing as moral neutrality, and therefore call for the state to endorse traditional values and lifestyles, laissez-faire conservatives denounce any form of government intervention in the private realm as an illegitimate intrusion on individual liberty.

In sum, women of the New Right are *not* a homogeneous entity; rather, the New Right encompasses a range of individuals who hold diverse—and even opposing—views about human nature, men and women's roles, the function of government, and the ideal society. While the two worlds converge through shared symbols, in reality the New Right speaks a common language devoid of any common meaning.

This schism within the New Right is historically based. Lipset and Raab's classic study of the American right from 1790 to 1970 finds a continuous marriage of interests between two groups: those based in the less-educated, lower economic strata, highly religious, intolerant of religious and ethnic minorities, and drawn to the non-economic issues of right-wing movements; and those rooted in the highly educated, higher-income strata, less religious, tolerant of minorities, and committed above all to economic conservatism.[5]

Further, studies of the Old Right of the 1950s disclose a similar split. Various terms have been used to capture this division within the Old Right, including the fundamentalist right vs. nineteenth-century liberals,[6] religious fundamentalists vs. ultraconservatives,[7] pseudo-conservatives vs. economic conservatives,[8] the practical right vs. sophisticated conservatives,[9] and the radical right vs. the old guard.[10] There is a striking similarity to these studies. Again, we find a partnership between those motivated by religious belief and those primarily concerned with economic issues. Drawing upon these various studies, the profile of the religious right reveals a movement of less-educated manual and semi-skilled workers of the lower middle class, typically Southern, raised on farms or in small towns, and most often of Baptist or fundamentalist background. Activated by their concern with the breakdown of religion in modern life, this group is portrayed as intolerant, as moral absolutists. Viewing Communism as the earthly manifestation of the Devil, the religious right aimed to save America from Communism in part by attacking the ecumenical movement.[11]

The economic conservative faction of the Old Right is characterized by more affluent, more highly educated, middle-class Protestants from old Republican families, usually belonging to the Episcopal, Presbyterian, or Congregationalist denominations and concentrated in the business and professional class. Activated in reaction to the New Deal and the Communist movement of the 1930s, this segment of the right was rooted in a political-economic ideology based on opposition to bureaucracy and nostalgia for the Golden Age of small farmers and businessmen;[12] economic conservatives embraced self-government and self-reliance,[13] along with strict construction of the Constitution, individualism, and isolationism.[14]

This cleavage within the right is also evidenced in the conservative intellectual movement in America. Nash's study of conservative intellectuals since 1945 actually reveals three distinct groups. The first group are the classical liberals or libertarians, who promote the free market, private property, limited government, self-reliance, and laissez-faire and who resist the threat of the ever-expanding state to liberty and free enterprise. The second are the traditionalists, who are dismayed by the erosion of values and the emergence of a secular, rootless mass society; in reaction to the state as the collapse of moral authority, they call for a return to traditional religious and ethical absolutes. The third are the militant anti-Communists, ex-radicals disillusioned by the left and alarmed by the despotism of the Soviet Union.[15]

Linked to the New Right, this third strand corresponds to today's neoconservatives. Primarily academics and writers who rejected the politics of the Democratic Party during the late 1960s, neoconservatives are converts from the left, disillusioned liberals drawn heavily from Jewish, intellectual circles of the East Coast.[16] Nash argues that anti-Communism acts as the cement that glues together these three strands of the conservative intellectual movement.[17]

In short, the division between social and laissez-faire conservatism in the contemporary right is historically rooted in both the mass base and the intellectual leadership of the Old Right. Thus, despite claims that what is new about the New Right is its attention to the social issues,[18] in fact social conservatism is *not* a distinguishing characteristic of the New Right. The issues may have shifted from temperance and Darwinism to ERA and school prayer, but non-economic issues have typically played a part in right-wing movements.

But if social conservatism is not a distinguishing characteristic of the New Right, what *is* unique about the New Right is the new activism of women. It is not entirely clear whether the lack of attention to women in the Old Right is due to the small number of female participants in the movement or to the male bias of the researchers.[19] Because so little data exists on female activists in the Old Right, there is no way of knowing how women of the Old and New Right compare in terms of number of participants, degree of involvement, or social background. It *is* clear, however, that, unlike the Old Right, women in the New Right are a visible presence as members and leaders throughout the conservative movement.

New research, particularly by feminist scholars, specifically focusses on women's involvement on the right. While these studies are a welcome and necessary addition to our knowledge, virtually all of the research focusses exclusively on female participation in anti-feminist activities.[20] Typically, conclusions are reached about "right-wing women" based on involvement in anti-ERA or anti-abortion organizations. Yet this is a limited portrayal of women of the right. By only focussing on women involved in the social issues, these scholars overlook important areas of female participation.

Once we include the diversity of women's activities on the right, a different picture emerges. Comparing social and laissez-faire conservative women, we find important differences between the two groups. For example, social conservatives view feminism as an anti-family force, as a symbol of the narcissism associated with the "Me Decade" of the 1970s, and as an attack on the status of the home-maker. Laissez-faire conservative women, on the other hand, do *not* consider feminism to be a threat. Rather, laissez-faire women actually support part of the feminist agenda.

These varying views of feminism are intricately connected to each world's view of gender—that is, the "proper" roles of men and women in society. Social conservatives envision gender as a divinely ordained hierarchical ordering in which men have natural authority over women. Women's roles are essentially defined in terms of support for men and a general orientation toward others. In line with traditional notions of gender, women are characterized by their roles within the family—as wives and mothers. Men are the breadwinners; women are the nurturers, the caretakers. Laissez-faire conservatives, on the other hand, hold no such notions of male authority, female submission, or women's "natural" orientation toward others. In fact, these very notions are antithetical to the laissez-faire conservative world view. Like many feminists, laissez-faire conservative women believe there are few natural differences between the sexes. Extending their view of human nature to women as well as to men, they envision both sexes as rational, self-interested, and autonomous actors. Like men, women must be able to climb to the height of their talents in a marketplace free from outside interference.

It is essential to recognize these differences *among* women of the New Right in order to shatter the illusion of right-wing women as a monolithic group. Further, there is a prevalent assumption that anti-feminist women are "a brainwashed flock,"[21] "lackeys" of men.[22] Commonly, such women are assumed to be victims of "false consciousness," unable to identify and to act in their own interest as women.[23] Ironically, despite the fact that laissez-faire conservative women are closer to feminists in their view of gender, it is actually the social conservative woman who *does* act in her own interest as a woman.

Far from suffering from false consciousness, in fact the social conservative woman is well aware of her status *as a woman* and acts to defend that status. It is just that the social conservative woman's view of women's interests is at odds with a feminist view of women's interests. Clearly, the preservation of traditional gender roles is at the very core of the social conservative woman's activism. In contrast, the laissez-faire conservative woman acts in defense of her self-interest in the marketplace, not to protect her interest as a woman within the family.

To borrow a distinction from Marx, while social conservative women act as women "for themselves," laissez-faire women remain women "in themselves."[24] That is, while gender identity is central to the political involvement of the social conservative woman—that is, she acts to protect women's interests within traditional bounds—laissez-faire women do not recognize their collective interest as women; at the core, their activism is not motivated out of concern regarding gender. In short, the social conservative woman recognizes her commonality with other traditional women and seeks to protect women's place as a group. Laissez-faire women, however, do not act as members of a sex; rather, they seek to protect their freedom as self-interested "members" of the market.[25]

In focussing on female activism, a word of caution is in order. This book does not aim to compare the motivation of women to that of men on the right. There is no analysis of the contrasting styles or beliefs of male and female activists. It may well be that the two world views presented here are as true for men as they are for women. In fact, given the continuity between the findings of this study and earlier research on the right, I presume that the basic division of beliefs *does* hold for men as well as for women of the New Right, although, if we were to compare men and women, we might uncover differences between the sexes in terms of the emphasis placed on particular beliefs within each world view. For example, I suspect that while the symbols of Communism and Big Government are equally salient for men and women in both camps, the symbol of Feminism, which evokes much more response among social conservatives, is more directly relevant to social conservative women than to social conservative men.

But men's perceptions are not my interest here. Just as the multitude of studies on men draw no conclusions about the particularities of a "male perspective," I am not arguing that women of the right represent a distinctly "female voice." Statements of this sort necessitate a different type of methodology, a study based on a detailed comparison of the population of women on the right to the population of men on the right. The focus of this study, however, is comparing women with each other to examine the differences which emerge among women of the right in order to move beyond the association of right-wing women solely with anti-feminist activities.

In focussing on women, I include analysis of the variation in perceptions of gender, feminism, and "women's issues" as well as the more "traditional" political concerns. One might speculate that such issues are more germane to women and therefore may take priority and be more clearly articulated by women versus men on the right. Again, it would take a comparative study of men and women on the right to understand such gender differences. An interesting area for future research would be uncovering the areas of convergence and departure among men and women on the right. For example, if female social conservatives act to protect their interests as women, do male social conservatives act to protect their interests as men? Or is there a separate base for men's involvement, perhaps motivated more directly by religious conviction? Also, do laissez-faire men share part of the feminist vision or are there differences between laissez-faire men and women regarding "women's issues"? Because our knowledge of right-wing women has been so limited to date, there is a real thirst for answers to questions such as these, opening up many areas for future inquiry.

Methodology

This study aims to move beyond survey analysis in order to grasp the internal logic of the ideology that attracts women to the right-wing cause. To understand the variation of belief among women of the right, we must try to view the world through their eyes; in Herbert Blumer's words, we must "get inside their worlds of meanings."[26] Rather than considering those active on the right pathological, that is, having personality disorders or being social isolates, as is so commonly assumed in the literature,[27] this study seeks to understand how an individual might meaningfully adopt right-wing values and beliefs.

Three methodological approaches are used to penetrate the styles of thought that characterize women of the right: intensive interviews, participant-observation, and a textual analysis of organizational materials. The categories of social and laissez-faire conservative derived from these three sources of data are used as *ideal types*.[28] In reality, a given individual may not fit within the exact bounds of the ideal type; that is, individual cases may be more mixed.

Nor are the actors themselves necessarily aware of or self-conscious about this subjective meaning. One interesting pattern in the research was the variation in response by activists to the categories of social and laissez-faire conservatism. As the differences among women emerged from the data, I began asking women I interviewed for reactions to these proposed types. Social conservative women denied the existence of any split on the right, arguing that the division was being falsely imposed. In contrast, nearly all of the laissez-faire women acknowledged the division. In fact, many of the laissez-faire activists initially responded to the study by asserting, "Now don't group me with Phyllis Schlafly. I don't agree with those Moral Majority types." Perhaps laissez-faire women are more finely tuned into the long-standing divisions within the right, while the social conservative activist, newer to the political world, assumes others on the right share her perceptions and beliefs.

Deciding how to define "conservative" or "right-wing" was a particularly difficult issue because one of the general "tenets of conservatism" is a rejection of the "isms" of ideology, of abstract and universal principles. A true understanding of any conservative movement must be firmly grounded in the historical reality of the time.[29] No consensus exists on the exact boundaries of the New Right. Generally, when people use the term "New Right" they refer to a network of people and organizations that came into prominence in the mid-1970s, including conservative politicians such as Jesse Helms, Orrin Hatch, and Jack Kemp, conservative think-tanks such as the Heritage Foundation, general-purpose organizations such as the Conservative Caucus, the National Conservative Political Action Committee, and the Committee for the Survival of a Free Congress, as well as the religious sector, including prime-time preachers, the Moral Majority, and groups working against such issues as abortion, gay rights, and pornography.

All the activists in this study are self-identified and labelled by others as conservative. Activists included in the sample either were referred to me by others after I explicitly stated that I wanted to talk to women of the New Right or because of their affiliation with organizations identified as part of the general movement called the "New Right." The entire sample supported the 1980 election of Ronald Reagan, with nearly all criticisms falling to the right of Reagan's policies. Many of the women interviewed worked for or supported the 1964 presidential campaign of Barry Goldwater as well. Thus, the organizations and political beliefs represented in this study range from the conservative branch of the Republican Party to the more "extreme" ideology of such groups as the Libertarian Party and the Moral Majority.

The one group consciously excluded were women whose primary or sole affiliation was with the right-to-life movement. This was done both because of the abundance of data available on anti-abortion activists[30] and, more importantly, because abortion is a

complex issue, drawing in many single-issue activists who are motivated by strong religious convictions but who do not align themselves with the conservative movement as a whole. This does not
mean, however, that women included in this sample did not take
strong stands against abortion, or even that they did not campaign
against abortion; it merely means that their political work extended
beyond the abortion issue to embrace other conservative activities as
well.

Intensive Interviews. I conducted in-depth interviews with thirty female activists. The interviews ranged in length from one-and-a-half
to four hours.[31] Confidentiality was assured; therefore, throughout
the book, details about individual women have been altered to protect their identity.

The interviews aimed to understand the history and motivation of
women's involvement as well as the central issues of concern to the
activist; thus, the interviews sought to uncover how and why each
woman is trying to influence the world through her activism, the
values and beliefs she holds dear, the main components of her world
view—in short, to understand her political ideology.[32]

Organizations represented by this sample include the following
(multiple affiliations are, of course, involved): American Legislative Exchange Council, College Republicans, Conservative Caucus,
Eagle Forum, Family Forum, Free Congress Foundation, John Birch
Society, Libertarian Party, Moral Majority, Morality in the Media,
Pro-Family Forum, Republican National Committee, Republican
Party, Women for Constitutional Government, Women's Republican Club, and local anti-busing, anti-tax, and anti-gun control organizations.

Participant-Observation. I also took extensive field notes during
participant-observation at conservative conferences and organizational meetings, including Phyllis Schlafly's Over the Rainbow Celebration of the defeat of ERA (July 1, 1982, Washington, D.C.);
Family Forum II: Traditional Values Work, a national conference
held in Washington, D.C., July 27–29, 1982, co-sponsored by the

Moral Majority and the Free Congress Foundation; the Conservative Political Action Conference (February 17–20, 1983), co-sponsored by the American Conservative Union and Young Americans for Freedom; and settings associated with the John Birch Society, the Libertarian Party, and the South Shore Pro-Family Forum.

Participant-observation adds a further dimension to the perceptions gained through the interviews. Surrounded by their peers, those attending meetings and conferences often express themselves in a freer and heartier manner than in a one-to-one situation. This allows another view of the central symbols and beliefs valued by groups of people who share a political ideology.

Analysis of Organizational Materials. I also examined the printed literature of organizations affiliated with those interviewed as well as literature obtained at conferences and meetings.[33] This textual analysis aimed at discovering the ideological appeals central to different types of organizations in order to understand the similarities and differences among right-wing groups. I focussed on such questions as: what are the main problems America faces? who or what is perceived to be the source of these problems? are moral or economic solutions called for in addressing these problems? and how are the family and the role of women viewed within the literature?

All three sources of data are used throughout the book to illustrate the two worlds of the New Right. While the interview data is solely female, the other two sources of data are disproportionately male. As is commonly the case, among the left as well as the right, women tend to be under-represented both as speakers at conferences and as authors of printed materials. Unfortunately, to limit sources only to the writings and speeches of women at this point in time would severely limit the available data. However, whenever possible, I have relied on female sources. Further, I have tried throughout the book to use excerpts from the interviews in discussions that rely on the speeches and writings of men in order to give voice to the female activists. Because both social and laissez-faire conservative women readily identify themselves with men, it is safe to say that in their view the reliance on male sources poses no contradiction to the telling of their story. This statement in itself adds further testimony to the worlds of women of the New Right.

Comparing the background of the women interviewed reveals the varying social bases of each type. In particular, while all activists interviewed are white, there are notable differences between social and laissez-faire conservative women with regards to age, religion, education, marital status, and occupation.

Regarding age, the overall sample includes women ranging in age from their late twenties to late fifties. Social conservative women tend to be somewhat older than laissez-faire conservative women, with the average ages being forty-five years and thirty-eight years respectively.

Religious affiliation also distinguishes the two groups. While the sample as a whole is disproportionately Catholic, due to the location of the majority of the interviews in Massachussetts, the social conservative group is virtually all Catholic and fundamentalist Christian, while the laissez-faire conservative camp is divided between Catholics and more ecumenical Protestants, with a minority of Jewish constituents.

There is also a difference between the groups in terms of level of education. While the sample overall is highly educated, with nearly all women having completed a college education, laissez-faire conservative activists hold more post-graduate degrees than do social conservative activists.

Additionally, differences show up in terms of marital status and occupation of the activists. Overall, there are slightly more married than single women; within the sample, slightly more of the single women fall within the laissez-faire conservative group. Of those married, all but two have children. The laissez-faire group includes two divorced women who are living with men, as well as another woman living with her fiancee, a lifestyle not found among any of the social conservative activists. With regards to occupation, while the clear majority (90%) of the sample are employed outside the home, all women who are full-time homemakers are located within the social conservative group. Half of the overall sample hold jobs directly tied to their political beliefs, for example, employment in conservative organizations, as Reagan administrators, and so on. The laissez-faire group, however, includes more women who have training and/or who hold professional positions distinct from their political work, for example, engineer, college professor. For further discussion of the varying backgrounds of the two groups, see Chapter Six.[34]

The critical issue in carrying out this research was gaining the trust of women of the Right. Despite the fact that I identified myself as a sociologist and from Harvard, two ready signs of a confirmed liberal from a conservative viewpoint, I was able to build trust through my role as an interviewer. Being a graduate student granted legitimacy to my position as a "seeker of knowledge," thus placing me in a non-threatening position. In reality, I *was* a novice: having grown up in a liberal Jewish home, I was very much asking to be taught a new perspective on the world. It was also beneficial to have familiarized myself enough with the issues to be able to ask intelligent questions, while still remaining "uneducated" to all the details, thus genuinely being eager and thirsty for new information; in short, the key was knowing enough without knowing too much.

Also, I built trust by adopting a non-argumentative approach in the interviews. While I would push to clarify ideas and beliefs, I did not assert my own opinions, judgments, or values nor did I try to debate ideas. If asked, of course, I would state my own doubts or disagreements, but generally I defined my own role entirely in terms of listening and absorbing the other world view. I believe this approach, more than anything else, bridged the gap between me and the women I interviewed. Because many activists on the right have been met with hostility and constant rebuttal by liberals and the media (interchangeable terms in conservative eyes), the fact that I conveyed an honest attempt to understand the opinions and values of the women I met in a non-aggressive manner was met with a welcome and open response.

The issue of presentation of self created different problems at the meetings and conferences than were raised during the interviews. On the one hand, it is much easier in a large group of people to remain anonymous, to be an observer par excellence. In one case, at the Moral Majority conference, the issue was additionally eased by the fact that at registration one was handed a badge of identity—a red ribbon was given to the conference organizers, a white ribbon to those exhibiting materials, a yellow ribbon to the media people, and a blue ribbon to those attending as participants. I assume that part of the reasoning behind this arrangement was immediately to identify the media, who are perceived as liberal and antagonistic to those on the right. In any case, to be recognized visibly as a participant raised other problems, for example, whether to take part in the applause and ovations for speakers with whom I did not agree, or how to respond to requests to sign petitions on conservative issues. Thus, participant-observation involved a constant process of negotiation of my role. The most difficult negotiations occurred during meals or in casual conversations when I had to decide how much of my role to disclose. The main problem involved a delicate balancing act between building trust and gaining acceptance while not misrepresenting my own position.

The aim throughout this study has been to try to suspend judgment, to quiet the voices within in order to allow those outside to be more audible. While I recognize that it is never completely possible to wipe clean the slate, to be free of presupposition, it is nevertheless necessary to attempt to do so. The ability to empathize with roles different from one's own, the degree to which the researcher is able to separate the observer role from her own ideological commitments, will always be integral concerns of fieldwork. The inherent limits faced in attempting to carry out such work, all the same, should not prevent us from trying to take the role of the other, to step into someone else's shoes, to view the world through their eyes.

Finally, let me comment on what can and cannot be learned from a study of this kind. Obviously, one must be cautious in generalizing from the small sample in this study to the population as a whole. While the interviews with local activists took place in Massachusetts, a state that is disproportionately liberal and Irish Catholic, the field data from conferences and the textual analysis do draw upon a national pool of activists. Moreover, because the basic division in political beliefs at the heart of this analysis is consistent with the findings regarding the dual social base and ideological tensions historically present in the American right, there is reason to believe that the findings here are true for the New Right as a whole. In fact, other analysts of the New Right have sketched out ideological strains that parallel the division found here regarding social and laissez-faire conservatism.[35] Nonetheless, any conclusive statements about the overall distribution of right-wing beliefs requires a national study based on survey analysis.

The nature of this study, however, rests not in survey analysis but in the tradition of Max Weber. The aim is to attempt "an interpretive understanding of social action insofar as the acting individual attaches a subjective meaning to it."[36] The intent is to uncover these meanings, to delineate the varying bases of activism, to interpret the world views of women of the right. The hope of this work, however, is not just to enrich ongoing sociological debate; it is to deepen, as well, our understanding of some of the crucial issues of our time and of people trying to come to terms with the changing world around them.

CHAPTER TWO

The Two World Views

Social conservatives and laissez-faire conservatives look at the world from separate vantage points, each yielding different visions of both the country's history and the current problems facing the nation. Further, telescoping in through these two lenses, the two worlds of the New Right also yield varying perceptions of men and women's roles in society.

The Social Conservative World View

I am in Washington at Phyllis Schlafly's Over the Rainbow Celebration of the defeat of the ERA. The day begins with an invocation to Jesus Christ. A middle-aged to elderly audience, all white, predominantly women, fills the hall. Name tags reveal representatives of Florida, Tennessee, Alabama, and Pennsylvania. A woman nearby wears a large cross around her neck and a pin on her dress, a gold bar fastened to a pair of tiny white gloves.

The woman sitting next to me introduces herself. She is perhaps in her late forties or early fifties with jet black hair. She is from Alabama. In the course of our conversation she tells me that her son was recently divorced by his wife. It seems the wife "bought the women's lib stuff about having her own career" and ended up leaving him. She took their one daughter with her. The woman explains that in the Scriptures it says that if your wife leaves you, you may remarry; so, since it wasn't her son's fault, he may marry again.

The start of the program brings an end to our conversation. Throughout the speeches the woman responds with mutters of "I declare." When Senator Jeremiah Denton is introduced with the story of his blinking an SOS while being held as a prisoner of war in Vietnam, she leans over to me and whispers, "How precious." The audience punctuates the address with calls of "Amen."

In line for the lunch buffet two women behind me talk. "When I was growing up we never *heard* of abortion or illegitimate babies or homosexuality. There weren't such things. Now look what's happened to society . . . and the crime rate has gone up so much." She argues with a young woman from Ireland who begins raising questions about the high defense budget. The first woman responds: "But we have to be strong. Look at Europe. They've got Bulgaria and Yugoslavia and Poland and. . . ." I hear more Southern accents than I have since I lived in Texas. Nearby a woman gleefully remarks to her friend, "I've got to get one of those bumpers stickers with 'Anti-ERA—NOW.' Isn't that great? And we'll drive over and park right in front of the NOW headquarters in Birmingham!"

I sit down at a table with two women and a young man. The older woman introduces herself and her daughter, both from Arkansas. The man is an undergraduate from Michigan working as a summer intern for a congressman. The mother asks him, "Have you been to the seminaries yet? Oh, they're tremendous. I had never gone but my husband took me. He says, 'If I could have half a million dollars or a look at the seminaries, I'd take the seminaries.' " She subsequently introduces the man to others who sit down with us as "this nice Christian man studying political science." She asks him if his congressman has signed the school prayer bill. She talks of the Arkansas struggle against ERA, saying, "I think anything that's good and Christian doesn't get in the media. . . . We had our celebration victory on the Capitol steps [in Arkansas]. . . . We were thanking God and the papers reported it and the way they say it, it's making fun of that! . . . [During the fight against ERA] I went back and read everything and I can't believe it didn't pass when it went through in '75. They had all the votes for it but it was a miracle! God didn't want it to pass so He stopped it in various ways."

The afternoon sessions address how to build a militarily strong America, a physically strong America, and a politically strong America. There is an evangelizing style to the meetings, a constant equation of the Soviet Union with Evil, the Devil, Satan. The day ends with Phyllis Schlafly introducing all the women across the country who were leaders in helping to defeat ERA. Many of them, in turn, present her with gifts. One STOPERA chapter gives her a prayer rug with an eagle embroidered on it, an emblem of her organization, the Eagle Forum. The conference closes with everyone singing "God Bless America."

Vision of America: The Religious Lens

Every ideology has a central lens through which it views the world. Events and objects come into focus through this lens, filtering reality, forming images of meaning. The central lens of social conservatism is religion, specifically Christianity or at times the Judeo-Christian tradition. Vision is refracted through this religious lens, coloring all perception.

In looking at America through this lens, social conservatives see a country founded upon religious beliefs and deeply rooted in a religious tradition. Tele-evangelist Pat Robertson,[1] speaking at the Family Forum conference, puts it this way: "When this nation here was founded, we embraced *Christian* principles. . . . There was a deep settled spiritual conviction [among the members of the Jamestown colony] that this land belonged to Jesus Christ." He tells stories of the deep religious concern of the Founding Fathers, how they went down on their knees in prayer at the Constitutional Convention:

> Out of [the Constitutional Convention] . . . came the finest in-
> strument of self-government ever struck by human hands. It
> wasn't just human hands. It was a divine instrument. And that
> instrument *assumes*, ladies and gentlemen, it *assumes* throughout
> *all* of its pages the existence of God, the existence of the Bible,
> the existence of spiritual principles. And these men attempted,
> under God, to form a nation that was governed and ruled by

eternal principles. They weren't coming up with new things out of the sociological research of the latest professor of the University of Philadelphia. They were looking at the Holy Bible.[2]

The Declaration of Independence also is seen essentially as a religious document. A statement in the *Phyllis Schlafly Report* asserts:

> The Declaration of Independence is the official and unequivocal recognition by the American people of their belief and faith in God. It is a religious document from its first sentence to its last. . . . The nation created by the great Declaration is God's country. The rights it defines are God-given. The actions of its signers are God-inspired.[3]

As "God's country," the United States is believed to profit from her special relationship with the Divine. First of all, America's economic system is rooted in biblical principles. Jerry Falwell, founder and president of the Moral Majority, claims that the free enterprise system, ownership of property, and business competition are all clearly outlined in the Book of Proverbs.[4] Second, America is uniquely favored within God's plan. The Revolutionary War is seen as an act of Providence directed and won by God for the purpose of bringing the United States into being.[5] God's pro-American stance is also evidenced in Phyllis Schlafly's declaration that the atomic bomb is a "marvelous gift that was given to our country by a wise God."[6] In short, because of America's religiosity, Divine Will has destined America to a special role within the universe.

Looked at through this religious lens, the family stands at the center of one's field of vision. The family is the building block of society, the foundation upon which all of culture is maintained. The family provides the moral foundation for all of civilization. Thus, the strength and stability of families determine the vitality and moral life of society.[7]

The most important function performed by the family is the rearing and character formation of children. As the socializer of children, the family instills children with moral values. Onalee McGraw, a national leader of the pro-family movement,[8] writes:

The family is the core institution that decisively determines the nature of society itself. . . . In our free and pluralistic society, the family has traditionally been understood as the primary source of moral authority for the developing individual. The moral authority anchored in the family is by its very nature dependent on a consensus of core values within society.[9]

Besides being the source of moral authority, the family is also beneficial to society in taming the pursuit of self-interest. The family demands that people act for the larger good:

The common good requires people to act out of motives larger than their own narrow self-interests. Unless people are capable of self-discipline, of placing restraints upon their appetites and desires, the common good cannot be maintained. The disposition of self-restraint and selfless action is first learned in the family.[10]

Implicit in this image of the family is the social conservative conception of human nature. Humans are creatures of unlimited appetites and instincts. Left on their own, they would turn the world into a chaos of seething passions, overrun by narrow self-interest. Only the moral authority of the family or the church restrains human passions, transforming self-interest into the larger good. The ideal society is one in which individuals are integrated into a moral community, bound together by faith, by common moral values, and by obeying the dictates of the family, the church, and God.

Thus, the family unit is inextricably bound to society itself and is essential in civilizing and socializing individuals. Because the family is so central to society, social conservatives feel that it is imperative to protect and sustain the family unit. Former Congressman John LeBoutillier urges: "We need once again to recognize that America is only as strong as is the American family. . . . We need to realize that the true strength of this nation is measured only by the number of 'happy firesides' across the land."[11]

Accompanying this reverence for the family unit is fear of the decline or weakening of family life. The fear is that any attack on the family will ultimately cause the deterioration and collapse of all of civilization. It is out of this need to protect the family—to maintain the moral authority of society—that social conservatives view with dismay the affairs of contemporary America.[12]

America's Historical Shift: Moral Decay

While America was founded with God's grace and has flourished with His blessing, an historical shift has occurred that threatens America's standing. Of chief concern, America has moved away from God. Pleasure and prosperity have replaced biblical principles as the priority of the nation.

One account dates the decline of Christian influence in America to the repeal of Prohibition in 1933.[13] Virginia Bessey, on the other hand, speaking at the Family Forum conference, pinpoints the root of this historical shift to the 1950s:

> Until the close of perhaps 1950 America was accepted as being a Christian nation. We had a definite standard against which we could measure our whole existence, our actions, our laws, and our lives, a set of Judeo-Christian principles that had not changed to fit the times or convenience's sake. . . . They were our foundation; and there existed up until that time a very moral consensus in this country. . . .
>
> This country was then very much family-oriented. Though divorce, living together outside of marriage, abortion, homosexuality were not uncommon then, they were at least seldom defended in theory. There were moral absolutes that were recognized; and agencies of public expression, including the media and school system, honored these values. Then, unfortunately, over the last twenty years this Judeo-Christian moral consensus has been threatened, challenged, and often times shattered.[14]

Whether one dates this shift to the 1930s or to the 1950s, the picture is clear: the moral absolutes that govern the nation are in disarray. America has somehow moved off the path to God, away from the biblical principles adhered to by the Founding Fathers. This shift has led to erosion of the family unit. While in the past the family has been stable and strong, "a haven in a heartless world," contemporary America is plagued by an attack on the family, a deterioration of the basic unit of society.

The overwhelming image is of *moral decay*. References to moral decay pervade social conservative ideology, for the signs of decadence abound: sexual promiscuity, pornography, legalized abortion, and the disparagement of marriage, family, and motherhood.

One social conservative activist interviewed, a woman involved in Morality in the Media,[15] describes contemporary America in the following way:

> Is it freedom when you can't get your own view represented and there's only one side? Is it freedom when you can't walk down the street at night? Is it freedom to kill a baby who has no choice? History has proven over and over again that a country can be destroyed by *moral decay*, from within. That's what's happening to this country today. Sex hasn't been invented by this generation, you know.
>
> Why do you suppose Rome crumbled? Because of moral decay. And the saturation is so total because even the poorest of the poor have a TV today. The very poor and the very rich have always had loose morals. The very poor because they couldn't help it and the very rich because they had nothing better to do. But now it's middle America, the mainstream. It's like a strong tree. It can withstand a lot, many things, but when you destroy its roots— We're destroying the roots.

This fear of the moral disintegration of American society is also expressed by a woman active in a local pro-family group:

> I think our society is in decay. Everyone is so concerned about themself, the me generation. I see people around here taking aerobics or so concerned about fertilizing their lawn. Meanwhile

the whole world is crumbling. It's as if I had one son who was on drugs, one daughter pregnant, another son doing some kind of criminal activity, and I looked around and said, "Well, I think I'll go do some gardening."

But this is the time to stay close to home, to protect the family in these times of trouble. There are too many humanists running around. All these people jogging and so concerned about *themselves*. . . . You have mothers who want to go out and have a career, children who know their parents don't have time for them so they turn to other kids for advice, and husbands who think it's okay for them to have extracurricular activities. The family is falling apart.

This historical shift that has pushed America off the path to God and on to the road to degeneracy has, then, left the country in disfavor with God. With the advance of moral decay, America may no longer be blessed. In a sermon for the Moral Majority, Dick Vignuelle exhorts:

God's not going to sit by and twiddle His thumb. . . . When you have a parade of 20 percent of the people in San Francisco saying: "I'm a homosexual and I'm proud. . . ." God destroyed Sodom and Gomorrah for that very thing. . . . God's just going to let that earthquake take place that they've been threatened with and just push them right out in the Pacific Ocean. . . . You think God is smiling on America when America is thumbing its nose at God saying, "We don't need you any more. In fact, you're not even there". . . .

Can you believe that with the military hardware the U.S. has, that we sent eight helicopters [to Iran] when we should have sent eighty and three of them collapse? I think God's trying to say something to us, folks. . . . We better get back to a moral base upon which this nation was founded before it's too late.[16]

Clearly, social conservatives see moral problems as the root of America's ills.[17] Moral problems are not only key, but they take precedence over all other issues. Ed McAteer, founder of the New Right organization the Religious Roundtable, addresses this primacy of the moral realm:

> I speak from my heart as well as my head. I personally deeply believe that our economic woes, our military woes and our political woes are not really our woes. Those are not our problems. They are a result of our problem. Our problem is a moral, spiritual problem. All of these others are a result of that problem, and so therefore I am 180 degrees positioned against those who say that the only thing to handle is the economic problem.[18]

A national pro-family leader interviewed echoed this view:

> Of course, from my perspective worrying only about economics and defense is sort of like building a house on a slippery mountainside with no foundation. Then along comes a rainstorm; it'll just wash the house right down the road. But if you had a foundation, you could get the whole thing anchored. So I would say the biggest problems are moral. If the social order would get cleaned up, the economic problems could be resolved more readily. Because if people were in a more stable society, they wouldn't have the frantic thirst for more material goods that they have. They'd be willing to have a more modest lifestyle in order to achieve something later on for their kids. And so if you had a stable social order, a lot of the other things would fall into place.

All of America's problems, then, pivot around the decay of this moral foundation. But it is not simply that moral problems supersede other problems; *all* problems, in fact, are moral problems at base. This is clearly articulated in a speech by George Gilder given at Phyllis Schlafly's celebration of the defeat of the ERA:

> The crucial problems of the poor in America are *not* material. This is something the churches must come to understand. . . . The poor in America are richer than the upper fifth of all people

during most of America's history. They're some of the richest people in the entire world. . . . The crucial problems of the poor are not material but are spiritual. . . . The real need of the poor in America is spiritual revival and ultimately that spiritual revival has to come from the churches. That's why the churches *do* have the crucial role. But not the role that Ronald Reagan is talking about when he said poverty could be abolished in America if just each church brought in ten people and paid them money and ful-filled their material needs. We don't have any material poverty of that kind. The reason these ghettoes look terribly impoverished is because broken families live slovenly lives. It doesn't matter how much money they have. . . . [The answer is] for each church to convert ten poor atheists to the Church.[19]

Because poverty is rooted in an impoverishment of spirit and *not* in the material world, poverty must be solved through the moral realm. Hence, social conservatives call for spiritual renewal and the revival of prayer to help restore America. Others call for repentance.

Yet beyond prayer and repentance, social conservatives also call for action in this world, for concrete political involvement. To this end the Moral Majority claims to have registered 2.5 million new voters for the 1980 elections alone.[20] Through this political action social conservatives hope to push America back on her righteous path. They see themselves as having a special mission: to restore America to health, to regenerate religious belief, and to renew faith, morality, and decency. This sense of mission is vividly conveyed in a story told by one of the speakers at a local pro-family conference:

The other night there was a meeting in my community of the Mass. Citizens for Life [anti-abortion organization]. . . . I couldn't go so I asked my wife if she would go to represent the family. When I came home that night I asked my wife, "How did it go?" and she said: "Not too well. They expected a hundred or so people to come and had set up for that number. You know how many came? Only ten." And you know what I said to her? I said, "So why are you upset? Do you know how many apostles there were? Twelve. And do you know how they felt when they started out?" You see, we are the apostles. We are the anointed ones, the chosen few. . . .

You know, I believe that years from now people will look back on American history . . . and they will see us as having turned the tide. And they'll say, "Thank God they came along when they did and made America turn back." They will see us as the vanguard. And we *are* the vanguard. *You* are the vanguard. *You* are the salt of the earth. It is up to us to work onwards.[21]

Clearly, social conservative political activism is deeply rooted in religious conviction. In seeing America as corrupted by moral decay, the social conservative activist is motivated to clean up this country, to regenerate America. One woman involved in the promotion of school prayer puts it this way:

You know, it's like people who overdose on drugs and then get their stomach pumped. You wouldn't do that to someone who just ate a regular meal. But maybe we need to have our stomach pumped. . . . Sometimes you need to do this to save lives. . . . One day someone will thank me for saving them. . . . Maybe that's what we have to do. The world is degenerating. I'm not a political person. But I believe in the Truth. If that means I have to do some political things, I will.

Another woman, active in the pro-family movement, called me up after the interview to add the following: "I want to emphasize that the base of my whole involvement is moral reasons; the belief in morally right or wrong acts is a strong motivating factor for my involvement. I hope that came across but I just want to make sure that that is stated."

Moral conviction is the source of these women's activism. Such conviction grows out of perception through the religious lens. In their vision of America, past and present, social conservatives are taking a firm stand to ensure that their hopes for the country, and not their fears, are realized in the coming years. As Connie Marsh-

ner, one of the leading figures of the pro-family movement, puts it:
"The battle lines are being drawn. There is forming a constituency
in this nation for policies that will be based not on fulfilling the
economic needs of people but on a return to traditional moral
values." [22]

The Laissez-Faire Conservative World View

It is the second day of the Conservative Political Action Conference.
Several hundred people sit in the ballroom waiting to hear Secretary
of State George Shultz. The vast majority are men, men in suits.[23]
The women present are also professionally dressed in business suits,
grey wool and tweeds, pumps, pearls and pin-stripes. There is a mix
of ages; many middle-aged people but also those younger, members
of Young Americans for Freedom. There are no crying babies,
no mothers nursing in bathrooms, as at an earlier Moral Majority
conference.

I find a seat. People nearby argue over the regulation of gas. A
gold watch with Nancy and Ronald Reagan posed as the face adorns
the wrist of the woman in front of me. The man across the aisle
wears a tie with the liberty bell on it; seated next to him is his
briefcase emblazoned with "Libertas."

In the afternoon we hear discussions of "The Re-Arming of
America," "Monetary Policy," and "The U.S. as Leader of the Free
World" and an address by Caspar Weinberger. During the question
and answer period following Weinberger's address, a man waits to
speak before the microphone. He holds a briefcase, one side bearing
a sticker declaring "I'm proud to be a farmer," the other side a
sticker asserting "ERA—Yes!".

On the third day of the conference speakers discuss "A Midterm
Assessment of the Reagan Administration," "Taming the Federal
Leviathan," and "Economic Recovery: Putting America Back to
Work." During the morning session Representative Jack Kemp[24]
addresses the conference. He is introduced not only as a political
leader but also as a football hero, "a man with a vision of America

where the American dream has been restored in a country which is once again a land of opportunity, where an individual with guts, intelligence, and creativity goes as far as his abilities can take him." Kemp explains that Redskins quarterback Joe Thiesman was supposed to introduce him, but unfortunately couldn't make it. He uses football metaphors to discuss the need for America's defense, America's strength, and America's victory.

As I leave the convention hall at lunchtime, I overhear a conversation between two women, fashionably dressed, in their mid-forties. One woman complains about the lack of women represented at the conference. The other woman murmurs her assent: "Yes, it *is* very male oriented."

In the afternoon Secretary of the Interior James Watt addresses the conference. Two young men behind me discuss how drunk they got the night before, making bets on how much they can hold. Watt speaks of America's greatness and of the heavy hand of oppression that snuffs out political liberty, of the one enemy of spiritual freedom, which is government. He receives prolonged applause and a standing ovation.

That night is the final dinner, featuring Jeane Kirkpatrick. At my dinner table is a middle-aged blonde woman from Pennsylvania seated with the winner of the National Reagan Lookalike Contest. Throughout the meal people come by to pose for photographs with the famous face. Two older men at the table continue to discuss various kinds of ammunition. After dinner the program of the evening opens with the Pledge of Allegiance and a prayer. As I reflect on the events of the past few days, I realize that the only renewal I've heard mentioned is economic renewal, and the only miracle discussed, the miracle of capitalism.

Vision of America: The Lens of Liberty

While religion is the central lens of social conservatism, laissez-faire conservatives view the world through the lens of liberty. Events and objects are filtered through this lens, coloring all perception. Laissez-faire conservatives identify their roots in classical liberalism; the meaning of liberty derives from this tradition.[25] While liberalism in contemporary America signifies the New Deal, the Democratic Party, and the welfare state, classical liberalism of the nineteenth century is quite different from this modern American version.

Classical liberalism is associated both with the *economic* liberalism of laissez-faire and with the *political* liberalism of the minimal state based on constitutional law. Laissez faire, as articulated by Adam Smith, contends that the self-regulating market, unrestrained by monopoly or political intervention, creates a natural harmony in the social order. Smith upheld the economic liberty of individuals, based on free contract, believing that the free labor of each individual adds to the entire wealth of a nation. The utilitarianism of James Mill and Jeremy Bentham is also associated with classical liberalism. In particular, the utilitarian adherence to maximum free choice for the individual and the belief in society based on "the greatest good for the greatest number" are key components of the political liberal tradition. Political liberalism was also influenced by such figures as John Stuart Mill and John Locke, who upheld the political rights of the individual—for example, freedom of speech and freedom of religion—and who argued for constitutionalism with a doctrine of separation of powers.

In promoting individual political rights, classical liberals not only sought protection for civil liberties but also sought to ensure individual *property* rights. The right to own property was embraced as a sacred entitlement, an essential ingredient in the attainment of human liberty.

The good society, then, according to classical liberalism, maximizes individual liberty and the pursuit of individual self-interest. An Invisible Hand is assumed to be at work in the marketplace, efficiently and beneficially regulating the rational pursuit of self-interest, thereby achieving social harmony, that is, the greatest good for the greatest number. Thus, classical liberalism calls for an unfettered market, free from regulations, and a minimal non-interventionist state. The laissez-faire ideal is a self-contained system that functions in equilibrium as long as there is no tampering or outside interference.

Many of the tenets of classical liberalism are present in the world view of laissez-faire conservatives[26]—in particular, the economic liberty of the free market and the political liberty of individuals. As with classical liberalism, the concept of liberty is inextricably bound to the concept of the individual. In fact, while the family stands at the center of the social conservative field of vision, the individual is at the center of the laissez-faire conservative lens. As the primary element of society, the individual is seen as an autonomous, rational, self-interested actor. Rather than viewing humans as creatures of unlimited passions that require moral restraint, laissez-faire conservatives view humans as beings endowed with free will. Individual initiative and self-reliance are hailed as hallmarks of human nature. Hence, the larger good is not ensured through the maintenance of moral authority; rather, the public good is best served by the pursuit of self-interest. In Jeane Kirkpatrick's words:

> Liberalism sees the individual as the unit of action, believes each individual is best able to judge his own interest, defines the public good in terms of the interests of individuals, relies on individual initiative and individual activity to maximize wealth and achieve the greatest good for the greatest number, and conceives of history as made by the purposes and actions of individuals.[27]

Looked at through this lens of liberty, all of human history is interpreted as the expansion or inhibition of individual voluntaristic action. The end of serfdom is linked with the emergence of free trade.[28] Progress and wealth are associated with the uninhibited pursuit of self-interest. Only when government is limited does liberty flourish.

America is awarded a special role in history as the cradle of liberty. Praise is lavished on the early settlers for the spirit of inventiveness and self-reliance that resulted in the founding of the new nation. The American Revolution is exalted as a revolt against "enlightened despotism," interpreted as a symbol of the rejection of Old World tyranny, a milestone in the struggle for human liberty:

A "can-do," problem-solving attitude has typified the American spirit since the days of the early settlers. . . . It should never be forgotten . . . that the principles of free enterprise, of individual freedom and initiative, of the liberty of each citizen from the overwhelming burden of state control, and of open democracy are undoubtedly the most revolutionary set of political ideas in the history of mankind.[29]

The Declaration of Independence and the Constitution are revered, not as religious documents, but rather as sacred symbols of the spirit of human liberty. For example, the Statement of Purpose of Young Americans for Freedom extolls the Constitution for upholding the ideals of limited government, the free market, and the separation of powers.[30]

America as a symbol of the triumph of liberty is also heard in the voices of the activists interviewed. One woman, who heads a national conservative organization that advises legislators, puts it this way:

I still like to drive along the Virginia side of the Potomac River and look at the Capitol at night. Because it's not only the capital of the United States—and I have a lot of respect just for that, for the country—but it's really the capital of the free world. I always say, "As long as the light's on in the Capitol, we know we're all right." Because you know if this capital ever goes, that's it for the free world.

Another woman, locally active in an anti-tax organization, says:

I think we have to work to preserve this country and some basic values. Like freedom. If we don't protect this country and what it stands for, there won't be any places in the world with these values. You know, my family came over here from Ireland. . . . And my grandparents didn't have any money, but they worked hard and saved. This country was built by immigrants. New York was built by immigrants. And that freedom is what we must protect.

In viewing America as the heritage of liberty, laissez-faire conservatives interpret America's position in the world as a direct result of the pursuit of freedom. The successes of the nation are not attributed to abundant natural resources but to the unleashing of human creativity through the guarantee of freedom of speech, association, and trade and the right to the product of one's labor.[31] As in classical liberalism, political rights are linked to property rights; both add to the wealth of nations. Jeane Kirkpatrick comments:

> It is especially encouraging to note the growing awareness in the world that economic liberty, far from being an obstacle to material well-being, is a precondition for it. As the experience of the Western democracies and the newly industrialized countries has shown, wealth is a consequence of freedom. It is created by innovation and experiment, by human intellect and effort; by the activity, in other words, of free creative individuals.[32]

In stark contrast, then, to the ideal world of social conservatism, in which moral authority restricts self-interest and thereby integrates individuals into a community, the laissez-faire ideal poses a society in which natural harmony exists through the very pursuit of individual self-interest. Individuals left to their own initiative will be creative and productive. The aim of the good society, then, is to elevate the potential of humans by bringing this nature to fruition. At its best, human society is the sum total of individuals pursuing their own interest, relating through free exchange.

America's Historical Shift: The Attack on Liberty

Despite these disparate views of human nature and the ideal society, social and laissez-faire conservatives both share a fear regarding the future of America. Laissez-faire conservatives, too, look with alarm at the state of contemporary America. While laissez-faire conserva-

tives do not perceive America as slipping off the path of righteousness, they are as disturbed as social conservatives by the current direction and spirit of the country. They are also troubled by America's
departure from her founding principles. But it is not moral decay
that is of utmost concern; rather, it is the perceived attack on liberty.
For example, a pamphlet published by the Freeman Institute warns:

> The Founding Fathers put together a system of government
> that was so effective in promoting freedom and producing pros-
> perity that it became the hope of the world for the next 150 years.
> By 1905, this tiny nation of the U.S., by following the Founders'
> formula and with only 6% of the world's population, was pro-
> ducing over one-half of the world's wealth.
>
> However, beginning in the early 1900s, the whole world, in-
> cluding America, began experimenting with other formulas that
> have been tried repeatedly during different times in history. As the
> U.S. followed these failure formulas, more than 100 major prob-
> lems developed as the principles of the Founders were abandoned.

Using the name "Freemen" as "referring to those who were responsible for preserving the rights of human liberty," that is, the
Founding Fathers, the Freeman Institute set up a constitutional semi-
nar called "the miracle of America" to make people aware "of the
importance of America's charter of liberty."[33]
Concern about the current spirit of the American people and
expression of the need to return to this country's founding principles
are evidenced as well in the voice of a local activist, a member of
the Libertarian Party who is involved in reforming public education:

> The last twenty years have seen an increase in a general liberal,
> progressive thought. Everyone is concerned about altruism, pro-
> moting those who can't help themselves. Meanwhile look what's
> happened—the talented, the gifted, are overlooked. We have all
> kinds of programs and attention toward the handicapped. It's not
> that we shouldn't. It's just that in the meantime we've overlooked
> the gifted of our country. Now in our public schools they'll bring

in special teachers to help all the handicapped and everyone else. But what do we do for those with talent. . . .

People today are no longer proud. We've learned to be ashamed of our talents. We hide what we've achieved. There's nothing wrong with achieving, with wanting to improve yourself. That's what this country was built on. That's how cities and towns were built.

In stark contrast to the social conservative woman, who reacts to the current obsession with self, the lack of attention toward others, this activist opposes the *altruism* rampant in society, which translates into a loss of achievement. The call, then, is not for a return to spiritual faith, to religious devotion, or to the path of right living, but rather for a strengthening of individual initiative, self-reliance, hard work, and pride.

Correspondingly, while social conservatives root America's problems in the moral realm, laissez-faire conservatives point to the economic realm as the base of America's problems. Hence, calls for economic recovery and the need *above all* to address America's economic problems are present throughout laissez-faire conservative ideology. For example, when asked to name the most important problems facing America today, laissez-faire conservative activists unanimously select issues related to the economy. One Reagan administrator, who works in the Department of Health and Human Services, says:

I think the economic issues are more important [than the social issues]. . . . I don't think the Moral Majority is the mainstream. . . . But I do think the economy comes first. The economy is the basis of the whole thing. Economic needs, a strong fiscal base. The economy gives stability. Once you have a sound economy, then values come up, the need for a greater good. But right now, we need to work on the economy.

In the laissez-faire conservative world view economic issues take precedence over social issues; the economy supercedes the moral realm. As one local activist, involved in several Republican organizations, puts it:

> Definitely the economic issues [are most important]. Everything else is connected to the economic issues. Crime, for example — well, teenage unemployment. I think if they would lift the minimum wage for some jobs, they could train teenagers; they could give them jobs so they could earn a little money and meanwhile learn some skills. . . . The pocketbook is the main thing. . . . I think those people for the social or the moral issues are really a minority. That's not what most people are upset about. It's really the economic thing people want to change.

Further, just as social conservatives believe moral issues do not simply supersede all other issues, but see all issues as moral at base, so do laissez-faire conservatives believe all issues are affected by the economy. As a Reagan administrator who works in the Department of Education comments:

> I think the economy is the major issue because if we don't get it straightened out, then we don't have control. It's just such a pervasive concern; it impacts on every other area. The inability to get the budget under control impacts on defense policy, and the inability to get the budget under control impacts on the ability of the working class to buy homes, or make job changes, or the decision for women isn't even a decision any more — am I going to stay home or not stay home? Because I *have* to go out and work because we can't live on one income. So how am I going to put the kids through school? It's just got to be a major concern. You just *have* to have the economy under control.

Closely tied to economic concerns are concerns about defense. After the economy, defense is the second problem named most often by laissez-faire conservative activists. Another Reagan administrator states:

I think the economic issues are most important. . . . We've already
reduced the rate of inflation. Before the economy has always been
fixed. . . . It's like putting a Band-Aid on a cut, but beneath the
Band-Aid the cut is still festering. This is the first big tax cut
that's ever been done. . . . [But] if you don't have a good defense,
you can forget everything else. We need a strong defense.

While there is consensus among laissez-faire conservatives about
looking primarily to the economic realm, and secondarily to defense,
in seeking to protect liberty, there are internal divisions among them
regarding how the issues are posed and especially regarding the proposed solutions to America's problems. One issue of primary contention is how much government involvement is needed, particularly in
regards to defense. This issue is at the heart of a split within libertarianism. Libertarianism represents perhaps the "purest" expression
of laissez-faire conservative belief, and thus provides a microcosm of
the issue of debate within the larger constituency.

Libertarianism promotes the maximum in voluntaristic action.
Ayn Rand, a libertarian writer who inspired a cult following during
the 1960s, advocates "the virtue of selfishness," believing individuals
left to act in their own best interest spontaneously achieve the
greatest good. Libertarians oppose any form of coercion, defined as
"the initiation of force or fraud by one individual against another."
They uphold the right of individuals to exercise complete freedom
with regards to their own life, liberty, and property.

An activist involved in public education, who is a member of the
Libertarian Party, explains libertarianism in these terms:

> We believe in objectivism. You've heard of Ayn Rand? She be-
> lieved in the primacy of reason and non-initiation of force. The
> primacy of reason is Man as a thinking being, that we should rely
> on our own thinking abilities as opposed to not thinking, being
> uncritical. . . . The non-interference principle means as long as
> our rights don't infringe on someone else's they should be
> guaranteed. . . .

The Libertarian Party is a capitalist party. We believe in free enterprise, in individual rights and freedom as fundamental, what this country was founded on. . . . I think economics is key. . . . We believe in the individual, individual initiative and individual rights. Otherwise you have socialism, Communism, and fascism —totalitarianism.

In short, libertarians embrace freedom of action as the highest principle and view private enterprise and property rights as essential components of individual liberty. Any interference with individual liberty is considered illegitimate, with particular skepticism expressed toward the abuse of governmental power. The 1982 Libertarian Party Platform began:

We, the members of the Libertarian Party, challenge the cult of the omnipotent state and defend the rights of the individual. We hold that all individuals have the right to exercise sole dominion over their own lives, and have the right to live in whatever manner they choose, so long as they do not forcibly interfere with the equal rights of others to live in whatever manner they choose.[34]

In order to protect liberty, as defined in these terms, the Libertarian Party called for such measures as the repeal of victimless crimes, the right to choice in abortion but opposition to any government funding of abortion, the abolition of the CIA and the FBI as agencies of covert surveillance, a drastic reduction of taxes, total elimination of the property tax, and the removal of all government impediments to free trade.

Yet not all libertarians agree on how to define intrusion on liberty, on where the exact boundaries of legitimate government should be drawn. As another activist in the Libertarian Party explains:

There are really two segments within the Party. . . . The limited state group . . . believes that we have to reduce government, but that government should only serve three purposes: judiciary, police, and defense. Then there are those of us who believe in absolutely reducing government; we're anarchists really. I think we could turn over all functions of government to private hands.

The exact boundary between governmental power and individual liberty is the main area of contention among libertarians, with debate revolving around the extent to which governmental activity is compatible with individual freedom. Recognizing the need for a limited role of government to protect property rights, ensure contracts, and defend the nation against foreign aggressors, the *minarchist* faction of libertarians argues for a return to the minimal state of classical liberalism. Believing defense is one of the few legitimate functions of government, minarchists argue that the protection of liberty requires expanded defense expenditures. *Anarchocapitalists*, on the other hand, take an isolationist position; because the state enjoys a monopoly on the legitimate use of force, anarchocapitalists argue that even limited government is a potential tyrant. Hence, this faction rejects even the minimal state, believing the costs of government far outweigh its benefits. Murray Rothbard, a leading figure of anarchocapitalism, maintains that the entire public domain should be transferred to private ownership, including streets, the police, the courts, and even defense.[35]

Clearly, all those who fall within the general category of laissez-faire conservatism do not adhere to the principles or proposed solutions called for by libertarians. The larger question of how much government involvement is needed to solve America's problems, however, is an issue of controversy. Despite this internal debate, the laissez-faire conservative world view unites people who share the belief that liberty and limited government go hand in hand. Looking through this lens of liberty, laissez-faire conservatives do not seek to return America to her moral and religious roots through spiritual renewal; rather, they look to the economic realm in returning America to her heritage of economic and political freedom.

The laissez-faire conservative world, then, stands in distinct contrast to the world of social conservatives. It is marked as much by what is absent from its ideology as by what is present. One noticeable difference between the two worlds is the lack of nearly any reference to religion throughout laissez-faire conservative ideology. A poignant example of the differences between the two worlds is visible in one of the few references to the Bible that *is* made. In speaking about inflation at the Conservative Political Action Conference, Representative Jack Kemp refers to the story of King Solomon rebuilding the Temple:

> He needs fir trees. He needs cedar trees. . . . In order to get the cedar trees from Tyre in Lebanon, he enters into a long-range agreement with King Hiram. They come to the agreement that . . . in exchange for the trees, he would deliver 20,000 measures of grain and 20 measures of oil . . . predicated on the fact that each of them were honest in their trade. . . . The measure was absolute.
>
> Ladies and gentlemen, we need a measure again in this country. You need it in the world today. You can't have trade and peace and stability in a liberal democratic free enterprise-oriented world until this country helps lead the way back towards that kind of stability. . . . We should . . . restore a measure, a standard, a value to our money.[36]

In short, the Bible is invoked to argue for free trade, for the stability of free enterprise. Hence, while social conservatives lament the decay of America's moral foundation, and plead for a return to traditional *values*, laissez-faire conservatives decry the departure of America from her economic foundation and from the tradition of liberty and accordingly call for a return to *a value*, a standard for the essential mode of exchange —money.

Finally, in stark contrast to the pro-family activist who stresses that her entire involvement in politics rests on the belief in morally right or wrong acts, one laissez-faire conservative activist, reflecting on the various ways people get involved in politics, explains:

> [People involved on the social issues] are not protecting their financial interest. There's just no reason to do it, except sheer honor. . . . The economics people, of course, are always accused

of acting in their personal best interest. I don't see anything wrong with that. If we each one acted in our personal best interest, we would all be better off.

Clearly, both types of activists act out of strong convictions. But whereas morality is the source of social conservative activism, belief in self-interest and protection of the individual is the mainstay of the activism of laissez-faire conservatives.

Through the Telescope: Perceptions of Gender

One final way of distinguishing between the two world views is to telescope in on the perceptions each ideology has of the proper roles of men and women. The examination of perceptions of gender, and consequently of how each views sexual discrimination, offers a crystal-clear illustration of the underlying assumptions at the heart of each world view.

Looking first through the social conservative lens, one sees a strict division of gender roles as decreed by the Scriptures. Gender is envisioned as a hierarchical ordering with God and Christ at the top, followed by the man, and then the woman. According to Jerry Falwell:

> God Almighty created men and women biologically different and with differing needs and roles. He made men and women to complement each other and to love each other. . . . Scripture declares that God has called the father to be the spiritual leader in his family. . . . Good husbands who are godly men are good leaders. Their wives and children want to follow them and be under their protection. The husband is to be the decisionmaker and the one who motivates his family with love. . . . He is to be a protector. He is to protect them not only from physical harm but from spiritual harm as well.[37]

While male and female roles are each respected as essential and complementary components of God's plan, it is clear that women exist to support men in their positions of higher authority. A woman's strength is to help a man be all God intended him to be. In short, the man is meant to lead, to maintain authority, and the woman is meant to assist, to submit to his authority. Pro-family leader Connie Marshner states: "Life is a lot more sane and livable if you know where you stand. Women need to know that somebody will have the authority and make the decision, and that your job is to be happy with it." [38]

A woman's role, however, is not simply to help her husband but to support others. Her function is to meet the needs of others, using the talents and abilities the Lord provided. [39] In a speech at the Family Forum conference entitled "The New Traditional Woman," Connie Marshner expands upon this view of women's role:

> A woman's nature is, simply, other-oriented. . . . To the traditional woman self-centeredness remains as ugly and sinful as ever. The less time women spend thinking about themselves, the happier they are. . . . Women are ordained by their nature to spend themselves in meeting the needs of others. And women, far more than men, will transmit culture and values to the next generation. There is nothing demeaning about this nature: it is ennobling. [40]

This belief in women's natural orientation to others is reflected as well in the voice of a local pro-family activist:

> Being a mother has enhanced my life *so much.* [My children] really brought me out of myself. Before I had children I was always worried about how my hair looked or my clothes, but now I no longer worry about that as much. I'm no longer self-centered. It feels good because now I put six people ahead of me. I don't think about myself all the time. Other people join the Peace Corps or do volunteer work for the same reason—to do something good for others, to get out of their selfish existence —

but I think being a mother answers it all. In the Peace Corps you have to leave the country after it's over, but here it's lasting. I am giving something important to my children and to future generations.

Also, whereas other women go to aerobics class or cake-decorating class, I don't do anything but my political activities and my family. I mean what is more important? Sure, I'd like to get my body in shape. But what difference is it going to make to my grandchildren whether or not I take an aerobics class? . . . I am leaving behind a legacy to them. So I really see all this activism as a part of being a housewife. Cleaning house is part of the short-run goals of being a housewife; but my activism leaves something for the long run.

The time and energy devoted to political activism is interpreted as part of the self-sacrifice and altruism essential to the female role. Being a housewife includes cleaning up the political world as well.

The ideal of masculinity, in turn, is to provide guidance and spiritual leadership for the family. As one woman, active in the promotion of school prayer, puts it:

God made Man and He made Woman to complement each other. I like it that way. . . . Since I've been born again, I've come to realize what a real man is. A *real man* is like Jesus. . . . Jesus was the type of man who other men emulated and tried to be like. . . . And women adored Jesus. They'd follow him all over. Because he respected them. Even bad women. In *Luke*, prostitutes, bad women in society, loved Jesus because he said "I love you anyway." . . . Look at the men who founded this country. They were all real men—George Washington, Thomas Jefferson, John Adams. They were real heroes. They all believed in God.

The social conservative world, then, is rooted in a firm conception of the proper roles of men and women, which, divinely ordained, are essential to the survival of the family and to the maintenance of a moral, ordered, and stable society. Men and women have clearly

defined, separate functions. Because gender is delineated in such un-
ambiguous terms, any blurring of these roles is viewed as a threat.
One local pro-family activist expresses her fear of this threat in the
following story:

> You know, tonight we took the kids out to Papa Gino's for dinner.
> While we were sitting there, these three girls came in dressed up
> in baseball outfits. They looked just like boys. From the back you
> couldn't tell the difference. They had it all down—even drum-
> ming on the table [imitates a drum-player]. And the way they
> walked, everything! They were about fourteen. I mean, here's my
> twelve-year-old son sitting there and what is he to think? What
> effect does that have on my son to see this sameness? He won't
> be able to tell the difference between the sexes seeing things like
> that.

The ultimate fear underlying this concern over confused gender
roles is the fear of homosexuality. Hence, one social conservative
warned, "The increase in homosexuality is just one of the social
disorders that is an outgrowth of gender-role blurring." Instead, she
calls for a reaffirmation of gender differences and cooperation between the sexes:

> To demean men is to sow the seeds of our own destruction. How
> can a man learn to wisely lead and nurture a family unless there
> is respect and cooperation? . . . We must work together, men and
> women, to enhance and value each other and thereby teach chil-
> dren that their gender is a gift from God to be used and nurtured
> with eternal circumstances.[41]

In order to reaffirm the essential line dividing the sexes, Reverend
Jerry Falwell sermonizes about the super-masculinity of Jesus. De-
nouncing the portrayal of Christ as having long hair and wearing
flowing robes, Falwell asserts: "Christ wasn't effeminate. . . . The
man who lived on this earth was a man with muscles. . . . Christ was
a he-man!"[42]

While the social conservative lens clearly reflects a man's world distinct from a woman's world, no such distinctions are visible through the laissez-faire conservative lens. While discussion of gender is common among social conservatives, there is a notable absence of commentary on men and women's roles among laissez-faire conservatives. There is particularly no mention of divine roles, of the need for male authority and female submission, or of women's natural orientation toward others. In fact, these very beliefs contradict the fundamental values at the base of the laissez-faire conservative world view. Listen, for example, to the words of one woman, active in public education, speaking about her view of gender:

> I believe women used to be considered property; that was terrible. I *do* believe in differences between the sexes. We're not all the same. There are biological differences. For example, I can't do all the things men can do in terms of strength; but difference does not mean inferiority. I think women are strong, competent, able. Women have to get over their roles as shy, pretty, helpless, and always nice. Men who are successful and competent get really scared and threatened when they discover a strong woman. I've had people treat me that way.

Later, this activist comments:

> The other day when I was collecting petitions, it really made me mad; I could see why women want the ERA! All of these women would say, "Gee, I can't sign. I'd have to talk it over with my husband." Or "No, my husband votes in our family." Aren't they thinking people?

In short, the social conservative vision of a hierarchical ordering of authority based on gender is antithetical to the laissez-faire conservative world view. Rather, the laissez-faire conservative faith in human nature, self-reliance, and free will, and belief in the liberty and autonomy of every individual, extends to women as well as to men and is at the base of the laissez-faire attitude toward gender.

One woman interviewed, who heads an anti-tax organization, re-
acted to my description of this study by saying, "Why study *women*
in politics? After all, women are no different than men." Later, she
adds: "When you come down to it, some men are aggressive; some
women are aggressive. Some men are shy; some women are shy. It's
only because people *expect* particular reactions or traits in men and
women that it is so. We are really only people." In contrast to the
social conservative activist previously quoted, who praised the selflessness of the mother role, this tax reform activist responds to *her*
days as a homemaker by saying:

> Ontological guilt—do you know what that is? The feeling that
> you're not doing enough, that if only you could do more, get
> something more from your life—that is what I felt as a home-
> maker. I felt I was not working to my capacity. Now I have really
> found myself. I never feel as if I haven't done enough. Every
> moment is consumed in my work, which is a fulfillment of my
> beliefs.

Whereas social conservatives perceive a natural other-orientation
in women, laissez-faire conservatives uphold the belief that both
men and women are self-interested actors, capable and responsible
for autonomous action. Where social conservatives view a chain of
command with men delegating authority to women, laissez-faire
conservatives regard such submission as abhorrent, believing each
individual has a right to self-determination.

This difference between the social and the laissez-faire conservative perception of gender results in fundamentally different perspectives regarding sexual discrimination. Because social conservatives
adhere to a hierarchical ordering, they believe positional differences
between the sexes do not imply inequality, and therefore deny the
existence of discrimination. For example, Connie Marshner, speaking at the Family Forum conference, argues:

> Feminists like to blame everything on men. . . . Women are
> second-class citizens, they say, because men degrade women. But

it is important to put things in correct perspective. Women earn
fifty-nine cents for every dollar earned by men—you have heard
this quoted as a rallying cry. But women themselves choose to
work part-time, or only temporarily. . . . When you factor in the
part-time and temporary nature of the work, the fifty-nine cent
statistic falls apart. It becomes approximately eighty percent
parity. . . . Only eighty percent, feminists would still screech, why
not one hundred percent? They would say it is because women
are discriminated against. . . . They would not entertain the idea
that women may not want to work as hard or that in school they
may not want to take as challenging courses. Such ideas would be
heresy to a feminist.[43]

Similarly, Phyllis Schlafly claims that "the fact that there may be
only eighteen women out of 535 members of Congress does not
prove discrimination at all. . . . The small number of women in
Congress proves only that most women do not want to do the things
that must be done to win elections."[44]

In both accounts, the gap in wages or the disproportionate number
of men and women are seen as outcomes of women's choice. If
individual women truly wanted to study as hard, work as hard, or
campaign as hard as men, such disparities between the sexes would
disappear. It is for this reason that Schlafly concludes, "The claim
that American women are downtrodden and unfairly treated is the
fraud of the century."[45] Instead, Schlafly insists that females are in
a favored position in America, the privileged beneficiaries of the
Christian tradition of respect for women, based on the chivalry and
honor bestowed on Mary, the mother of Christ.[46]

In a similar vein, a national organizer also acknowledges women's
favored status, claiming that being female only adds to a woman's
chances:

Let me clue you in—it's a great advantage being female. I get
away with things I could never do if I were a man! You know, I
get in to see corporate leaders; I get through to people on the
phone. I'm sure that it would be a lot easier for some of these men

to brush off another man than to brush me off. I just think that it's a great advantage. I'm so glad I'm a woman. There's not a thing in the world that I wanted to do that I couldn't do.

While the social conservative perception of gender results in this denial of discrimination, laissez-faire activists are much more inclined to conclude that sexual discrimination exists. Contrast Schlafly's statement regarding the small number of women in Congress with a statement made by Jeane Kirkpatrick in her book *Political Woman*: "The men who control access to the inner citadels of legislative power resist the inclusion of women."[47] In the conclusion to her study of female legislators, Kirkpatrick argues that in order for more women to become involved in politics it will be necessary

to abandon the notion, still supported by some religious denominations, that men are the natural governors of society, . . . that femininity is inexorably associated with the submissiveness of female to male. . . . What must also go is the expectation that the male will have prime responsibility for the financial support of the family and the female for its nurturance.[48]

Recognition of the discriminatory treatment of women in politics is also evident in a story told by the libertarian activist involved in reforming public education:

Once I was on this panel debating the Mayor and he argued against my comments about waste in government by saying, "When was the last time you cleaned out your refrigerator? Didn't you throw anything out?" And then, "Why aren't you home with your children?" I got the audience on my side because I said, "Gee, it's embarrassing. I can't remember when the last time was that I cleaned my refrigerator. Actually, I think my husband did it." I went up to him afterwards and said, "Why did you have to say something like that? My husband is at home with my son and he's perfectly capable of taking care of him." I hate that kind of attitude.

Another woman, also active in the Libertarian Party, says she thought discrimination was exaggerated but still exists. She reports:

> I once worked for a corporation. I came up for a promotion. It was between me and this man. They gave it to him. I asked my boss, "Was I qualified to get the promotion?" and he said, "We gave it to him because he has a family." I said, "I didn't ask you if he had a family, I said was I qualified." I quit two weeks later. I figure any place that doesn't value me and my work doesn't deserve me. Those places lose all their most productive people. If you don't reward them, they'll go somewhere else. . . . Sure, there's discrimination. But I'm not going to get upset over a person's attitude about women or blacks. I can go somewhere else. Also, you can boycott a place so that other people know about it.

This story illustrates not only the laissez-faire perception of discrimination, but also the reaction to such bias. Consistent with her beliefs, this activist responds to the situation in voluntaristic terms; on her own initiative she decides to leave the job and enter the free market to choose another one.

Another conservative activist who also reports discrimination reacts in a similar way:

> I've been discriminated against on jobs several times. My first job I was discriminated—really sexual harrassment—only not directly. They kept telling me how wonderful the former secretary was and then I found out that she was sleeping with a man on the Board. They told me I wasn't outgoing enough, I was too shy. I believed them at first until someone told me, "No, that's not it." They fired me. After five months.
>
> So I *do* see the discrimination, but I'm not sure what you can do about it. Or another time I wasn't hired and a man was. But it's just my word against his, so what can be done? I read a lot of women's books—*Men and Women of the Corporation, Games Your Mother Never Told You*—to learn about it. I think that's how

women can deal with it—to really understand the psychology of organizations. I think if I understand how things are run and what I'm up against—by understanding the psychology of the situation I can make my way.

Again, the response to discrimination is individualistic; by truly understanding how corporations work and the psychology of the situation, this woman hopes to combat injustice.

As can be seen, while social conservative women deny the existence of sexual discrimination, laissez-faire conservative women are far more likely to see and to name such discrimination. In contrast, then, to the social conservative activist who rejoiced in the advances she could make through being female, one laissez-faire activist commented on *her* political achievements by saying, "I survived because I learned how to do my homework. A man can get away without doing any homework, but I did mine."

Yet while laissez-faire conservative women are closer to feminists in their recognition of sexual discrimination, they do not recognize the institutional basis for sexual inequality nor do they call for collective responses or government action to remedy injustice. While they do not blame women for creating these conditions, as social conservatives do, they do place responsibility for change on individual women and not on men, on government, or on collectivities of women. In short, laissez-faire conservatives are consistent in their adherence to individualism, both in their perceptions of gender and in the proposed solutions to discrimination.

To conclude, examining the variation in perceptions of gender and sexual discrimination magnifies the underlying assumptions that differentiate the two world views. The social conservative world is constructed around a divinely ordained hierarchy of authority; it is an integrated moral community based on the complementarity of male and female roles. In stark contrast, the laissez-faire world is made up of autonomous, self-interested actors. It is a world in which both men and women, unconstrained by external interference, following the dictates of their own initiative, are equally free to climb to the height of their talents, thereby producing wealth and harmony for all.

Conclusion

There are two worlds among women of the New Right. The world of the social conservative woman is distinct from that of the laissez-faire conservative activist. Where one looks through a religious lens, and sees the family at the center of vision, the other views the world through the lens of liberty, with the individual standing firmly in the foreground. Where one sees a hierarchy of men and women, the other sees the sexes standing equal and alone. Where one perceives America as contaminated by moral decay, the other sees an assault on the most precious of liberties.

Amazingly, despite the very different beliefs that separate these two worlds, it is through the naming of the forces that threaten America that the two constituencies converge. In locating who or what is responsible for America's historical shift, the two groups are able to unite into a single cause. It is the potency of political symbols that allows the disparate perspectives of social and laissez-faire conservative women to come together in forming the New Right.

CHAPTER THREE

Communism

Every ideology projects sharpened images, symbols that evoke the precious beliefs of that world view. In the foreground of the social conservative world, for example, stands the family, the basic unit of society, a symbol of the moral foundation of civilization. Yet symbols also reflect what is most deeply feared and abhorrent, representing images of a world contrary to one's own. For both social and laissez-faire conservatives, Communism represents this inverted image. Just as fear and opposition to Communism was the hallmark of the Old Right of the 1950s, so Communism remains the central symbol of threat within the New Right of the 1980s. Yet while social and laissez-faire conservatives share an emotional response to this symbol, Communism evokes disparate meanings within the context of each world view.

Through the Social Conservative Lens

Through the lens of social conservatism, Communism looms as a major threat to all that is valued and held dear. Communism symbolizes a way of life diametrically opposed to the world of social conservatives, posing the extreme fear of where America is headed as she veers off the path of righteousness and morality.

The psychological reaction to this symbol, the fear Communism evokes, derives from its substantive meaning. Communism symbolizes a threat in two ways: it promotes the destruction of the family, and it promotes atheism. In this way, Communism represents the very inversion of the social conservative world view.

Communism symbolizes a threat to the family because the eradication of the family unit is perceived to be a main Communist goal. This view is exemplified in a speech given at the Family Forum conference:

> We may say today, without any fear of contradiction, that very, very many contemporary families are demolishing themselves. . . . There are those who organize, activate, and stimulate all of these factors working against the family. Of all of them we should mention first of all International Communism, the great promoter of the destruction of the family unit, which they aim at not only by their preaching but also by the destruction of all those things that are bulwarks and protections of the family.

One way, for example, in which Communism destroys the family is by attacking the natural basis of relationships within the family. The speaker continues by describing the efforts of the French Socialist Party: "The socialist aim is to completely eliminate any difference between the sexes, between the ages, and between all authority. They wish to introduce into the family from the earliest age class warfare because there can be no domination of superior over inferior."[1] Communism, which for this speaker clearly is interchangeable with socialism, symbolizes a force of decay because it seeks to destroy the basic unit of society by threatening to level all relationships based on inequality. Rather than a natural hierarchy of authority, so central to the social conservative world, Communism poses a radical reordering of relationships based on the elimination of domination.

Further, Communism also aims to discredit the authority of the Word of God. Communist takeover is accompanied by the destruction of churches, the killing or imprisonment of preachers, and censorship of the Bible. Thus, Communism also symbolizes atheism.

"Godless" and "atheistic" are epithets commonly linked with Communism.

An activist involved against pornography speaks of her fear of the spread of Communism, the way in which Communism threatens religion:

> I have a map at home that shows how since 1917 countries have become Communist one by one. . . . Every year one by one they are taken over. Africa is nothing but a hotbed of countries that are vulnerable to Communism. Now South America and Mexico are very poor people and they're prone to Communism. And Cambodia is annihilated, the boat people trying to leave. And why do they build a wall in Germany—to keep them in? If it's such a great country, why do they need a wall? It's sinister, really. . . .
>
> I saw a film on "Our Lady of Fatima". . . . Our Lady of Fatima came at a time when the Bolshevik Revolution took place to warn people that if we didn't stop Russia, she would spread her atheistic ways. She predicted World War II. She performed a miracle which was witnessed by 75,000 people in Portugal, a country teeming with Communism. They were trying to destroy religion. . . . She showed how Russia would become so powerful and devour the rest of the world—how we're having wars because of our sinfulness, the sins of the flesh. God hasn't done this. We've done this to ourselves. So if we go back to God's way and the Commandments . . . then the threat of war— If we pray for the conversion of Russia, then things will change.

Ultimately, Communism symbolizes the very embodiment of Evil; the Soviet Union is associated with Satan himself. Brigadier General Albion Knight reveals this true meaning of Communism in a speech at the Over the Rainbow celebration. Referring to the nuclear freeze movement, he comments:

> [The nuclear freeze activists] will tell you that the only solution is a one-world government and to abolish the nation state. . . .

The hard-core leadership is socialist or sometimes Communist. The people are being used, most of them are innocent. . . . They're being told "There is no hope" . . . , make the best deal with Satan that you can. . . . Therefore, you must give in and make your agreement with the Soviet Union. . . .

Jesus at the time of the Temptations did not sign a SALT agreement with Satan. Jesus in the Gospel of Matthew also said there won't be any one-world government either. . . . There will still be good nations and there will be bad nations and there will be judgment. . . . We are required by the Bible to resist Evil, to resist Satan.[2]

The image is clear; the lines are drawn. On one side stands Evil: Communism, the Soviet Union, Satan; on the other side stands Good: Christianity, America, and God.

Since Communism symbolizes the antithesis of everything that social conservatives hold most sacred, conflict between the superpowers represents a battle between Good and Evil. At the center of this battle are two contrary ways of looking at the world. Ed McAteer, president of the New Right organization the Religious Roundtable, conceptualizes the conflict in these terms:

I believe that there are really two philosophies at warfare, contending for the minds and the allegiances of men. One of them, on the Left, represents the Soviet Union and says that there is no God. Minor premise: Man is good. You ask the question . . . if man is really inherently good, explain to me the lying, the cheating, the hating, the exploitation. The answer would come back, always: man's environment. Take him out of a Toyota, put him in a Cadillac. On the other side, the philosophy that I adhered to was that of Western Civilization, headed up by the United States of America. It operated on the philosophy that there is a God. Minor premise: Man is imperfect.[3]

Thus, Communism represents not only the inversion of religious faith, but also an inverted view of human nature. While religious

Americans recognize and accept the inevitability of Man's[4] fallen state, Communists assume humans are influenced by their environment and therefore are perfectible.

Because Communism poses such a fundamental threat to assumptions regarding God and Man, social conservatives are fearful for the future of America. A godless society is conducive with the aims of the Soviets. The lack of faith and the perversion rampant in contemporary America leave the country morally weak, dangerously susceptible to infiltration. A society that lacks moral integration is easily divided, ripe for Communist takeover.

In expressing this fear of Communist infiltration into American life, social conservatives echo the cries of the Old Right during the McCarthy years. Yet there is an important difference. In turning their attention toward Communist influence in domestic life, social conservatives of the New Right rename Communism. The main enemy within America is called Secular Humanism. While Communism poses a threat from without, Secular Humanism is actively at work within the country, chipping away at America's moral foundation. Thus, the symbol of Communism is infused with new meaning.

What Is Secular Humanism?

In June of 1984 Republican Senator Orrin Hatch of Utah added a paragraph to the Education for Economic Security Act, legislation that earmarked $75 million for magnet schools in communities undertaking desegregation. Unnoticed until the bill was passed, the amendment prohibited the use of federal magnet school funds for "any course of instruction the substance of which is Secular Humanism." The bipartisan supporters of the bill, including liberal Democrats Daniel Patrick Moynihan of New York, Claiborne Pell of Rhode Island, and Thomas Eagleton of Missouri, all admitted no knowledge of the amendment nor did they know the meaning of "Secular Humanism." What *is* Secular Humanism?

The concept of humanism dates back to Protagoras' statement in the fifth century B.C., "Man is the measure of all things." Much of modern humanism developed out of the eighteenth-century Enlightenment, which embraced critical thought and science and the belief in human reason and progress.

When social conservatives speak of Secular Humanism they are specifically referring to the Humanist Manifestoes published in the United States. "Humanist Manifesto I," first published in the *New Humanist* in 1933, was signed by over thirty men, most prominent among them John Dewey. The introduction claims the document was "designed to represent a developing point of view, . . . a new philosophy." The Manifesto begins by acknowledging that science and economic change have fundamentally altered traditional beliefs. Religion in the modern world must reconcile itself with this new knowledge and experience or risk losing its significance and power to solve human problems. In short, religion requires new meaning and purpose to meet the needs of the twentieth century. The document proceeds by detailing the new purposes of religion, placing emphasis on human needs and enhancement of life.

"Humanist Manifesto II," published by the American Humanist Association, appeared in *The Humanist* in 1973. Reacting to the previous forty years' events—of war, the rise of totalitarianism, the persistence of poverty and racism—the second manifesto reaffirms that traditional theism is "an unproved and outmoded faith." Declaring the ultimate goal to be "the fulfillment of the potential for growth in each human personality," the authors set forth a set of common principles, "a design for a secular society on a planetary scale" as a vision of hope for humankind.[5]

Like Communism, Secular Humanism, as embodied in these manifestoes, symbolizes the inverted image of the social conservative world. Jerry Falwell states: "Humanist Manifesto I and Humanist Manifesto II openly deny the existence of a Creator, urge abolition of national sovereignty in favor of world government, and embrace complete sexual freedom, abortion, homosexuality, and euthanasia. . . . Humanism promotes the socialization of all humanity into a world commune."[6]

Similarly, Phyllis Schlafly warns: "Humanism works for the establishment of a 'secular society,' a 'socialized economic order,' world government, military disarmament, and population control by government."[7] In short, humanism actively seeks the same goals as Communism: a secular society based on one world government. To social conservatives, humanism is a secular religion that is replacing traditional religious faith.

As a competing religion, Secular Humanism is based upon fundamentally different tenets than is traditional belief. Of key import, Secular Humanism places people, and not God, at the center of the universe. This is abhorrent because it denies biblical truth; rather than accepting Man as the unique product of God, humanism views the human being as the highest animal, produced by chance. Further, placing humans at the center of the world not only defies belief in Creation, but also leaves Man to his own resources, without divine guidelines by which to live. Thus, humanism replaces the absolute right and wrong of God's laws with relative values and standards freely chosen by the individual. Pro-family leader Onalee McGraw speaks of this danger:

> In humanism, self-fulfillment, happiness, love, and justice are found by each man individually, without reference to any divine source. In the Judeo-Christian ethic, there is and can be no real self-fulfillment, happiness, love or justice on earth that can be found which does not ultimately issue from Almighty God, the Creator and Sustainer. . . .
> Secular humanism is defined as a religion that denies the existence of God and bestows that role to the individual. It grants maximum individual autonomy and implies the right to make life and death decisions.[8]

The view of human nature implicit in Secular Humanism also contradicts traditional religious faith. Social conservatives believe that while Man is created in the image of God, he disregarded God's love and instead chose the route of temporary pleasure. Thus, Man is fallen, a sinner, and will remain a sinner until death.[9] Secular Humanists, however, believe Man is basically good and is the master of his own fate. In social conservative eyes, humanists "believe the fiction that it is possible to pull oneself up by one's own bootstraps, that one can voluntarily change one's fallen, human nature into a beneficent feeling of universal brotherhood."[10]

As with Communism, the contrast is clear: on one side stands traditional Christianity, which accepts Man's fallen state; on the other side is Secular Humanism, based upon belief in human perfectibility. Rather than accepting the sinfulness of human nature, humanists place faith in the ability for self-improvement, the achievements of individual initiative.

Further, social conservatives accuse humanists of failing to recognize Man's spiritual nature. Rather than elevating Man's spirit, Secular Humanists promote the supremacy of the intellect, affirming Man's control over the universe through reason and mind alone. Rejecting supernaturalism, humanism attempts to create a heaven on earth, thereby renouncing God and his law.[11]

Through such faith in reason, Secular Humanists exalt, as well, belief in scientific truth. This, too, is opposed by social conservatives:

> [Secular Humanism] postulates that science is the sole source of knowledge. More accurately stated this means that we can only *know* what our five senses can tell us as we subject things to the scientific method. This, of course, is a closed system which denies divine revelation, miracles, and the personal divine intervention of God in the affairs of man.[12]

Rejection of this humanist faith in reason, the intellect, and scientific knowledge is most notable in the continual attacks social conservatives make on psychology. For example, behaviorist psychology is charged with reducing Man to a bundle of reflexes in which the environment conditions all behavior. This reduction of Man solely to his biological element denies the existence of Man's soul:

> In this view, man's uniqueness is reduced to mere biological and environmental determinism. Consequently, man has neither inherent worth nor natural dignity beyond that which he grants to himself or that which other men grant to him. Man's ultimate value and worth must, therefore, be determined by society,

culture or politics. . . . In this dismal view, man is utterly alone, bound by his own subjective consciousness.[13]

Rather than recognizing the moral order that transcends Man's material being, psychology reduces humans to isolated individuals, merely responding to the immediate social and political world. Without ties to bind individuals together into a moral order, this image of individuals alone represents the feared society of social conservatism, a chaotic world of anomie.

Further, social conservatives reject psychology for its inherent notion of perfectibility. For instance, one author charges: "By making man self-actualizing, Maslow and others have made man God."[14] Similarly, Lawrence Kohlberg is attacked for his theory of moral development; such theory is seen as denying the existence of moral absolutes inherent in the Judeo-Christian ethic. In short, psychology represents the ultimate secularization of human nature, the scientific disenchantment of the world.

As can be seen, Secular Humanism represents a competing belief system centered on Man, which rests on a view of human nature that is diametrically opposed to traditional religious belief. While Secular Humanists view Man as good, as perfectible, and uphold Man's ability to reason, social conservatives view Man as fallen, as sinful, and uphold the spirit or soul of Man as supreme. As one woman puts it, "Taking the advice of a secular humanist on proper human behavior is like signing up to learn hop-scotch from a teacher whose legs are paralyzed."[15]

Yet the social conservative critique of Secular Humanism reveals the fissure between the two world views, for the humanist view of human nature clearly resembles the tenets of laissez-faire conservative belief. Social conservatives reject what laissez-faire conservatives uphold: the voluntaristic element that allows humans self-determination. The social conservative antipathy toward individuals' being the sole determinant of their fate is the very ideal of the laissez-faire conservative world. Like humanists, laissez-faire conservatives also exalt human reason and intelligence, cherishing the individual's ability to control his or her own destiny. In fact, the dreaded image of the social conservative world in which Man stands alone is embraced as the ideal world of laissez-faire conservatives: each individual, standing on his or her own two feet, unencumbered by outside interference, is left free to achieve the height of their talents.

The Social Consequences of Secular Humanism

The danger Secular Humanism symbolizes does not merely reside in its variant conception of human nature. Secular Humanism poses a threat because of the *social implications* of this inverted world view. In particular, Secular Humanism is blamed for providing the philosophical base for the self-centered, hedonistic culture characteristic of present-day America. By placing people at the center of the universe, humanism reduces human life to a meaningless existence in which the only important thing is for individuals to make themselves happy in the here and now. This fosters the philosophy of "Do your own thing," captured by the slogan, "If it feels good, do it."[16]

The primary import humanism places on the individual, combined with the absence of divine guidance and moral absolutes, means that every person decides individually the standards by which to live. The outcome of Secular Humanist belief, then, is a world without shared meaning or values, an egoistical society of permissiveness:

> The Humanists' "man", as nothing more than a material accident, out of nothing, going nowhere must begin all thought and action in self-centeredness which automatically moves through alienation, despair and into desperation which must either quietly destroy the individual from within or seek relief in some form of violence against other individuals or groups. It is entirely due to an accumulation of the old and new emphases upon the teachings of Secular Humanists that our time has been defined as the ME generation.[17]

This image of the humanistic culture of narcissism is one of despair. The individual is lost in a world without absolutes; loosened from the moral bonds tieing him to others, he wanders alone, seeking some sense of meaning, desperately craving a sense of purpose and self-worth.

Yet juxtaposed next to this image of despair is an image of temptation. The hedonism and materialism of Secular Humanism is dangerously alluring, seducing individuals away from moral absolutes. According to Rebecca Myer, a member of the Coalition for Decency:

> No family is immune to the tragedy of divorce, teenage rebellion, peer pressure, or the temptations of a permissive culture which glorifies youth, sexual attractiveness, and the material accouterments of the "good life." . . . Far too many of us, deceived by the siren of the "Me First" philosophers, are unwilling or unable to hold onto values and ideals which have stood the test of time for thousands of years. We succumb to the temptation to "be me" or "do my own thing" regardless of the effect that decision has on anyone else. The "now generation" has lived as if there were no tomorrow, no day of reckoning.[18]

The Battle Against Secular Humanism

Because Secular Humanism represents such a fundamental threat— to religion, to the family, to society itself—and because of the temptation Secular Humanism poses to traditional lifestyles, the social conservative world is cast in Manichean terms. The need to oppose the humanist threat is portrayed as a battle: "The battle for the mind is between atheistic, godless humanism and basic Christian consensus . . . , moral values or anarchy, one or the other. . . . Either God exists and has given man moral guidelines by which to live, or God is a myth and man is left to determine his own fate."[19] All issues can be reduced to right and wrong, black and white. As JoAnn Gaspar, a national pro-family leader, put it: "I believe there are angels, and I believe there are devils. All men of good will should agree on abortion, homosexuality and pornography as being bad."[20]

In a world colored in such absolute hues, there are no shades of grey. Social conservatives reject any notion of moral neutrality, believing it is a myth that faith in humanism is any more neutral or scientific than faith in God. The battle then entails exposing the supposed neutrality of Secular Humanism. In a speech at the Family Forum conference, Virginia Bessey reveals the reality beneath so-called neutral values:

> One of the reasons that is given to justify the changes [in the family] is a word coined "democratic pluralism." In other words, what the point of this "democratic pluralism" is saying is that we should not in democracy impose one set of values over another on anyone. . . . This lack of values has been held up in colleges as the ultimate in freedom or fairness. . . . Don't force your values upon us, they say. . . . However, if you stop to think about that logically, every decision that we make and all laws are based on some set of values. While tolerance has been called for that all points of view can be expressed, again simple logic tells us that the very nature of democratic pluralism, as they call it, implies *conflict*. Instead of neutrality in the views of various groups, in practicality what happens is the group that maintains the social order and social power maintains power.
>
> And that is what's happening today. . . . What is happening today is that those who support the belief in the religion of what we have come to know as "secular humanism," that man is the measure of all things, have gained the power. . . . Humanism is so much prevailing in our educational system to such a degree that no mention of God, religion, and certainly not even a whisper of prayer are admitted in schools.[21]

In short, Secular Humanism labels itself as neutral, tolerant, and pluralistic, but to those believing in moral absolutes, in a God-given truth, it is none of these. Rather, Secular Humanism represents a deviation from Absolutes, from Truth, from God. And any deviation from the absolute standards threatens the collapse of all values. This distrust or fear of straying from the Absolute, wading in the murky waters of relativism, is clearly articulated by Pat Robertson:

For decades at the leading universities the leading intellectual was John Dewey. John Dewey was a cultural relativist. John Dewey did not believe there was anything such as an absolute. . . . He did not believe in God. He did not believe in Judgment. . . . The corollary of this is that if you do your own thing, it's okay. So there is no restraint on human behavior whatsoever as long as it doesn't hurt somebody else. So adultery is okay as long as you folks don't hurt anybody; fornication is okay and homosexuality is okay and abortion is okay. . . . I mean do your thing, baby, I mean if you want to smoke grass, smoke it; if you want to snort coke, snort it. . . . Because after all there's no judgment. So the question is: "How do you adjust to your lifestyle? Does your behavior reflect a good self-image?" I'm okay, you're okay sort of thing. I mean that is the prevailing cultural view being taught in *most* universities.[22]

The underlying image is clear. The denial of an absolute truth reduces everything to relativity; marriage, the family, God, and the Ten Commandments are all relative to individual desires. Once one moral code is defied, all of society will crumble as all other codes are called into question. Once the bonds on human conduct are let loose, there is no telling what will be unleashed. Without a blueprint for conduct, Man is left to his own doing; and Man left on his own is a creature of passions, emotions, desires, and instincts. With no restraints imposed upon him, he succumbs to all temptations; he remains untamed, in a state of nature.

What is striking about this vision of the decadent society is how close it comes to the ideal society of laissez-faire conservative belief. The humanist dictum that social conservatives abhor, "Do your own thing as long as it doesn't hurt anyone else," closely parallels the libertarian ideal upholding the maximum in individual liberty without force or fraud. Again we see that what is abhorrent to social conservatives is upheld by laissez-faire conservatives. The social conservative hell is the laissez-faire conservative heaven.

The reality of the social conservative world is stark. The time is now. The crisis is whether traditional values will be preserved before decadence takes over. America stands on the brink of destruction:

> It is time that we faced reality. We are in trouble as a nation. We are very quickly moving toward an amoral society where nothing is either absolutely right or absolutely wrong. Our absolutes are disappearing, and with this disappearance we must face the sad fact that our society is crumbling.[23]

Finally, the battle becomes one between God and the Devil. Ultimately, like Communism, Secular Humanism symbolizes the modern manifestation of Satan: "In our day, one of the tools by which Satan keeps men's minds darkened is the teaching of secular humanism. . . . Today Satan-endorsed secular humanism coaxes Christians to join its ranks as it ignores God, His changeless word, and His people, the Church."[24]

And so the forces of decay that are seeping into America's institutions, corrupting her morals and turning her people away from God, are finally revealed to be the Devil Incarnate. America's decline as a world power is interpreted as a sign of Satan's triumph.[25]

Once the world is reduced to such Manichean terms, the seeds are planted for growth of a full-fledged conspiracy theory. The first sign emerges with the expression of a "we/they" mentality. Senator Jesse Helms captures this perspective during a talk given at the Over the Rainbow celebration:

> [Judeo-Christian beliefs] are being attacked by those who do not share traditional religious beliefs but who aggressively promote a strict and intolerant secularism. You've met these forces in the battle over the ratification of the ERA. These forces just do not view the world as our Founding Fathers did. Where *we* see a reasonable tradition in exempting women from the harshness of infantry, servitude, war, *they* see some strange kind of oppression. Where *we* see obvious differences in men and women requiring a few legal distinctions, *they* ignore the differences and end up with

a monstrosity called "homosexual marriage." Simply put, they hold values alien to those that make up the American heritage.[26]

From an expression of some amorphous "they," the force soon becomes an organized group with a defined intent, seeking power: "Secular humanism is a dangerous ideological system because it seeks to impose its ideology through the organs of the State."[27] Secular Humanists are then perceived to be infiltrating the government and other key institutions of American society. In Congress, the Supreme Court, the Cabinet, and other public institutions, humanists are working tirelessly to replace Christian principles with the amoral concepts of Secular Humanism. Pro-family leader Rosemary Thomson, commenting on her and her husband's political awakening, states, "Suddenly we understood that a subtle new religion, humanism, had been embraced by an elite group of leaders in government, education and media."[28] Similarly, Betsy Barber Bancroft warns her sister Christians, in a manuscript entitled, "The Prudent Woman's Guide to Secular Humanism":

> Most Christians are well aware of the deterioration of morals and the resultant distress of the traditional family unit in our nation. Most are not aware of the role which humanists in public schools, book publishing, government rehabilitation services, social "sciences," and tax supported sex "education" have played in this revolution of behavior.[29]

Secular Humanists are organized and purposive. In the most extreme version, Secular Humanists are envisioned as a vast network, united in their desire to take over America, to corrupt the American way:

> More often than not dedicated Christians are pathetically ignorant of the *source* of the moral decay and related problems which are consuming this nation's once-great spiritual strength. Dedicated humanists, on the other hand, know exactly what they wish to

destroy in our nation's conscience and practice. They are militant, well-educated, entrenched in positions of power and influence, and highly motivated.[30]

Another publication warns of the outcome of the humanist effort:

It is quite clear from the humanists' own writings and actions that they intend for the most intelligent members of the species . . . to rise to the top and become an oligarchical dictatorship. The intellectual elite will determine the best course for all, and the rest had better follow.[31]

Finally, this conspiracy theory of Secular Humanism is summed up by social conservative leader Tim LaHaye:

It is all very simple. . . . We are being controlled by a small but very influential cadre of committed humanists, who are determined to turn traditional moral-minded America into an amoral, humanist country. Oh, they don't call it humanism. They label it DEMOCRACY, but they mean humanism, in all its atheistic, amoral degeneracy.[32]

The images here are assuredly frightening. Similar to the McCarthy scare of the 1950s, which envisioned the internal infiltration of a Communist conspiracy into the government, the media, the schools, and the other institutions of society, so now Secular Humanism is named as the force silently creeping through the halls of America's institutions, quietly eroding the nation's strength. Yet Communism and Secular Humanism are intertwined. Jerry Falwell warns: "Since World War II there has been a continuing infiltration of socialism onto the campuses of our major colleges and universities. As the Bible and prayer were removed, they were replaced with courses reflecting the philosophy of humanism."[33]

Together Communism and Secular Humanism are subverting the Christian American way of life. Both represent the inverted image, a diametrically opposed world view, the feared society. Hence, the battle against Communism *is* the battle against Secular Humanism. If moral Americans can only invert this inverted image, replacing Secular Humanism and godless Communism with religious faith and moral living, America will be returned to the path of righteousness, restored to her favored place within God's plan.

Through the Laissez-Faire Conservative Lens

Communism represents as much of a threat to laissez-faire conservatives as it does to social conservatives. Yet, while both groups share an emotional reaction to Communism, the substantive meaning of Communism is quite different when seen through the lens of the laissez-faire conservative world.

First, Communism threatens economic liberty. As an economic system, Communism stands in stark opposition to the fundamental principles of laissez-faire. Secretary of State George Shultz, speaking at the Conservative Political Action Conference, warns:

> We must recognize that *our* way of looking at economic organization in terms of the marketplace, in terms of freedom of enterprise, has a rival, and that rival is the command economy approach. I have found in travelling around the world as a businessman and in my present capacities that it is widely recognized, *increasingly* widely recognized, that the command economy approach to economic development doesn't work. . . . Everywhere it is associated with human repression.[34]

The command economy approach of Communist regimes fundamentally challenges the central tenets of laissez-faire conservative belief by opposing capitalism and private property. While laissez-faire conservatives embrace a market economy, based on free contract between individuals, as yielding the greatest goods and the maximum freedom, the state-controlled economy of Communist regimes is seen as coercive control, which reduces productivity, denies individuals the right to the fruit of their labor, and limits individual freedom. Also, by rewarding group output and not individual productivity, Communism destroys individual incentive and initiative.

Second, Communism poses a threat to political liberty. Referring to Communist countries as "captive nations," laissez-faire conservatives view such regimes as anti-democratic, dictatorships that impose their will on the majority through the force of the state. In Jeane Kirkpatrick's words:

> In not one country where a Communist revolution has occurred have the citizens been permitted free elections, a free press, trade unions, free speech, and freedom to emigrate without official obstacles. In not one country where Communists have come to power have the "objective" conditions ever been judged such that the "vanguard" could safely turn over to the "toiling masses" control of their government, economy, society—control, that is, over their lives.[35]

Communist regimes not only curtail the political rights of individuals but also deny the very existence of the individual. Instead of respecting and elevating the individual to the height of her humanity, Communism crushes the individual through the power of the state. One woman, a national Republican organizer, explains the Marxist vision in these terms: "There's the notion that society is greater than the individual, that man exists for the social unit. Crudely, you see that practiced in the Gulag Archipelago society where they say, 'You're expendable.'"

Another woman, active in a college conservative organization, projects a similar image of Communist domination in discussing childcare:

> I'm not for childcare like Russia or Sweden has it. In Russia if you have a living grandparent, the child cannot get childcare. The grandparent is required to take care of the child. Or in Sweden they're taught that the state is first, that the state comes before the

parents. I don't believe that. . . . Also, that scares me because it reminds me of Nazi Germany where the state comes first above all.

This activist associates the Swedish welfare state and communism with totalitarianism in general; all impose state control at the expense of the individual. Similarly, Jeane Kirkpatrick comments: "Totalitarian utopians attribute no independence or intrinsic value or reality to individuals. Persons matter only as examples and members of a collectivity."[36] Rather than believing that the *individual* is the best judge of her *own* interest, Communism considers the revolutionary vanguard of the *proletariat* or the *Communist Party* to be the best judge of the *collective* interest.

View of Human Nature

It is this neglect of respect for the individual, above all, that laissez-faire conservatives find appalling. In failing to uphold the individual as the sacred unit of society, laissez-faire conservatives believe that Communists misjudge the basic nature of human beings. Rather than bringing human nature to fruition, Communism is the archenemy of human potential; it crushes individual initiative, stifles voluntarism, and imposes the will of the collective on that of the individual. The comrade of the Communist cadre has no place in the laissez-faire world of autonomous, self-interested actors. Laissez-faire conservatives reject the notion that individuals are merely cells of a larger organism; they are repelled by the idea that individuals should surrender themselves to "the common good" imposed by some greater authority.

In contrast, then, to social conservatives, who abhor Communism for levelling all relations, thereby destroying the natural hierarchy of authority, laissez-faire conservatives denounce Communism for imposing collective authority over individuals, thereby destroying individual autonomy and self-determination.

As can be seen, Communism symbolizes the very inversion of all that laissez-faire conservatives hold most dear: limited government, property rights, individualism, and liberty. Communism strikes at the very heart of laissez-faire conservative belief. Accordingly, laissez-faire conservatives call for unity in fighting Communism. For instance, the Council for the Defense of Freedom seeks

> to bring together men and women who are dedicated to the cause of freedom and who recognize that communism is a serious threat to the freedom of mankind. [The Council] has exposed the failures of communism as an economic system and its fallacies as an ideology, and pointed out the superiority of the free enterprise system under a political system and a republican form of government which have given peoples living under it the greatest amount of freedom and the highest standard of living in the world.[37]

The battle, then, is not envisioned as one between Good and Evil, God and Satan. Rather, the battle is between collectivism and the individual, between state control and self-determination:

> This is the mightiest conflict in all human history. This is a major conflict between the only two major philosophies of government there have ever been. One government ruled from the bottom up, with the final decisions in the hands of many, the United States and other democracies are the best examples of this in history; the other governmental form rules from the top down, with the final decision in the hands of the few. This type of government is self-selected, self-appointed, and self-perpetuating, with the Soviet Union and China as our best historical examples.[38]

The Battle Against Communism

In viewing Communism as a major threat, laissez-faire conservatives are committed to opposing Communism and summon their fellow Americans to join battle in the defense of liberty. Believing that national security is threatened by the international Communist movement, laissez-faire conservatives reject as an impossibility any policy of appeasement toward Communism. In order to preserve liberty the United States must maintain her strength; all aspects of foreign and military policy must therefore be directed toward achieving victory in the cold war.

Anti-Communist Foreign Policy. Two strategies are called for in achieving this victory. First, laissez-faire conservatives call for a foreign policy based on a rigorous anti-Communism. Rather than seeing the Soviet Union as devouring the world through the spread of godless humanism, laissez-faire conservatives see Soviet expansionism purely and simply as the erosion of liberty, the triumph of left-wing totalitarianism over freedom. The Soviet entry into Afghanistan, for example, is interpreted as one more example of the Communist menace acting to extinguish freedom.

The lines are clear-cut: either one sides with Moscow or one doesn't. Accordingly, laissez-faire conservatives urge alliance with countries that oppose Communism and favor severing ties with those countries perceived to be allies of the Eastern bloc. Either the principles of laissez faire are supported or they are undermined.

The issue of China and Taiwan offers a good example. Basically, laissez-faire conservatives are critical of a policy of appeasement toward China, viewing "Red China" as an ally, not a foe, of Moscow. Instead, laissez-faire conservatives favor policies that support Taiwan. The rate of growth, higher standard of living, and democratic freedoms evidenced in Taiwan, in contrast to China, demonstrate the superiority of the free market over Communism. Jeane Kirkpatrick praises the alternate model of development evidenced in Taiwan, in Singapore, and in South Korea: "Rather than impose command economies on captive peoples, they emphasized market forces, free trade, and individual initiative. Where others had sought to make the state the motor of economic development, they encouraged the private sector through tax concessions to both corporations and individuals." [39]

Thus, a foreign policy based on anti-Communism also implies encouraging the spread of free enterprise. The United States should favor those countries that have adopted economic policies emphasizing market orientation based on stimulation of the private sector.

Only by strengthening individual initiative and incentive will self-reliance, high productivity, and the maintenance of a free market be ensured. The protection of free trade is at the heart of the matter. One author arguing against alliance with China claims it is wrong to cooperate with a totalitarian dictatorship based on a completely different set of human, political, and economic values from those of the United States. Further, he argues:

> The security of the vital sea lanes of the Pacific depends on access to bases and friendly military forces in that whole region of the China seas and the straits passages from the Pacific into the Indian Ocean and to the Persian Gulf. That is the key strategic problem of our time — protecting trade and free passage in the world sea lanes.[40]

Clearly, it is not simply laissez faire in Taiwan that is central; rather it is protection of *American* business interest in the Pacific. Again, the appeal is couched in terms of totalitarianism versus freedom.

The fight to protect liberty and democracy from dictatorship is a key rallying cry in calls for an anti-Communist foreign policy. The world can clearly be divided between those fighting for freedom and the foes of freedom. Those opposed to the regimes of Nicaragua, Poland, and Afghanistan are "freedom fighters" and are linked with the Founding Fathers, who fought for American liberty. No such label is given to the people fighting tyranny in South Africa or Chile. In deciding who falls on which side of the fence, laissez-faire conservatives argue that right-wing authoritarian regimes are preferable to left-wing authoritarian regimes. In their view, the United States shares a common hatred of Communism with the right. Further, under rightist regimes property rights are respected and order prevails, conditions essential for economic growth. Thus, democracy is more likely to develop out of regimes on the right than out of those on the left.

It is for this reason that Jeane Kirkpatrick berates the double standard toward dictatorships implicit in American foreign policy. She argues that there is a mistaken assumption that because Communists are engaged in a struggle between rich and poor, between the oppressors and the oppressed, that Communist regimes do not have to be judged by the same standards as other undemocratic elites. Thus, American liberals denounce human rights violations in Chile, Bolivia, or Guatemala, while ignoring the serious violations of basic human rights committed, for example, by Cuba.[41]

Build-up of Defenses. Besides stipulating a foreign policy centered on anti-Communism, laissez-faire conservatives call for the build-up of American defenses. In appealing for increased military expenditures, they claim that over the last decade the balance of military power has shifted in favor of the Soviet Union. Citing facts and figures to show the superiority of Soviet defense, they argue that, "by losing our military edge, we have become vulnerable to hammer and sickle blackmail."[42] Or, in the words of one national activist: "We are so behind the Russians that it's destabilizing the international situation. . . . It's like a bully in the schoolyard. He'll only pick on the one who he knows he can beat up, but he wouldn't pick on a stronger one. The Soviet Union is trying to test the U.S."

Yet besides the claim to Soviet superiority, there is a more basic reason for this pro-military stance. Recurrent throughout laissez-faire conservative ideology is a deep-seated distrust of the Soviet Union. This distrust is evidenced, for instance, in another statement made by the activist just quoted:

There's no question that the most destructive issue is detente. Peaceful coexistence to the Soviet Union is different from what we want. Pretty soon they'll be marching into Europe. We've been lulled into thinking detente is what we want. That's a bunch of bullshit that we can live as brothers, everyone peaceful. We need to rebuild militarily.

At base, Communists are believed to achieve victory through pure power and deception. Despite any unilateral or bilateral agreements, the Soviets live by their own rules. Laissez-faire conservatives point to numerous broken treaties as the basis for their suspicion of Soviet intentions. This is a major reason behind opposition to the nuclear freeze movement. As Congressman George Wortley states, writing in support of the Young Americans for Freedom's effort to counter "freeze propaganda": "Despite the fact that the Soviets have broken every major arms limitation agreement, enslaved Eastern Europe, and are currently fighting "proxy wars" through their Cuban clients in Africa and the Americas, nuclear freeze backers still advocate the dismantling of our defenses."[43] Simply stated, one local activist puts it this way: "The nuclear freeze . . . is unrealistic because the Russians have abused treaties so many times, we really can't trust them."

Not only would a nuclear freeze lock the United States into a permanent position of nuclear inferiority, but also, without any means of verification, a freeze would depend upon trusting a regime that never lives up to its promises. Thus, laissez-faire conservatives are skeptical about Soviet sincerity in promoting arms limitation. The nuclear freeze movement is viewed as a Communist ploy, a Soviet-backed effort to ensure Communist supremacy: "Upon closer examination of the so-called "peace movement" one thing becomes abundantly clear: the peace movement in America is an integral part of Soviet foreign policy. . . . It is a well developed and carefully implemented strategy aimed at gaining and maintaining a Soviet global military dominance."[44]

Carrying this one step further, political scientist Stefan Possony, speaking at the Conservative Political Action Conference, warns:

> The goal of the propagandists probably is to transform the peace
> movement into a surrender movement. . . . KGB agents, usually
> posing as journalists, manipulate major mass organizations. They
> have contacts with intellectuals, professionals, media people, poli-
> ticians, Congressmen, and with American institutions like
> academics. In their disguise they sermonize American tourists
> about the alleged devotion of the U.S.S.R. to peace. . . . Thus,
> professional propagandists of the CPSU are trying to influence

Americans who are involved with the peace movement. This is an incontrovertible fact.[45]

To avoid having to rely on Soviet trust, many laissez-faire conservatives support President Reagan's Strategic Defense Initiative or "Star Wars" strategy of funding research for the use of sophisticated technology in space that will act as a defensive screen to thwart Soviet missiles. The hope is that this defensive shield will override current Soviet superiority in long-range ballistic missiles. Best of all, it does not require any assumption of trust of the Russians.

In sum, laissez-faire conservatives call for increased defense and the exploration of new military strategies and techniques to protect the Free World from Communism. Reviving the slogan originally voiced by Senator Barry Goldwater, laissez-faire conservatives promote "peace through strength." As Mickey Edwards, chairman of the American Conservative Union, puts it: "The world was never a more peaceful place than when the U.S. had a national defense second to none." [46]

The Libertarian Alternative. Yet there is a faction of laissez-faire conservatives who dispute this belief that the chief way to fight Communism is through increasing the military budget. Specifically, there is a wing within libertarianism that contends that true loyalty to the principles of laissez-faire means *non-intervention* in foreign affairs and a *cutback* of defense spending. This approach is evidenced in a section of the 1982 Libertarian Party platform that reads:

American foreign policy should seek an America at peace with the world and the defense —against attack from abroad—of the lives, liberty and property of the American people on American soil. . . . The principle of non-intervention should guide relationships between governments. The U.S. government should return to the historic libertarian tradition of avoiding entangling alliances, abstaining totally from foreign quarrels and imperialist adventures, and recognizing the right to unrestricted trade, travel and immigration. . . . We view the mass destruction potential of modern warfare as the greatest threat to the lives and liberties of the American people and all the people of the globe.[47]

The statement calls for complete disarmament and an end to all foreign aid. In another libertarian publication, the author reiterates this isolationist approach, referring to defense ploys as "macho swaggering" and calling for an end to increases in both entitlement programs *and* defense spending.[48]

A female activist in the Libertarian Party explains this approach to foreign policy:

> Libertarians don't believe in alliances. We do believe in free trade, though. We're not exactly isolationists. I'm about 80 percent pacifist. . . . My own opinion is for unilateral disarmament. But then you have others in the Party, for example, this friend of mine, who wants a National Guard. Even though we disagree so much on this, we were able to work out a platform that was mutually agreeable. Because even though I would like disarmament, that means I can disarm just one person—myself. Everyone else has the right to bear arms. I can't tell anyone else to disarm. Ideally, people should [be able] to defend what they believe in.
>
> In a libertarian world, government would not be able to do two things: declare war and make alliances. . . . As it stands now, the neutrality act forbids people to offer to fight for undeclared wars. Then it goes and sends men to fight for things they might not even believe in. If everyone could decide for themself, people could form their own armies and volunteer. For example, I might have been driven to go to Afghanistan. If I could be persuaded from what I read to do that, I don't think there'd be any problem getting people to defend what they believe in.

In a sharp departure from those advocating increased government involvement in defense, this libertarian clearly places voluntarism and individual self-determination above the government's right to intervene. Again, the dispute involves the legitimate boundaries of government authority.

Another libertarian proposes that, rather than increased government spending on defense, the material foundation for military strength rests on a vigorous laissez-faire economy. A free market leads to competition, resulting in the rapid development of new technology by the most efficient means. He concludes:

> In general, libertarians believe in the power of the free market to prevail against the unfree nations that might pose threats to us. By allowing our own society to blossom fully in freedom and laissez-faire, we can confidently hope to surpass our enemies in material wealth and power—making it fruitless for them to attack us and inspiring them, by our example, to overthrow the bonds of tyranny for the bounty of liberty.[49]

In short, the abundance and freedom produced by a capitalist economy will be enough to ensure victory over Communism.

Yet while there is internal debate about whether Communism is best fought through increased defense or through increased isolationism, laissez-faire conservatives are united in their belief that, above all, the free market must prevail. Hence, while anti-Communism is the backbone of foreign policy, laissez-faire conservatives oppose any restriction on trade with Communist countries. In their view the Soviet grain embargo had little value and only hurt the American farmer. Russia, in fact, was able to make up for the deficit by purchasing grain from other countries. In the process, some American allies became middlemen, reselling American grain to the Soviets, thereby reaping all the profits.[50]

This view of commerce in strict adherence to a free market, based on individual actors unhampered by any form of intervention, is consistent with the principles of laissez faire. In contrast, the social conservative position on trade with the Soviets is evidenced in Phyllis Schlafly's comment:

> "Everybody's doing it" is the standard excuse offered by the sinner to excuse his sin. Group responsibility, egged on by peer pressure, is presumed to provide the fig leaf to hide individual

guilt for a wide variety of sins. . . . Likewise, "everybody's doing it" is the slogan with which U.S. businesses justify selling high technology to the Soviet Union.[51]

There is clearly disagreement between the laissez-faire position, which upholds free trade, and the social conservative position, couched in religious terms, which demands limitations on sales to the Soviets.

In the laissez-faire conservative world, Communism looms, threatening to destroy limited government and individual liberty. The battle against this threat entails a vigorous anti-Communism with regards to foreign policy, combined with protection of the free market. In addition, many laissez-faire conservatives call for increased defense. By rebuilding the country's economic and military strength, America can once again return to the principles of the Founding Fathers and maintain her place as leader of the Free World.

Conclusion

As we have seen, Communism poses as much of a threat to the world of laissez-faire conservatives as it does to the social conservative world. Yet the fundamental meaning of that threat is entirely different. The contrast in ideology is marked as much by what is absent as by what is present. For laissez-faire conservatives, Communism is not perceived as endangering the family or religious belief. There is no mention of the dangers Communism poses to belief in God or to the moral order. Rather, Communism symbolizes a threat to the very principles of laissez faire, to economic and political liberty.

Hence, although the Soviet Union represents the foe of both worlds, for social conservatives the Soviet Union is the Devil Incarnate, while for laissez-faire conservatives it embodies the total loss of individual freedom. Similarly, while social and laissez-faire conservatives share a distrust of the nuclear freeze movement, both believing it to be a front for Communist infiltration, they cast the threat in different terms. Where social conservatives see the freeze as a demonic plot led by the forces of Evil and immorality, laissez-faire conservatives see it as a ploy by Communists to weaken the United States militarily, bringing them one step closer to achieving worldwide domination.

CHAPTER FOUR

Big Government

"Get government off our backs" is a phrase often associated with the New Right. While Communism represents the feared society, Big Government signifies the present state of American society, America on the road of decline. Both social and laissez-faire conservatives share this sense of decline and oppose Big Government, but their objections and their intents remain distinct.

Through the Social Conservative Lens

In looking at present-day America, social conservatives contrast the current American government with the legitimate role of government. One refrain heard throughout social conservative ideology is that the United States is meant to be a republic and not a democracy.[1] Claiming that the Founding Fathers feared majority rule, social conservatives believe the government was actually set up *against* democracy. Pure democracy is envisioned as mob rule, the tyranny of the masses. In a speech at the Over the Rainbow celebration, Senator Jeremiah Denton refers to democracy as presented in Plato's *Republic* in the following way:

> It was a kind that was so democratic that the leaders were ap-
> pointed by lot. They would rule according to the whims of the
> mob. And the animals roamed in the streets because there was a
> complete feeling of liberty—you know, do your own thing and
> I'll do mine. There was a good deal of chaos. That form doesn't

last very long and you work down into that form called despotism.[2]

Democracy is equated with a mass of individuals, unrestrained, each pursuing his or her own desires. Liberty represents the unleashing of moral bonds, the anarchy of a society based on "do your own thing," in which Man's primal instinctual nature is unfettered, resulting in chaos. This dreaded image of liberty unbound clearly parallels the ideal society of laissez-faire conservatism.

Instead of this vision of democratic chaos, America as a republic is a government of law in which checks and balances restrain mob rule so that order prevails. But just as the mob must be kept in check so, too, must the government. The Founding Fathers established the Constitution both to check mob rule and in recognition of the dangers of unrestrained governmental power, to limit the scope of central government.

But America has made a wrong turn; the government has moved dangerously beyond these legitimate functions. Rather than look to God as the provider, Americans now look to government. Thus, America has taken the first step on the road to socialism. Departing from the original principles of the Founding Fathers, government now challenges religious faith. In an impassioned speech to the Family Forum conference, the Reverend James Robison preaches:

> Do you know what our socialist society is doing right now? It's bringing judgment on evildoers. Would you like to find the evildoers? There's a mirror not too far from here down the hall. . . . We are the evildoers. . . . We didn't want to be our brother's keeper; we wanted Washington to take care of our brother. We didn't want to take care of mother and dad, grandmother and granddad; we wanted the government to take care of mother and dad and grandmother and granddad. . . .
>
> It is a sin against God when you lift up your eyes to the Hill [Capitol Hill] from whence cometh your health, you think, rather than lifting up your eyes to the hills from whence in fact *does* come your health. Because God and God alone is our source. And God

and God alone we ought to depend upon, not Man. When we depend upon Man then God has cursed this man who trusts in Man. . . . Whenever we have a problem now we turn to Washington; we say "Sure, they've got the solution."[3]

Rather than being the servant to humanity, government has now become the master. Rather than trusting in God to solve problems, people depend on Fallen Man, in the form of government, for the answers.

Besides seeing this dependence on government as sinful, social conservatives see Big Government as promoting immorality and usurping traditional authority. In these two ways Big Government contributes to the erosion of religious belief and threatens the security of the American family.

Big Government as Promoting Immorality

One chief way in which Big Government promotes immorality is through recognition and support for Secular Humanism. Secular Humanism is being imposed as the state religion through tax-supported public schools and through government funding of humanist organizations and activities. Citing Supreme Court decisions that recognize non-theistic belief as a form of religion, social conservatives argue that the separation of church and state is being violated by this imposition of the religion of Secular Humanism through public institutions.[4]

Children are being indoctrinated into Secular Humanism through public education. Mel and Norma Gabler, two leading social conservatives associated with the effort to weed out humanist influence in public education, comment:

It is important to realize that textbooks were about 97% Christian/ moral when our nation was founded. . . . However, the Christian/moral influence was gradually eliminated on the pretext that the State has no right or authority to teach religion. This vacuum has been filled with the philosophy/religion of humanism, faith in man rather than God. Today textbooks are nearly 100% amoral or humanistic.[5]

For over twenty years the Gablers have devoted their life to what they call "book reviewing," pleading their case before the annual textbook committee hearings in Texas. Texas is one of the most influential states for textbook publishing. With an estimated $60.3 million in textbook purchases in 1982, Texas represents the fourth largest state market in the United States. Its statewide selection policy (rather than local adoption procedures) means that decisions made in Texas have far-reaching results. Texas law allows public comment on proposed books before they are approved for use. Through this open screening process it is possible for anyone in the state to challenge any part of a textbook being considered for adoption. Until the 1980s the Gablers monopolized the Texas book selection process. For example, in 1974 they helped persuade the Texas board to put a statement in all textbooks dealing with evolution, identifying evolution as "only one of several explanations of the origin of humankind . . . in a manner which is not detrimental to other theories of evolution," that is, Creationism.[6]

The Gablers' efforts have sparked the involvement of other concerned parents. Using the Gablers' guidelines, for example, in 1986 parents in Church Hill, Tennessee, objected to a reading series approved by the state. They took issue, for instance, with a first-grade reader in which the storyline read: "Jim cooks while the little girl reads." One parent complained, "True, the little girl cooks after Jim, [but it has already been] planted in the first grader's mind that there are no God-given roles for the different sexes." Pitted against the local school board, these parents brought their case to the federal district court, declaring their right to shield their children from books they deem to be anti-Christian. Michael Farris, the general counsel for Concerned Women for America, the Washington lobby that financed the Tennessee plaintiffs, commented: "There's a widespread feeling amongst conservative Christians that the religion of secular humanism has permeated public education."[7]

Besides promoting immorality through Secular Humanism in public schools, Big Government also directly funds humanistic organizations. Social conservatives have on record and are quick to name hundreds of liberal organizations supported through tax dollars, all seen as bastions of humanism. Frequently mentioned organizations that receive government monies include Planned Parenthood, the National Organization for Women, the National Urban League, Americans for Democratic Action, the National Welfare Rights Organization, the United Farmworkers, the Southern Christian Leadership Foundation, and the American Association of University Women; an often-cited case is a government grant that sponsored a Gay Community Rap Center and a dance program entitled "Leaping Lesbians."

One activist interviewed, a national organizer for Phyllis Schlafly's organization, the Eagle Forum, explains opposition to government funding in the following way:

> The battle comes down to "Is this the federal government or the state government or any government's responsibility to fund these things or should they be left to the private sector?" . . . For example, the NOW got over $400,000 last year through the Department of Education. We look at that and we say, "That's a sham. That's ridiculous. . . ." People are simply calling for the enforcement of the laws of our land. . . . The Legal Service Corporation actually tried to put in affirmative action laws for homosexuals. . . . People don't want to see that. They don't want to see funding of Planned Parenthood. They don't want to see funding of abortion. So what they're saying to the government is "Get out of that."

Besides corrupting morals through the promotion of Secular Humanism, Big Government also promotes immorality through its own programs, in particular, through the welfare system and the tax system. Some social conservatives consider the very principle of welfare morally wrong:

> There is a moral issue in welfare money. It's immoral to take money from people who work and give it to those who won't

work. . . . We're not forcing our morality on others. This is God's morality, not ours. Our laws were founded on God's word and not on Man's will.[8]

Further, welfare encourages immorality by "rewarding" illegitimacy. For example, New Right spokesman George Gilder equates the increase in government welfare programs with the rise in black illegitimacy rates. He argues that the government offers so many enticements to black teenage women, for example, legal aid, food programs, housing subsidies, that they cannot pass up the "good deal." Similarly, he maintains that the tax system promotes immorality by rewarding particular lifestyles:

> The tax burden has shifted from single people and from groovy people without any children to a couple trying to raise the next generation of Americans. . . . But if you're willing to leave your children in a daycare center and go out to work, the government will give you $800 right off the top, a pretty good deal. . . . So the government very much wants you to leave your kids in daycare centers. But if you raise your children yourself, you have to pay for it through the nose. However, that's nothing. If you could really kick out your husband and go on welfare, the government will give you $18,000 in benefits every year. . . . If Brezhnev in Moscow had tried to design a welfare program, a tax system to undermine America and destroy its vibrancy and its productivity and its future, he could not conceivably have been shrewd enough to design such a sinister arrangement as our current compassionate liberals have contrived for us.[9]

In short, the government both directly funds Secular Humanism and indirectly endorses lifestyles that deviate from traditional religious values. In social conservative eyes, then, the increase in the size of government has been accompanied by an increase in immorality. As Tim LaHaye puts it, "We have a situation now where government is condoning what God condemns."[10]

Big Government as Usurping Traditional Authority

Big Government also usurps traditional authority. Besides appropriating God's role as Provider, Big Government encroaches upon the traditional authority of the church, the family, and the neighborhood. Responsibilities traditionally designated to the family, for example, care for the aged, the religious upbringing of children, or those designated to the church, such as, relief for the poor, increasingly are monopolized by the state. Social conservatives react particularly vehemently to government intervention in areas formerly under the jurisdiction of the family. In their view, the helping professions have invaded the family with their therapeutic techniques, depriving parents of their legitimate functions. This "human service bureaucracy" of psychologists, sociologists, social workers, and other "experts" claim to know what is best for family life. These social service professionals have now become an entrenched segment of society, claiming new needs and further government intervention as a self-serving device to ensure their continued demand.[11]

The public schools are not only the locus for the fight against Secular Humanism but are also a major battleground for the struggle between governmental and parental authority.[12] Three issues are of particular concern: control over schools attended, control over curriculum, and control over values.

One area of concern focusses on who determines which schools children attend, the government or parents. Busing has been a catalyst for much social conservative protest. As one national pro-family leader explains:

> Social conservatives are concerned with being able to control their own lives when you come right down to it: that their children have the access to the sort of education which the parents would like the child to have, that the children are able to go to school in a neighborhood that's convenient to the parents so that they can go to school and learn with kids and also they can play with the children.

In fact, many women previously uninvolved in politics have been drawn in through the busing issue. Once involved, their commitment deepens as they learn about other issues. One local pro-family activist discusses her initial involvement through opposition to busing:

> I got involved when the busing issue came up. . . . It was not because of being racist that I objected. I have to explain that because so many people, as soon as you tell them you're against busing, accuse you of being racist. At the time I only had one child, two-and-a-half years old, so I wasn't active for my own children. It was "What can be done to one person, can be done to me." My sister was involved and that got me interested. . . . So I got involved on that one issue and little did I know then that that would begin ten years of activism!
> . . . Now I'm working with a pro-family group. The latest thing has been the Reagan decision on family planning. As far as I'm concerned, he didn't go far enough. . . . You know, I've been in one of those teenage clinics. I went in one day and picked up their literature. And on it they say: "Free contraception available. We will remain confidential and will not require parental consent. Dispose of this properly." I couldn't figure that one out—dispose of this, as if that encourages them to hide this so the parents can't see it. I don't want my children to have access to this, to someone outside the family giving them advice. It encourages them to go to someone else. Also, why should part of my tax dollar go to sponsor family planning? Or litigation that supports homosexuality? I'd rather that part of *my money* go to get food on the table for my children. . . .
> Like busing, family planning takes control out of parents' hands. It's the government telling me what to do.

Clearly, the underlying concern in both busing and birth control is government intrusion into areas legitimately regulated by the family. This activist fears the loss of control over her children, believing the moral authority to guide her children's lives should rest in the hands of parents, not government.

Besides the issue of which schools children attend, a second area of concern focusses on the kind of education children are receiving, on who controls the curriculum. One high-priority issue is prayer in schools. The Supreme Court decision prohibiting school prayer is viewed as one more way in which God has been removed from the American way of life, further evidence of the triumph of atheistic Secular Humanism. Yet the issue of government authority is at stake as well. One Reagan administrator, working in the Department of Education, explains the issue of school prayer:

> I have a hard time with the prayer in school because I'm Jewish. When I was a kid I grew up in a Catholic neighborhood and went to a school where the New Testament prayers were read. Mother had to go up to the school and complain to the principal. It was taken care of. So I do have some personal experience of a little bit of a problem. However, even given my own personal negative experience, I don't want it dictated by the federal government and the Supreme Court. I think that people have the ability on a local level to handle local problems. . . . I just think that there are certain areas that the federal government has encroached into that there's just no need for federal involvement. . . . I mean where has our federal government shown that they have this wonderful expertise or the ability to do things better than local people do them?

The prohibition of school prayer is viewed as Big Government infringing on an area best left to local decision-making.

Federal appropriation of local control is expressed as well in the discussion of which textbooks and course materials should be used in the classroom. According to one activist involved against gun control:

> I think there is a Judeo-Christian morality, an ethic by which to live. I also think parents on a local level should be able to say what books their children read in school. If they think *Ulysses*, or some other book, has too much gutter language, and they don't

want their children hearing or learning those words, they should be able to censor that. Or if they want to teach their children about sex, they should be able to not want sex education in the schools. But within reason. I don't think that parents have the right to want a book that teaches racial antagonism in the schools; there, I think the school board has a right to override the parents. But for the most part, I think parents, not the school board, should have control over what values are taught in the schools. . . .

Or Creationism—I do believe Darwinism should be taught. I don't think it's depraved or disgusting. But it's a theory. It's not proven. It's one theory just like Creation is another theory. I think Darwinism should be taught along with other theories.

Clearly, efforts to monitor textbooks reflect a wish not only to counter Secular Humanism but also to return authority to its proper hands, to parents and the community.

A national Republican activist reiterates this need for local control:

Why should someone in Washington explain to anybody what they should learn? . . . [The textbook-burners in West Virginia] weren't suggesting that there ought to be government censorship. Just the reverse—they're protesting government censorship. . . . It's the duty of your parents and of your school.

From this perspective government censorship means federal intrusion into local decision-making. Instead, parents and the community are the rightful agents for control over the curriculum. Again, the underlying issue is who should determine children's education, federal bureaucrats and experts or parents and the community. As Alice Moore, a leader in the "back to basics" movement, sums it up:

What is at issue here . . . is simply who is going to have control over the schools, the parents and the taxpayers and the people who live here or the educational specialists, the administrators, the people from other places who have been trying to tell us what is best for our children. We think we are competent to make those decisions for ourselves.[13]

Another issue closely connected to control over the curriculum goes right to the core of the social conservative world view: situation ethics. Situation ethics raises the question not simply of the *content* of the curriculum but, more fundamentally, of who determines the *values* being instilled in America's youth. Connie Marshner explains "consequentialist" or "situational ethics":

> What are consequentialist ethics? Consequentialist ethics are commonly taught in the public schools today and indeed in far too many churches. Consequentialist ethics could be summarized by quoting from a bumper sticker I have seen occasionally: "If it will feel good, do it." Consequentialist ethics is the thesis that you can judge whether something is good or bad by its consequences. If having an abortion has the "good" result that you can continue your career, then the abortion is a "good" thing, a "right" thing to do. If living with John instead of marrying him brings the "good" result that you never argue about money because you each have your own, then living together is a "good" thing to do.
>
> In contrast, non-consequentialist ethics, which are traditional values, maintain that moral norms are not dependent upon consequences, but rather upon whether certain actions are right or wrong intrinsically. Hence the norms concerning these acts, once they are well-defined, are without exception.[14]

In short, situation ethics are determined by circumstances, not by moral absolutes. Such teaching results in indoctrination into a type of ethical relativism, a "moral supermarket approach"[15] to living.

The specific way in which situation ethics are promoted in the public schools is through *values clarification* programs. Hypothetical situations are posed for students and they in turn must consider, "What would you do?" The aim is to help the student analyze the complexities involved in any given circumstance in order to ascertain what the individual student feels is the best response. By posing situations in which the child has to decide for him or herself what is right or wrong, children are encouraged to discover their *own* set of personal values. This is abhorrent because it fosters the belief that *all* values are acceptable, undermining belief in the absolute moral values decreed by the Scriptures. Instead of faith in the *objective* truths of God, the individual is left to his or her own *subjective* conscience to choose the moral standards by which to live.

Values clarification also aims to introduce students to other cultures that hold different values. One critic explains:

> In one culture study, fifth grade children are led to discover the lifestyle of the Netsilik Eskimo tribe of Canada. What do they practice? They practice Cannibalism, infanticide, murder of grandparents, wife swapping, mating with animals—the most degrading things you can imagine. And what is the teacher to say about all this? She is not to make a value judgment. The children must decide with the clear implication that if the Netsiliks want to live this way, it is all right. The whole idea is that one culture is as good as another and the values of no culture are absolute.[16]

This acceptance of other cultures and belief systems as equally valid is perceived as denying or negating the absolute values sanctioned by God.

Besides undermining religious authority, values clarification programs also subvert parental authority, driving a wedge between parents and children. By regarding the individual as the supreme arbiter of the truth, such programs facilitate self-centeredness, implicitly assuming that the good life is one of self-fulfillment and self-actualization. Values clarification programs thus encourage introspection, elevate self-gratification, and result in a "do your own thing," narcissistic mentality. As a result of sponsoring self-interest by rearing the "Me generation," values clarification programs teach students how to rebel against parental authority. For example, the child learns to respond to parental prohibitions against premarital sex or drugs by saying, "But that's *your* value judgment." This destroys the natural hierarchy of the family in which parents have authority over children.

Situation ethics and values clarification programs are viewed as dangerous, then, because, instead of socializing children into traditional values, they instead encourage a questioning, disobedient attitude among the young. Inquiry, debate, critical thought, all threaten to replace blind faith with doubts and rebellion. The result: insurrection against parents, against traditional values, and against God. And once God is no longer the Absolute, people depend on Fallen Man, with all the dangers such trust ensures. Once one begins to question, the entire structure is in danger of collapse; despotism follows. Ultimately, textbooks and lessons that encourage students to challenge basic assumptions pose a threat to society itself. In Mel Gabler's words: "Is it any wonder that a culture which trains its young to have such inquiring minds will produce rebels who are ready to challenge *everything* that exists, even values older generations have come to honor and revere?"[17]

To prevent disaster, the Moral Majority calls for "a re-affirmation of parents' rights as the authority figures for children."[18] Control over schooling, over curriculum, and over values all must be returned to parental hands. In a call to activism, Onalee McGraw implores:

> When it comes to the real conflicts underlying all these school boards, [there] are basically conflicts in values . . . , conflicts in philosophy and purpose that have to do with how you view the nature of human beings and whether or not you believe there is a God and whether there is an order that He created or not and all of those . . . beliefs and values which Americans have always . . . held in common, even though they were from different religions and backgrounds.
>
> Once parental authority comes to be very seriously questioned, [we are in] very, very serious trouble. . . . However, more and more parents are realizing that *they* are the primary educators of their children, that *they* have a responsibility to form the moral

character of their children. . . . Otherwise, where is the moral imagination and the wisdom of the ages? How is it going to be passed on? . . . Parents have to take back and *claim* the responsibilities that *God* gave them for the raising of their children.[19]

The Battle Against Government

The battle against government is a moral battle, between educational professionals and parental authority, between federal intrusion and community standards, between Secular Humanism and traditional values. There is no such thing as "moral neutrality," no shades of grey. Every situation can be reduced to two sides. And depending on where one stands, the world takes on a different appearance. Like the Gestalt drawing that pictures either a lamp or two profiles, depending on one's viewpoint, so the political world shifts in appearance according to one's perspective:

> Some people would view an education devoid of any reference to a supreme being as religiously and philosophically neutral. Others, particularly those with strong religious convictions, are likely to believe that an education devoid of all references to God or an order of being higher than man constitutes a religion of secularism imposed on their children. Given the deep diversity of values and faiths existing in the U.S., there is no way that a single, monolithic value-free ethic can be taught without violating the rights of parents to the free exercise of religion.[20]

Thus, social conservatives claim that what liberals view as the separation of church and state —through taking prayers out of public schools, for example —they view as the domination of the religion of Secular Humanism. What liberals interpret as the protection of freedom of religious expression, social conservatives see as the prohibition of their religious values, which, they claim, represent those of the majority of Americans and of the Founding Fathers. While worship of God has been removed from the schools, sex education and other Secular Humanist instruction have been inserted into public education. In short, public funding of education is far from "morally neutral." "Moral neutrality" does not represent tolerance and acceptance of all religions; rather, it marks the triumph of Secular Humanism over traditional religious beliefs.

To social conservatives, then, the plea for liberal tolerance is hypocritical in that it disguises a real intolerance for the acceptance of any overt expression of traditional religious values. Phyllis Schlafly speaks to this perceived hypocrisy:

> When the issue is classroom obscenity, profanity, immorality, evolution, secular humanism or feminism, the liberals are ostentatious and self-righteous in waving the First Amendment to justify "anything goes" in the schools. The liberals tell the churchgoing pupils and their parents, "Too bad for your religious values; you will be forced to read the books and listen to the teachers." . . .
>
> The liberals insist that the First Amendment requires the good child to shut up and endure his embarrassment while classroom discussions include profane, blasphemous or obscene books; attacks on moral standards and on the child's belief that God created the world; and descriptive classroom discussions of fornication, homosexuality, contraceptives, and abortions as though they were normal and acceptable practices. It's time that we expose the double standard of the liberals who promote such anti-religious classroom authoritarianism, but who want to censor with a vengeance any child who dares to speak the name of God in prayer.[21]

It is only by comprehending this Gestalt shift that the social conservative perception of less government intervention can be understood. While a common charge against social conservatives is that they in fact demand *increased* government involvement in the moral realm, social conservatives adamantly reject this assessment. In their eyes, they seek to *remove* the government from the private sphere. The activists interviewed vigorously responded to this charge. A

Reagan administrator in the Department of Education explains the issue in these terms:

> See, a lot of people feel that social conservatives are saying that we want the government in the bedroom monitoring activities. I don't think that's true. I think what they're saying is the government *is* in the bedroom, the government is telling our fourteen-year-old daughters that they can use birth control and paying for the devices as well as the doctors et cetera. They're saying, "We don't want that. We want parental control. We don't want the federal government coming in and telling us what's good for us or what's good for our children!" I think it's just a question of who's writing the story, how it's portrayed in the press.

She continues by explaining her position on homosexuality:

> I believe that what anyone wants to do in the privacy of their own bedroom or their own home is completely up to them. . . . If you have somebody who is openly say an adulterer, a married woman who is *openly* having an affair with either a married man or a single man. . . . And this person goes out and says, "This is an alternate lifestyle. This is what I believe in and I'm going to advocate this." I think very few people would argue that this woman would be an appropriate person to be teaching elementary or junior high school students. Especially if she were in the classroom openly saying: "I advocate adultery."
>
> To me homosexuality is that equivalent. I don't believe homosexuality is an alternate lifestyle. I wouldn't want it being presented to my children, to my neighbor's children or my brother's children, as an alternate lifestyle. If a man or a woman were a homosexual and they kept that in the privacy of their own bedroom, fine, let them go ahead and do whatever they want. But if they're going to *advocate* that, as something which is good for my kids or somebody else's—I mean I don't have any kids but if I *were* to—then I think I have the right to say "I don't want them teach-

ing my kids." Or "I don't want them living in my two-family house."

In a similar fashion, a national organizer for the Eagle Forum asserts:

I don't know who wants more government legislation in moral matters. I know Planned Parenthood probably does. . . . They're teaching a moral view that's very offensive, and we resent that, that the government's paying for it. *We* recognize that this country's built on the Judeo-Christian ethic . . . and our attitude would be "Uphold the laws of the country." And don't fund these other things. What people do in private, you can't preach that in most cases. But certainly you don't promote it in public.

A third activist, a national Republican organizer, also rejects the charge that social conservatives are calling for more government regulation. She insists that social conservatives are committed to limited government, illustrating with the issue of pornography:

On the pornography I think this: realistically there's no way to stop it but should the government be encouraging and should the government be assisting in various ways to give it a certain low mailing rate and so on? No, I don't think so. Now there's a consensus that you and I can send private mail to each other but there isn't a consensus that I'm allowed to go out and try to undermine the morals of a large number of people. Now I may do that anyway. And if I do it by speech there's no way that you can get at me. If I am using government facilities to do it, then again I am enlisting the assistance of the taxpayer and so again we are saying "Get the government off our backs."
There's a privacy issue involved. If you want to make love and you're not married, that's *your* business, God's business, and if you want to do that in the privacy of your house it's certainly none of *my* business. But if you're going to take pictures of this and put it out on the public street where my little boy can see it, I'm going

to get you because you're invading my privacy. I have a right not to watch you do that. So it's interference again.

A fourth activist, a national pro-family leader, sums up the debate:

The social issues are very much concerned with reducing government and permitting people to have control over their own lives. That is why, let us say, in the school prayer that there is concern that the government has interfered with people's personal action, and is restricting people from what they want to do. And therefore, it seems to me, it's a case of . . . move government back out of the personal realm and let the people do what they want to do.

As can be seen, rather than calling for *more* government intervention, social conservatives see themselves as calling for the *removal* of federal intrusion in the moral realm. In their eyes, the government already is involved in such issues—by funding the dispersal of birth control to minors, by restricting prayer in public schools, by assisting pornographers and endorsing "alternative" lifestyles. All four women voice objection to such actions as offensive to those who believe in traditional values. All of them call for the transfer of decision-making on such issues from the federal to the local level. Finally, they raise the issue of the boundaries between the public and private spheres. In their view, what is done in the private realm is determined entirely by the individual. But once one enters the public arena, the moral consensus must be upheld; individuals must not violate such standards in public. Thus, the government has no right to endorse or use public monies to support activities that offend this "public morality," that is, traditional values.

From such a standpoint social conservative activism is not offensive action that aims to intervene in the private sphere, but rather defensive action in response to humanist/liberal intrusion on such moral issues. As Onalee McGraw puts it: "These [social] issues became political because liberal ideologues insisted on using the mechanisms of the state to impose their own values and policy goals on

American society without regard to the deliberate consensus of the American people." [22]

To summarize, Big Government symbolizes a threat to the social conservative world because of the government's advocacy of immorality and Secular Humanism and because government usurps the legitimate functions of traditional authority. Instead, social conservatives call for the de-funding of liberal and Secular Humanist groups, a curtailing of government intervention, and a return to local control with the reassertion of parental rights.

Ultimately, the battle against Big Government is a moral battle, a struggle between right and wrong. Big Government poses an image —a dreaded image —of a world in defiance of God's laws, a world torn up by children rebelling against parents, a world devoid of order and authority, a world in which humanist influence brings America one step closer to Communism. Only a return to religious faith, a reclaiming of traditional values, and the reassertion of parental authority can return America to the path of righteousness.

Through the Laissez-Faire Conservative Lens

Like social conservatives, laissez-faire conservatives contrast America's present government to the role of government originally intended by the Founding Fathers. The sole purpose of government, in laissez-faire conservative eyes, is to protect the rights of the individual. In Jeane Kirkpatrick's words:

> The government of the U.S. was founded squarely and explicitly on the belief that the most basic function of government is to protect the rights of its citizens. . . . These notions—that the individual has rights which are prior to government, that protection of these rights is the purpose of the very existence of government, that the just powers of government depend on the consent of the governed—are the core of the American creed. [23]

The protection of individual rights and freedom is intertwined with the preservation of social order. Whereas social conservatives equate the extreme of liberty with disorder, that is, mob rule, laissez-faire conservatives see an inextricable bond between liberty and order. The Young Americans for Freedom Statement of Principles asserts: "The purposes of government are to protect these freedoms through the preservation of internal order, the provision of national defense, and the administration of justice. . . . When government ventures beyond these rightful functions, it accumulates power which tends to diminish order and liberty."[24]

As with the classical liberals, laissez-faire conservatives fear that any extension of government beyond these functions will encroach upon the liberty of the individual and the functioning of the free market. Hence, the laissez-faire conception of the legitimate role of government is inevitably linked to belief in the *limited* role of government. Accordingly, capitalism is the one system most compatible with liberty; because free enterprise relies on securing *private* control of economic power, it necessarily limits the power of government.

Any expansion of government, therefore, interferes with the unrestricted pursuit of self-interest and with the ability of individuals to be autonomous, self-determining actors. In simplified terms, an increase of government is equated with a decrease of individual initiative and freedom. As one activist puts it, "The more the federal government makes decisions, the more that takes away from individual responsibility."

Because government and liberty are conceptualized in these zero-sum terms, laissez-faire conservatives harbor a deep distrust of government. External authority is suspect because it conflicts with individual autonomy and decision-making. Whether that authority takes the form of a priest, king, dictator, or bureaucracy, voluntaristic action is impeded when individuals are controlled by those outside themselves. Further, because government has a legal monopoly on the use of force, governmental power must be kept within strict limits. The Founding Fathers established the Constitution in recognition of this need to curtail federal power.

But America has departed from this heritage of limited government, moving away from the functions originally intended by the Founding Fathers. In one account, government involvement in the building of railroads in the nineteenth century instigated increasing regulations and creeping government encroachment.[25] Others point to Franklin D. Roosevelt's New Deal as a turning point in American government: "Since 1933, the federal bureaucracy has increasingly resembled a well-meaning but overprotective parent smothering her children under a blanket of welfare and regulation. Over the last 50 years, taxes have increased, government has swelled and the national debt has become an eleven-figure monstrosity."[26]

No matter when the exact turning point occurred, the image is clear: government has expanded dangerously beyond the limited role set forth in the Constitution. Instead, government has become a vast bureaucracy, a modern leviathan.

The equation of Big Government with bureaucracy pervades laissez-faire conservative ideology. Labelling bureaucracy "the fourth branch of government," laissez-faire conservatives point to the soaring rise in government spending, the increasing number of federal regulations, the growth of federal agencies, and the expansion of congressional staffs as signs of the government stretching its tentacles, ever extending into new areas.

Like the sorcerer's apprentice who, innocently seeking to ease his labor, discovers that the magic he has set in motion has instead turned into a nightmare, bureaucracy, in this image, conjures up a surge of government expansion, once set in motion, soon out of control. Government programs relentlessly grind forward, automatically escalating in cost and size year after year.

In rejecting the leviathan of government bureaucracy, laissez-faire conservatives heap particular scorn on those who oil the machinery of the bureaucracy, that is, the bureaucrats. Bureaucrats are considered to be self-serving parasites, living off the taxpayer's money. Antagonism toward government employees also rests on the belief that their authority is furthered at the expense of the American citizen. Aversion to this centralization of authority is voiced by a libertarian activist who says, "What we'd like is a country where everyone makes their own decisions. You'd have people deciding how they want to live. Now you have a bureaucracy taking over." With the growth of government, decision-making is transferred from elected representatives to unelected bureaucrats. Increasingly, nameless, faceless employees, rather than the American people, are determining the course of the nation.

Besides its propensity to dangerously expand and usurp individual authority, Big Government threatens freedom by interfering with economic and political liberty. In these two ways Big Government symbolizes a threat to the very foundations of the laissez-faire conservative view of the world.

Big Government as Attacking Economic Liberty

The growth of the federal bureaucracy represents an interference with economic liberty by disrupting laissez faire, that is, the rational pursuit of self-interest in the marketplace: "As Adam Smith's greatest work saw light in 1776, so his greatest fear is perilously close to realization today; that government would so grow in size, cost, and influence so as to stifle capitalism."[27]

One way Big Government stifles capitalism is through direct government intervention in the marketplace. For example, by bailing out large corporations in need of assistance, government acts to protect *particular* actors in the marketplace, thereby upsetting the workings of the Invisible Hand:

> The free market does not mean attaching big business to a government teat. It means letting the market—that is, people's voluntary choices—determine the direction of the economy, without help or hindrance from the government. It means corporations survive only if people voluntarily support them with purchases.[28]

Government-granted protection of particular sectors of the economy is illegitimate use of governmental power that disrupts the voluntaristic dynamic of the marketplace.

Government regulations not only create impediments to free trade but also stifle innovation, the vital spark to the entrepreneurial process. A local tax reform activist discusses the necessity for innovation:

I believe there's nothing wrong with using one's brains to get ahead. That's what this country is about. A person can look around and say, "Hey, I want that. I'd like to make more money. How can I do that?" They can realize: "I can go work for that person and make money." Then they can work and save and decide: "I want to be the boss." That's what this country was built on. Thomas Edison, for example. He was mad at the gas company because of a bill and he wanted to try to find another way so he could save. So look at what he invented—not just electricity, but the record industry! Think about all the money that brings in and all the people that employs. He did all kinds of things.

People should be able to use their talents and abilities without being hampered, to be able to rise to the best of their abilities. That's what this country is built on; that is freedom. I'm not talking about the robber barons. I don't think you have to step on someone to get ahead. Sure, there are always people who will step on others. But just because a man wants to make money or start a business doesn't mean he's bad. Today Thomas Edison would probably have restrictions or regulations holding him back.

In this view, government regulations restrict the economic liberty of laissez faire, which allows individuals to rise to their talents, to invent, and thereby to add to the wealth of the nation. This takes away from individual autonomy. As Jeane Kirkpatrick puts it, "Wherever government regulates, it supplants the judgment and preferences of private individuals with its own judgment, backed by its unique authority and coercive power."[29]

Besides hampering innovation, Big Government also interferes in the marketplace by inhibiting individual initiative, particularly through the welfare system and the tax system. One libertarian activist describes the importance of individual initiative:

I've done many things—I've waitressed, I've done all kinds of jobs. I was a go-go dancer in California. I've lived in a flophouse on the South End. When you have to get by, you learn how to survive. There is something to be said for learning how to start out on the bottom and work yourself up, to save a little. To know that you can do something to improve your situation, that your individual initiative works.

Affirmative action destroys that. And the minimum wage. The minimum wage is very destructive because it eliminates all the low-paid jobs. But those low-paid jobs are the way to start out. My grandmother came here and worked for eight months as an indentured servant to pay off her way over. She cleaned and housekept for a family to pay for her ticket. People in low-paid jobs can learn the work ethic and how to make a little and save and immigrants can learn the language, too.

Besides inhibiting initiative by placing obstacles in the individual's path to self-improvement, government also acts to stifle the pursuit of self-interest by giving away too many goods and services for free, thereby reducing the individual's will to work. Hence, a great deal of protest focusses on Big Government's welfare programs. As one local activist explains:

This generation has no pride. The Depression started it all. FDR didn't help end the Depression. He didn't have a plan. He just did whatever idea looked like it would work. It was the war that ended the Depression. But then people began expecting handouts. Now instead of relying on their own abilities and opportunity, people today expect the government to help them out. People used to hate charity when I grew up. They'd be embarrassed to take handouts; they'd take pride in being self-sufficient. To take responsibility for oneself and to have opportunity without restrictions—that's what this country is about.

Another woman, the libertarian activist involved in public education reform, reiterates this view of government as extinguishing initiative:

Look at those countries with a big public sector. Britain, for example. When I was a stewardess I became friends with some

British stewardesses. I would go visit their families. Ninety percent of British wages go to taxes! And you know what happened at that time? They had articles written about the brain drain. People with talent, the brightest ones, were leaving the country. Because whenever you give people something free, you kill individual initiative. Take Sweden. Why do you think Sweden has the highest suicide rates among young people? Because they provide *everything*—there's nothing left to do, life is meaningless. When people are given all these things they come to expect it. You're robbing people of their individual initiative. This country began on *voluntarism.* That's how everything was built.

Laissez-faire conservative opposition to welfare, then, is not based on belief that welfare is immoral or encourages illegitimacy. Dependence on government is not opposed because it denies the ultimate authority of God. Rather, welfare represents the replacement of self-reliance, the robbing of initiative. Under welfare systems, free will dwindles and life is meaningless.

This vision of welfare recalls the image of bureaucracy: once set in motion, soon beyond our control. Laissez-faire conservatives express fear that once welfare programs are in place, expectations and demands for such programs will result in an ever-escalating need:

> Spreading as weeds in a vacant lot, these programs have increased budget deficits and choked incentive. . . . We are a society as addicted to support as we are to alcohol and cigarettes. There has always been the struggle between the satisfaction of standing on your own and the comfort of relying on others. Those choosing the latter path diminish both the society and themselves. Unless the welfare state is destroyed, those unnecessarily receiving the crutch of government aid will never walk alone.[30]

Opposition to welfare is closely connected to opposition to high taxes: both are perceived as killing initiative. The tax system punishes savings and investment and thereby is a disincentive to output and production. Again, government interferes with market forces, crush-

ing the incentive to work harder, to produce. The libertarian involved in public education reform discusses the destructive results of
high taxes:

> The large middle class has suffered. All these people ten or twenty
> years ago believed they could work hard and save so they could
> move into a nice home. There's nothing wrong with wanting a
> nice home, a nice car, a nice vacation to take with your family.
> But now what's happened? Those same people find today that
> their paycheck is eaten up by taxes, there's nothing left. *That's*
> why over 60 percent of the electorate in Massachusetts voted for
> [Proposition] 2½!* People are tired of having their paycheck taken
> from them. . . . You know, the government is only you and me.
> When we pay to the government, that's just taking something out
> of our own pocketbook. . . . So we should have control of where
> our taxpayer's dollars go to.

In short, while both social and laissez-faire conservatives oppose
the tax and welfare systems, they do so for fundamentally different
reasons. Social conservatives view these systems as immoral, as encouraging alternative lifestyles that conflict with traditional religious
values. Laissez-faire conservatives, on the other hand, oppose these
same systems for strangling individual initiative, thereby depriving
the entire nation of greater wealth.

But laissez-faire conservatives oppose these systems for another
reason as well. The combination of high taxes and increased welfare programs fundamentally redefines the role of government. The
government is now a welfare state, acting to redistribute wealth. One
local activist explains her opposition to this new role of government:

> Liberals originally were for protecting the individual against gov-
> ernment intervention. Now there's a difference between a social
> and a political liberal. A social liberal is interested in equalizing

---

*In 1980 Massachusetts voters passed Proposition 2½, which slashed commercial and resi-
dential property taxes.

everyone, in trying to fit everyone into the same mold. So the government is used to even things out. Welfare, for instance. Why should I have money taken from me to pay for someone who doesn't need it? In the work I do, I see people who really need welfare. For those, I believe they should get it. These are people who aren't retarded or handicapped, but they just don't have it upstairs. They can't survive. I think those people deserve welfare. But then there are a lot of people, well I should say a few people, who make welfare a game, who decide they can get the best deal by beating the welfare system. Those people shouldn't get welfare.

It is this function of government as "used to even things out," that is, to redistribute wealth, that laissez-faire conservatives oppose so vehemently. Taxation of the productive American citizen combined with the plethora of welfare programs offered to the non-working, non-productive citizen, not only kills individual initiative in both but also moves government dangerously beyond the limited role intended by the Founding Fathers:

When government interferes with the work of the market economy it tends to reduce the moral and physical strength of the nation. . . . When it takes from one man to bestow on another, it diminishes the incentive of the first, the integrity of the second, and the moral autonomy of both.[31]

This compulsory transfer of wealth places human liberty in jeopardy. Such programs promote equality at the expense of freedom.

In opposing government as the redistributor of wealth, laissez-faire conservatives call for solutions that will return the state to its proper limited function and will at the same time encourage self-reliance and individual initiative. Some call for the implementation of workfare programs. One woman, active in college conservative organizations, explains her support for workfare:

A friend of a friend of mine has a child and was on welfare. They wanted to pay for her to put her child in daycare and then pay her transportation and schooling so she could be sent to key-punch school, so she could learn a skill and find a job. But she didn't want to. So she refused. Now she's a cashier part-time. I was really irritated with her and so were her friends. Here she could have learned a skill and she didn't. I resent that. Someone that's disabled should be able to collect welfare, but others should work for it. . . .

I think workfare is a good idea. For example, they started a program where they wouldn't let people accept welfare unless they worked part time. They gave them jobs cleaning chairs in the school cafeteria or other kinds of things—jobs nobody else would do. And a lot of people didn't like those jobs so that gave them an incentive to look for something else; a lot of them got off welfare.

In her eyes, workfare teaches skills or at least provokes individuals to find alternative work to menial labor.

Others call for a transfer of welfare functions from public to private hands, returning the responsibility of aid to the needy to the charities and churches. As one libertarian activist explains:

People have always helped others. History proves it. If you look at history, you'll see that there have always been others to help out. In your temple, if some poor, starving family came to you, would you help them out? People will care for others. I'd much rather leave it up to individuals than to think the government will do something. Now as it is 70 percent of my paycheck is taken out for government. If I got that part back I'd put most of it—I wouldn't be honest if I said all of it—I like taking vacations and such, too —but I'd put a lot of it into charitable organizations. If the government stopped taking so much out of what people rightfully earn, people would have more to put into charities.

The call to make welfare a private function rests on the belief that people have a right to spend their earnings as they wish and trust

that individuals will voluntarily and sufficiently care for the disad-
vantaged.

Finally, there is a call for a return to the principles of laissez faire.
Capitalism itself is the answer to America's problems:

> The American way is that people work, they save a little money,
> that money adds up, the compound interest takes hold, by the
> time they retire they have a little nest egg and that nest egg sup-
> plies their needs in retirement. What is that nest egg? That nest
> egg is their work that's been magically transformed by capitalism
> into capital. . . . Free enterprise is all about the fact that the mar-
> ket and people make decisions that take care of their welfare. The
> government can't do it. And when they try to do it, they screw it
> up. . . . Let the [people] see the miracle of capitalism working for
> them. That's the way out of the poverty tract.[32]

Ultimately, then, laissez-faire conservatives place their hope in the
Invisible Hand of the free market to provide guidance to those problems now in the hands of Big Government. It is not religious faith
but rather, faith in the market that will answer America's problems.

Big Government as Attacking Political Liberty

Big Government is also a foe of freedom because it intrudes on the
individual's political liberty. The most common charge is that Big
Government illegitimately interferes in the individual's private life.
The libertarians are the most outspoken critics of Big Government
as "morals police":

> Big Government is bad for business, but it's also bad for our
> private lives. "Morality" cannot be imposed by force; it must be
> freely chosen to have any meaning at all. That government which
> is big enough to regulate our sex lives is big enough to regulate
> every other aspect of our lives as well.[33]

The activists interviewed also voice concern about Big Government's meddling in the personal arena. For example, the libertarian

active in public education reform explains why she opposes sex education in the public schools:

> While individually you or I might believe in educating our children about sex, a lot of people believe that is not the role of the schools. I personally think it's good to give children straightforward information on where they came from, on birth control, although I think I can do that myself. But there are other people who don't want their children to know at a certain age or want to do it themselves. Or like me — what if the teacher teaching sex education was particularly uptight or had a particular attitude towards sex? It's too private an issue for them to handle it. Also, if teachers take over that role soon people will give up responsibility. In a few years they might say: "Oh, well, I don't have to educate my children any more because the schools are doing that." But we are then giving up some individual responsibility.

Interestingly, while this activist would agree with social conservative opposition to sex education, she does so for contrary reasons, that is, because it may be taught in a repressive manner; also, her opposition is posed in terms of maintaining individual responsibility, not in terms of preserving the integrity of the family. Her differences from social conservatives are even more pronounced, however, when she discusses the position she supports as a member of the Libertarian Party:

> We're pro-abortion and believe homosexuality is a private matter which the government should not legislate. You know, anti-abortionists say we're pro-abortion, but we're not pro-abortion; we're pro-choice. It should be a woman's right to decide about her own body. We're pro-life.

It is not only libertarians, however, who delineate themselves as distinct from social conservatives. Other laissez-faire conservative activists also made clear these differences. For example, one activist, involved at the national level of the Republican Party, asserts:

I'm not a New Right social conservative. There *is* a difference between social and economic conservatives. I am personally against abortion, but I don't want a constitutional amendment banning abortions. I'm against school prayer. There's enough religion already in the schools. I'm an Orthodox Jew, and I personally find it offensive to read the King James Bible. I remember when I grew up my mother had to come to school and complain about them having me read Christian books. . . . I'm conservative on economic and defense issues.

Another activist, a local leader of the Massachusetts tax reform movement, also declared that she strictly defines herself as separate from social conservatives. While all conservatives may agree on the need for people to have more control over their incomes, she explains, the social conservatives "want to tell people how they can or cannot consume their incomes," for example, by controlling access to *Playboy* or other books and movies people may wish to see.

It is evident, then, that while social conservatives believe they are merely removing government from the private realm, laissez-faire conservatives perceive social conservatives as demanding increased government involvement in private matters. Against this, laissez-faire conservatives oppose Big Government intrusion into the moral realm, whether it be in terms of abortion, school prayer, or pornography. In their adherence to maximum free choice for individuals and protection of civil liberties, laissez-faire conservatives consider such government interference illegitimate and dangerous. Herein rests a potential conflict between the two world views. Where social conservatives look toward the state to restore traditional values, laissez-faire conservatives view any expansion of the state beyond its limited functions as an impingement on individual freedom.

Thus, for laissez-faire conservatives government expansion into *both* the public/economic realm and into the private/moral realm symbolizes a threat to the survival of liberty. Government should be returned to its limited size, with control focussed on a local level, and with government acting to enhance self-reliance, not to provide handouts or become Big Brother. Again, while all laissez-faire conservatives adhere to a view of limited government, there is disagreement about the exact boundaries of where government ends and tyranny begins. As one laissez-faire conservative activist states, in distinguishing herself from libertarians, "I don't believe in no government—that leads to chaos. Less government but not *no* government."

Yet, while it is important to recognize the divisions within the laissez-faire conservative perspective, it is equally as important to realize what unites those falling within this general world view. While laissez-faire conservatives may debate where the exact boundaries of legitimate government are drawn, none would object to the assertion made by Texas Representative Jim Collins: "The number-one problem in the United States is that we have far too much government."[34]

What is clear, above all, is that deeply intertwined with this rejection of Big Government is the desire to protect individual liberty. In a rousing speech at the Conservative Political Action Conference, former Secretary of the Interior James Watt declares:

> There's one heavy hand of oppression. It's called government. You can call it dictators, kings, warlords, or the Gestapo or whatever but it's excessive government that can snuff out political liberty. . . . The struggle is over political liberty and spiritual freedom. . . . The battle is for the form of government under which we will live.[35]

In opposition to this foe of freedom, this symbol of America's declining strength, laissez-faire conservatives call their fellow citizens to action, to join in the battle against Big Government and in defense of liberty:

> It isn't business vs. labor; it's freedom versus government power and oppression. . . . The current interventionist role of government is not being challenged in a fundamental way. . . . There is

so little respect, understanding and concern about life and liberty as our Founding Fathers understood it in Washington that it's hard to conclude anything other than that freedom is on the wane. . . . Growing numbers of Americans understand and desire freedom, and dedicated effort can make a difference. The measure of freedom that remains is still sufficient for us to turn the tide against the ever-growing oppressive government.[36]

Only an uncompromising dedication to individualism, the free market, and limited government will return America to her role as leader of the Free World.

Conclusion

Big Government evokes strong feelings among activists of the New Right. While both constituencies oppose the extension of federal authority over their lives, laissez-faire conservatives seek to return authority to the hands of the individual, believing each person should be the sole determinant of his or her own life. Social conservatives, on the other hand, view the total autonomy of individuals as narcissistic and amoral, the triumph of Secular Humanism. Instead, they seek to return the country to the authority of God, the Church, and parents. Further, social conservatives fear dependence on government because it represents the displacement of reliance on God with trust in Man, the Fallen. For laissez-faire conservatives, however, dependence on Big Government represents a substitute for individual initiative and reliance on self.

While social conservative and laissez-faire conservative women both claim to be motivated to political involvement by their opposition to Big Government, the fundamental meaning of this activism is distinct within the context of each world view. For example, one social conservative woman discusses how government interference was the impetus to her activism. Describing busing as her "baptism" into conservatism, she explains the motivation for her involvement:

I had been a schoolteacher. And then I quit to raise my family. Then during all the busing time — about 1973 — I began to get involved. My husband and I both saw what was happening in Massachusetts with the forced busing. You know, we're not against integration; I live in an integrated neighborhood in Dorchester. We're against the federal government forcing parents — telling them how to raise our children. We saw that our daughters would soon be affected by this. Now I see it as stopping government intervention in our lives. So we both felt we should get involved, to do something about this. . . .

You know, I was brought up like everyone else — "mother and apple pie." It took awhile for me to see things [as a conservative]. We see ourselves as pro-God, family, and the country. The issue that I see that connects these different causes is government intervention. The government should not have responsibility over our lives. I'm against the draft, too. . . . The government shouldn't interfere in young men's lives. If an earthquake happens, that's God's will. That we can't control. But the government has no right to tell someone what to do with their life.

The boundaries between governmental authority and the authority of parents and God is clearly of key concern.

In contrast, listen to the words of a libertarian activist who also names government interference as an important spark to her activism. She recounts a particular incident that had a radicalizing effect:

I remember one key event which had an impact on me. I was nineteen and dating a big black fellow from the Bronx. He designed missiles for the Vietnam War. No one thought anything of it then. It wasn't an issue. You have to remember, those were the Kennedy years. But there were some Southerners who couldn't understand what a cute blond thing was doing with a black man. They figured something was up. All we were really doing was sleeping together, the normal thing. One day two young guys came to see me to question me and they'd say things and I'd say, "How'd you know about that?" They told me: "We tapped your phone." Just like that! My jaw dropped down to the floor. That really hit me. Here I was only nineteen and realizing the government was invading my privacy.

Clearly, both the lifestyle of this laissez-faire conservative activist and her perception of what constitutes government interference are at odds with the social conservative view, rooted in religious belief, which argues that there is no such thing as moral neutrality regarding governmental action.

CHAPTER FIVE

Feminism

For social conservatives, another significant force of moral decay is Feminism. Along with Communism, Secular Humanism, and Big Government, Feminism symbolizes a threat to religion and to the family. Within the laissez-faire conservative world view, however, Feminism is not a potent foe of freedom eliciting strong emotional response. Laissez-faire conservative women actually share part of the feminist vision.

Through the Social Conservative Lens

In many ways the 1960s captured the social conservative vision of a society in decay, in chaos. The civil rights and anti-war movements, SDS and the Weathermen, the Yippies, hippies, and flower children, all symbolize the turbulence and social conflict that ripped apart the American dream during those tumultuous years. Signs of moral decay pervaded the 1960s — captured in the images of the blue-jeaned, beaded and bearded, long-haired youth, Timothy Leary and the LSD cult, Woodstock and communes, skinny-dipping and braless women, head shops and rock concerts, and ultimately captured in the image of a burning American flag. Further, the uprooting of traditional forms of authority also indicated "the rotting of America," as evidenced in the generation gap and the slogan "Don't trust anyone over thirty," or by the embrace of Eastern religion, yoga, Hare Krishna, and even occultism, and perhaps most radically designated by buttons declaring "God is dead" or "Question Authority." Such images capture the spirit of the times and also reveal the reason behind social conservative dismay provoked by such an era.[1] For these new images of the 1960s desecrated the sacred symbols of the social conservative world.

Yet there are two specific associations linked with the 1960s, and to Feminism as well, two signs that further imply moral decay. First, the 1960s is seen as the era that initiated an attack on the American family. While the Pill and the sexual revolution ate away at the traditional moral norms governing the family unit, the New Left—and later Feminism—launched an ideological attack on the family. Looking back on this era, one conservative critic notes: "The New Left revived the Marxist critique of the bourgeois family, viewing it as predicated on property relations, male supremacy, and the boredom of domestic bliss." By espousing "free love," the collectivization of childcare, and the elimination of the concept of illegitimacy, the New Left promoted the collapse of the nuclear family norm so that " 'Father Knows Best', 'Leave It to Beaver', and 'I Love Lucy' gave way to 'One Day at a Time', 'Three's Company', and 'Miss Winslow and Son.' "[2]

In addition to this ideological attack on the family, erosion of family life was augmented during the 1960s by the increased number of wives and mothers entering the labor force. Pat Robertson, speaking at the Family Forum conference, explains the consequences of such a trend:

> From the mid-sixties on it was necessary for women to enter the work force, not because they necessarily wanted to, but because they were forced to [due to deficit spending because of welfare programs]. . . . What did this do to the family? Twenty-five million children under school age are being dumped into daycare centers. . . . There's a lot of heady freedom to a fourteen- or fifteen-year-old who comes home who knows that his Dad won't be home 'till later and his mother won't be home so he's got his girlfriend with him and why not? I mean after all—a little grass here, a little sex there. Six hundred thousand teenage pregnancies

last year—what's happening? Well, the mothers aren't home. . . .
Divorces mean children are losing their role models; they're not
identifying with the proper spouse of the proper sex. You have a
rise in homosexuality. You have a rise in teenage delinquencies.
You've got a rise in rebellion in schools.[3]

In short, the 1960s ushered in not only an attack on the American
family by the New Left but also an internal erosion of the moral
bases supporting family life, particularly with the rising divorce rate
and increased number of working mothers.

The second corroding effect of the 1960s was a new emphasis on
self, the ushering in of the Me Decade of the 1970s. Social conservatives attribute this elevation of the self to the predominant ethic of
the 1960s, "Do your own thing." In addition, the 1960s brought with
it a new emphasis on rights, as every conceivable group grabbed for
its share of the pie in the name of "minority rights." This, too,
culminated in a heightening of self-interest. Finally, the popularity
of psychology during the 1960s, with stress on self-exploration, "I'm
Okay, You're Okay," and the multitude of new therapies also added
fuel to the fire of "Me-Firstism." The net result of these develop-
ments was the breeding of a culture of narcissism:

> The 1970s were characterized by an obsession with consciousness
> expansion, self-awareness, and a type of narcissism. The supposed
> new narcissism of the seventies expounded the ideas that within
> each individual there is a glorious talented personality, that each
> individual is possessed with an inner dignity that he alone can
> bring out in himself; each individual must think only of himself
> and do exactly what he or she feels like doing.[4]

In short, the 1960s fostered conditions favorable to the advance of
situation ethics and humanistic values. Increased materialism accompanied this obsession with self, as Americans sought immediate
gratification and instant credit to satisfy their appetite for consumption. Everyone sought something for nothing, as a plethora of books
advertising how to attain "The Joy of Sex" without guilt or how

to lose weight without dieting hit the bestsellers list.[5] Such self-gratifying trends symbolized humanism's materialistic appeal, tempting people away from the purity of spiritual belief and religious devotion.

Like the 1960s, Feminism also represents moral decay. Like the 1960s, Feminism is also perceived as a force attacking the American family. And, like the 1960s, Feminism, too, is associated with the new narcissism, the Me Decade. In addition, Feminism also symbolizes a threat because it represents an attack on the status of the homemaker and the extension of Big Government.

Feminism as Anti-Family

From the early days of the women's movement, Feminism was perceived as a force actively working against the family. Social conservatives charge feminists with renouncing the family as a source of repression and enslavement, a tool used by men to entrap and oppress women.[6] As one local pro-family activist puts it:

> The libbers want to abolish the family. That's what Gloria Frie —I mean Steinem says. "Women will not be liberated until marriage is eliminated." Have you seen the "Declaration on Feminism"? They state quite clearly there that they want to eliminate the family. That's why, when I hear people say they support ERA, I say to them, "Do you know what that means? Do you know what they want to do?" . . . The feminists want to abolish the family. But the family is the basis of everything. It is the foundation of our society; if that crumbles, everything else goes.

The national conference for International Women's Year (IWY) held in Houston in 1977 concretized the perception of Feminism as an anti-family force. Sponsored by the United Nations, the conference brought together women from all over the country to consider "women's issues." Social conservatives were shocked by the delegates' overwhelming support for such things as ERA, gay rights, federal funding of abortion, government-sponsored childcare, and contraception for minors without parental consent, all advocated in the name of "women's rights." Angry that the taxpayer's dollar was being used to fund a convention of feminists, the meeting in fact provoked activism by many women previously uninvolved in the political arena. One woman interviewed, now a Reagan administrator and national pro-family leader, explains her initial involvement in this way:

> There was the International Women's Year meeting back in '76 or '77 and Jean Stapleton was on television and said here was this grassroots meeting for women to go and talk about their concerns. So I went. I mean I had voted in elections but that was it. So I went down to the IWY meeting and heard all sorts of talk about this issue and that issue and the other issue I didn't know anything about. I guess then the fate of the ERA was fast and furious and "ERA—what's that?" I just didn't know anything. And I noticed that these people were very upset—I shouldn't say upset, but concerned. There was a whole slew of issues that people were just really—I hate to use the word "violent"—very enthusiastic about. . . . There was one group of women taking A, B, C, and D position and another group of women were taking X, Y, and Z position and I thought, "Well, now, why all this discussion, why all this controversy?" So then I started doing some studying.

IWY gave birth to a network of activists and organizations that called themselves the "pro-family movement." Rosemary Thomson, a leading figure of the movement, defines pro-family as a "person or group supporting legislation protecting traditional moral values, generally opposed to a range of issues, including ERA, abortion, gay rights, federal childcare, forced busing, etc."[7] If IWY gave birth to the pro-family movement, President Carter's 1980 White House Conference on Families (WHCF) solidified the movement, deepening the wrath of pro-family activists and drawing in further supporters. Thomson, named national Eagle Forum coordinator for the

WHCF by Phyllis Schlafly, declares: "IWY was our 'boot camp.'
Now we're ready for the offensive in the battle for our families and
our faith."[8] Another activist, also a pro-family leader, explains:

> The excesses of the feminist movement activated a lot of people
> who otherwise wouldn't have noticed that anything was going
> on—the IWY, et cetera. The White House Conference on
> Families activated a whole other group of people who had not
> been radicalized by IWY. . . . *Most* of the pro-family troops at the
> White House conference were new. That's fascinating because
> that got a whole new different segment of the population; those
> people are remaining active.

Social conservative critics charged that the conference was a
sham, employing biased processes of delegate selection to stack the
conference with "women's libbers" who sought to promote their
own agenda. But clearly the chief criticism raised by critics of the
conference centered on the definition of the family. The Reagan
administrator initially drawn in through IWY explains what took
place at the White House conference:

> There were two diametrically opposed definitions working at
> the family conference at the White House. One of them was the
> traditional family, that is, the family related by blood, marriage,
> or adoption. The other definition of the family is what I call the
> "groupie" or "roofers" definition of the family, those people that
> think that the family is anyone living under the same roof that
> provides support for each other *regardless* of blood, marriage, or
> adoption. These are two fundamentally different views that are in
> conflict. They're irreconciliable because the roofers, the groupie
> definition denies the existence of the traditional family. They
> don't recognize—they say *irregardless* of blood, marriage, and
> adoption. . . .
> When I was a delegate in Virginia I found out that's the defini-
> tion they were using. I found out that was the definition being put
> out by the American Home Economics Association. It's also the

definition that NOW uses and a lot of the gay community uses. I
hit the roof. . . . We've had this definition of the family for two
thousand years. I don't know of any existing society that works on
the other definition of the family. You need to have the biological
connection.

A local pro-family activist expresses a similar reaction to the
WHCF:

I went to the Conference on the Family in Washington. They
couldn't even come up with a definition of the family. So it was
changed to Conference on *Families*. But we should define what the
family is. And then anything that doesn't fit into that is a broken
home. The conference was biased from the start. You know, any-
time someone with a particular view, my political view, was
selected as delegates in a state, they reappoint them.

This battle over the definition of the family is a central focus of
social conservative concern. The conflict centers on what constitutes
a family, where the lines are drawn. On one side stand social conservatives, defining the family as persons related by blood, marriage,
or adoption; this, they contend, is the traditional definition of the
family. On the other side stand the feminists and humanists, who
include more diverse forms in the definition of family. In fact, Phyllis
Schlafly reports that Gloria Steinem worked for months to get the
White House Conference changed from "Family" to "Families" in
order to include alternative lifestyles.[9] Social conservatives reject
this acceptance of multiple family forms. In a debate held during the
Family Forum conference between leftist Michael Lerner and New
Right leader Paul Weyrich, Weyrich argued:

Where we disagree is in the effort to call a couple of lesbians who
are bringing up a child a family, calling a couple of roommates a
family, calling a couple of fornicators a family. These are families
. . . under your definition—garbage!! . . . It is ludicrous to call
acquaintances, neighbors, live-in types, and so on families. The

problem of not defining the family is that leads to the kind of perversion of thinking which has resulted in people trying to pass off
as legitimate families, illegitimate lifestyles.[10]

This same opposition to diverse family forms, with particular
animosity toward gay families, is echoed by Dr. Ronald Godwin,
vice-president of the Moral Majority, who objects to the placement
of "responsible, respectable kinds of families in with the homosexual
families and the lesbian families and all the perverse pollutions of the
definition." Yet Godwin also objects to what he calls the "pseudo-
historical" approach to the family:

> You'll hear many, many feminists and anti-family spokesmen
> today talking about history. . . . They'll tell you that down on the
> Fiji Islands, somewhere down on an island of Uwunga-Bunga,
> there's a tribe of people who have never ever practiced family life
> as we know it. But they also have bones in their nose and file their
> front teeth. And they eat rat meat for breakfast. They're some
> fairly strange, non-representative people. But they'll tell you
> about all the strange aberrations that have popped up in the human
> family over the centuries in various strange geographical locations.
> They'll tell you that in the nineteenth century in the backside of
> Europe such and such a thing went on. They'll deal in what is
> called pseudo-history. They'll try to build a historical case for the
> proposition that the traditional family never really was traditional
> and never really was a dominant force in all civilized societies.[11]

Once again, in upholding "traditional values," in this case regarding the definition of the family, social conservatives reject the acceptance of diverse cultural forms as equally valid and acceptable moral
standards by which to live. Instead, they assert one absolute standard
as the only legitimate code of behavior. Looking back on the White
House conference, Thomson reflects:

> The pro-family movement was, indeed, engaged in a spiritual
> battle —a struggle between those who believe in Biblical

principles and ungodly Humanism which rejects God's moral absolutes! . . .

Somehow, it was to the organizers of the White House Conference on Families as if the Lord had never spoken in history. As if He had never declared that taking an innocent life was forbidden. That parents were to train up a child. That sexual activity outside of marriage was fornication, and that homosexuality was an abomination to Him—sin, not gay.[12]

In this stark black and white world, Feminism is clearly intertwined with Secular Humanism. Both deny moral absolutes; both undermine the family. Feminism, too, is intertwined with Big Government. For it was the government-sponsored International Women's Year and White House conferences that allowed feminists and humanists to promote anti-family policies. Hence, in the battle to defend America, Feminism is a threat because, like the other forces of decay, it symbolizes an attack on the sacred unit of the social conservative world.

Feminism as the New Narcissism

Inextricably bound to the association of Feminism as anti-family is the perception of Feminism as an extension of the new narcissism, a symbol of the Me Decade. For in condemning the family, social conservatives argue, the women's liberation movement advises women to pursue their *own* individual interest above all else. Onalee McGraw explains: "The feminist movement issued an appeal that rapidly spread through our culture urging women to liberate themselves from the chains of family life and affirm their own self-fulfillment as the primary good." McGraw argues that the ultimate effect of such an appeal is the redefinition of the family unit:

> The humanist-feminist view of the family is that it is a biological, sociological unit in which the individual happens to reside; it has no meaning and purpose beyond that which each individual chooses to give it. Thus, the autonomous self, freely choosing and

acting, must satisfy its needs. When, by its very nature, the family exercises moral authority over its members, it thereby restricts the self in its pursuit of self-fulfillment and becomes an instrument of oppression and denial of individual rights.[13]

Instead of the family's being bound together by a higher moral authority, the family is reduced to a mere collection of individual interests.

Phyllis Schlafly reiterates this view of the feminist movement:

> Women's liberationists operate as Typhoid Marys carrying a germ called lost identity. They try to persuade wives that they have missed something in life because they are known by their husband's name and play second fiddle to his career. . . . As a home-wrecker, women's liberation is far in the lead over "the other man," "the other woman," or "incompatability."[14]

Schlafly illustrates the social destruction caused by women's liberation by quoting Albert Martin, who wrote a book discussing his own devastation when his wife of eighteen years walked out on him and their four sons, in search of her identity:

> An extraordinary emphasis on self is happening today across our nation, and this is why we continue to tear our marriages apart, splinter our families, and raise our divorce rates to new heights every year. The very core . . . is the enshrinement of individuality, the freedom of self, at the expense of marital union and social compromise.[15]

Thus, in social conservative eyes, when individuality and freedom of self extend to women as well as to men, marriage, the family, and society itself are threatened. The ultimate result of such a development is what Connie Marshner labels "macho feminism":

> Feminism replaced the saccharine sentimentalizations of women and home life and projected instead a new image of women: a

drab, macho feminism of hard-faced women who were bound and
determined to serve their place in the world, no matter whose
bodies they have to climb over to do it. This image provided the
plot line for such cultural weathervanes as *Kramer vs. Kramer.*
Macho feminism despises anything which seeks to interfere with
the desires of Number One. A relationship which proves burden-
some? Drop it! A husband whose needs cannot be conveniently
met? Forget him! Children who may wake up in the middle of the
night? No way! To this breed of thought, family interferes with
self-fulfillment, and given the choice between family and self, the
self is going to come out on top in their world. . . . Macho feminism has deceived women in that it convinced them that they
would be happy only if they were treated like men, and that included treating themselves like men.

Marshner concludes: "Feminists praise self-centeredness and call it
liberation."[16]

Feminism is a threat, then, because, when women pursue self-
interest, not only is the family neglected but also ultimately women
become like men. Hence, "macho feminism" is destructive because
if *everyone* pursues their own interest, no one is left to look out for
the larger good, that is, to be altruistic, to be the nurturer, the
caretaker, the mother. In short, the underlying fear expressed in this
critique of Feminism is the fear of a total masculinization of the
world.

Further, as "the most outrageous creation of the 'me-decade' "[17]
the women's movement is seen as one of the many groups ignited
by the 1960s, greedily grabbing for their rights. Feminist claims
of exploitation and oppression are perceived as illegitimate, as the
overreaction to common problems by another self-pitying group
jumping on the bandwagon of "minority rights." As part of this
"craze for equal opportunity," according to one critic, Feminism is
the "fight-for-your-right-to-do-anything-you-please-and-reject-all-
obligations philosophy."[18]

Carried to the extreme, this equation of Feminism with total self-
gratification interprets abortion as the ultimate selfish act, the place-

ment of a mother's desires above a baby's life. Ron Godwin, speaking at the Family Forum conference, portrays abortion in these terms:

> *Roe v. Wade* in 1973 gave mothers the right to rid themselves of unwanted children. Now as I speak this morning a recurring theme is going to occur . . . and that is that all of these changes that have occurred in the last few years are based on self-centeredness, on that which is convenient, on a principle of doing one's own thing, of doing that which is pleasurable and fulfulling to the individual.[19]

He predicts the next step will be infanticide, in which a small group of people will decide which child shall live and which shall die. Hence, at the extreme Feminism represents callous self-interest, women's fulfillment at the price of human life.[20]

Clearly, there is an interface between this view of Feminism and the evils embodied in Secular Humanism. Both are interpreted as emphasizing the self, as "doing one's own thing" without regard to divine laws. In Schlafly's words: "Just as humanism is based on atheism and the notion that man is at the center of the universe, Feminism puts woman at the center of the universe. They chose the word 'liberation' because they mean liberation from home, husband, family and children."[21]

Like humanism, Feminism denies biblical truth, ignoring the absolute moral authority of God: "The common denominator between hardcore feminists and humanists is rejection of God, the Father. . . . But in their final rejection of God, the most radical feminists set themselves up as a Goddess of feminist witchcraft."[22]

In fact, social conservatives recognize this interface between Feminism and humanism and perceive a conscious link between the two forces. According to Betsy Barber Bancroft, who calls women's liberation "the single greatest humanistic influence":

> Society at large has been made painfully aware of what a vocal minority of humanistically oriented women have defined as

the "rights" *demanded* by all women. . . . Present conditions demonstrate how the humanistic source of the so-called women's "rights" movement has predetermined the twisted course and the dark destination of that movement.[23]

Together, Feminism and Secular Humanism are casting a shadow over the American way of life.

Feminism as an Attack on the Status of the Homemaker

Besides Feminism as an anti-family symbol and as a symbol of the Me Decade, there is a third association linked with Feminism. In social conservative eyes, the feminist demand for women's self-fulfillment not only negates the traditional family but implicitly negates the role of the homemaker as well. By encouraging women to realize their full potential, Feminism assumes that women are not fulfilled through meeting the needs of husband and children.

Thus, Feminism represents not only a battle between a traditional and a non-traditional definition of the family but also a conflict over the very status of the homemaker. One woman interviewed, a national organizer for the Eagle Forum, explains how feminism devalues homemakers:

> The women's liberation movement really resents homemakers. There's a Chicago magazine out that gives great quotes about how they think it's an illegitimate profession being a homemaker. Now when they get a lot of media coverage saying things like that and they portray that they're working women and they scorn the homemaker . . . , that it's not intellectually satisfying . . . and you're just a glorified babysitter, et cetera, et cetera, they really caused the split to occur. They caused a resentment to grow between homemakers and working women. . . . The women who used to say, "I'm a homemaker" with pride now say, "I'm just a housewife." That's a terrible change in attitude. I don't think that's good at all.

Why it's really unfortunate is because girls getting out of college don't get the choice. They think they have to make long-range career plans. They have to go to graduate school. . . . They have to keep a job. They put their children in daycare centers. . . . To encourage a women to do that, you're going to find out too late that that isn't the best thing.

Feminism *implicitly* degrades homemakers by calling for women to seek fulfillment outside the home, which discredits those women who are fulfilled by being wives and mothers. Feminism *explicitly* belittles homemakers by labelling their work as drudgery, as mundane, as ungratifying, and as glorified babysitting. Feminism's call for women to go beyond the housewife role, to step into the male world of paid labor, denies the importance and the satisfaction derived by those content with their homemaker status. As one local pro-family activist explains:

> The feminists want all women to work. But all women don't want to work. I talk to women all the time around here who really want to stay home with their children. It's not because they're misled or not liberated. They honestly want to stay home with their children. I've seen women who have to work so torn up by having to leave their nine-month-old babies.

Or, in another pro-family activist's words:

> The women's liberation movement looks down on the housewife. She should be the most respected person as she is bringing up future generations. But women's liberation puts her down and says, "All she does is stay home all day and wash dirty diapers." ERA won't do anything for these women.

In this way, the conflict between feminists and homemakers is a tug-of-war between two lifestyles. There is not peaceful coexistence between those women following traditional ways and those women seeking new paths, new careers. Rather than the lifestyle of each being accepted and valued, social conservatives view feminists as promoting new roles for women at the expense of the old, thereby devaluing the homemaker's status:

> The women's liberation movement is forever bragging enthusiastically about the large numbers of wives who have moved into the labor force in the last several years. The feminists want to move all women into the labor force for their entire lives. The feminists see this goal as an end of "discrimination" against women. Of course, it would eliminate the career of motherhood and would require child-care to become a responsibility and probably a function of government.[24]

By denying the value of being a homemaker, feminists eliminate the element of choice involved in a woman's life. It is for this reason that social conservatives view with alarm feminist efforts to eliminate sex stereotypes in children's books—in their view, textbook censorship. As one activist, the Eagle Forum organizer, explains:

> The women's movement got together and they said you can't use words like "lady" or "homemaker" or those gender words. Homemaker is almost censored out of textbooks. They advocate showing the man in the apron and the girl reaching out to touch the snake on the sidewalk. It isn't as if both sides are portrayed. If anything we want *both* sides. We certainly don't want our side completely wiped out because in fact the majority of families today wouldn't want that. . . . I have no objection to women in career roles—that's *my* life and that's a valid choice but they're just trying to censor the homemaker role out of it and *that's* wrong. . . .
> Currently a woman can choose—she can go into a career, she has an equal pay for equal work law, she has equal opportunity laws. We think she should also be able to choose to be a full-time homemaker. It's not that we say that one is intrinsically better than the other. We say we recommend choice.

In social conservative eyes, it is not men who are to blame for degrading women, but feminists themselves are at fault for denying the worth of women's work in the home, for discrediting the house-wife role, and for disregarding the contributions women make in rearing future generations. Accordingly, Phyllis Schlafly responds to the feminist charge that women are treated as chattel by saying, "It is too bad that some women believe such falsehoods. This is the way the women's liberation movement deliberately degrades the home-maker and hacks away at her sense of self-worth and pride and pleasure in being female." [25]

Feminists also devalue women by measuring their worth purely in economic terms. For instance, social conservatives are appalled by feminist assessments of the monetary value of housework, believing such efforts reduce a relationship based on love to purely quantitative value. Similarly, Phyllis Schlafly argues that feminists are contemp-tuous of volunteer services performed by women because, "in their inverted scale of values, they judge every service by money, never by love." [26] Whereas feminists view men as taking women's volun-tarism for granted, not giving it proper value, social conservatives blame feminists for judging women's volunteer activities solely in terms of the economic rewards such work yields.

This perception of Feminism is evident in testimony Phyllis Schlafly gave to the U.S. House Social Security Subcommittee re-garding the elimination of dependent wives' benefits. Claiming that feminists complain "it isn't fair" for a dependent wife to receive as large a Social Security benefit as the working woman, Schlafly argues that feminists reduce women's work in the home purely to cash value, without recognizing the contribution homemakers make to society. She concludes:

> The feminist movement is trying to make the dependent wife obsolete. The proposal to eliminate the wife's and widow's bene-fits should be identified as what it is: a radical feminist proposal to punish the woman who chooses to be a dependent wife so she can care and nurture her own children.[27]

Feminists are viewed not only as denigrating homemakers for their lack of cash value but also as hostile toward homemakers, actively seeking to eliminate their very way of life.

In reaction, social conservatives uphold traditional values, traditional female roles, and the traditional style of life in which the homemaker is respected for the social contribution she makes. As one of the leading defenders of homemakers, Phyllis Schlafly argues that housewives make the most significant of contributions to society —by rearing moral, law-abiding, industrious citizens who form strong families of their own, the foundation for the future of the nation.

Further, Schlafly argues that the homemaker role is superior to paid labor. No amount of career success compares to the joy and satisfaction of motherhood. She advises homemakers to cherish their work for the amount of control and the rewards it allows them, more than most men are allowed at their jobs:

> If you think diapers and dishes are a never-ending, repetitive routine, just remember that most of the jobs outside the home are just as repetitious, tiresome, and boring. Consider the assembly-line worker who pulls the same lever, pushes the same button, or inspects thousands of identical bits of metal or glass or paper hour after weary hour. . . . The plain fact is that most women would rather cuddle a baby than a typewriter or factory machine.[28]

Similarly, the national organizer for the Eagle Forum states:

> It isn't evident to me that spending all day working for some big insurance company is all that rewarding, whereas working at home—I know that some people I know go to travelling seminars and they have hobbies. It seems to me that in some ways they have a more enriching day than the woman who is meeting some deadline.

In short, homemaking is an honorable career in and of itself. In defense of women's role in the home, Pat Robertson pleads:

> We've got to come back to the point of *Christian* marriage,
> *Christian* childcare, *Christian* families, and we've got to come to
> the point, ladies and gentlemen, where being a housewife is a
> noble profession and not something that's sneered at and looked
> down on by the emancipated ladies. That's very important. . . .
> Who rules our nation? Who is going to determine the next
> generation? It's not going to be the politicians and the presidents
> and the senators and the judges—it's going to be the mothers.[29]

Yet while feminists—and not men—are blamed for attacking the
status of homemakers and for degrading the traditional female role,
beneath this blame is also an underlying distrust of men.[30] This distrust is particularly evident in discussion of ERA. One reason for
opposition to ERA, for example, is that ERA will abolish the re-
quirement that a husband support his wife, thereby eliminating in
one stroke women's right to be full-time homemakers. One of the
most valuable property rights a woman now has is the right to be
provided for by her husband; ERA will eliminate this right. Whereas
now a wife has certain remedies if her husband neglects his responsibilities, such as purchasing goods on her husband's credit and letting
the store handle collection of payment, ERA will destroy such op-
tions. As one anti-ERA activist put it: "Marriage as a full equal
partnership is discrimination against women because the man is no
longer responsible for his wife. Under the Judeo-Christian tradition,
men *are* responsible. I did not get married as an equal partner."

Worst of all is the fear that men who stop loving their wives, or
who find a new woman, will be freed of all responsibility to support
their spouses. Phyllis Schlafly warns:

> Consider a wife in her 50's whose husband decides he wants to
> divorce her and trade her in on a younger model. This situation
> has become all too common, especially with no-fault divorce in
> many states. If ERA is ratified, and thereby wipes out the state
> laws that require a husband to support his wife, the cast-off wife
> will have to hunt for a job to support herself. . . . The most tragic
> effect of ERA would thus fall on the woman who has been a good

wife and homemaker for decades, and who can now be turned
out to pasture with impunity because a new, militant breed of
liberationist has come along.[31]

Similarly, Schlafly cautions that current Individual Retirement
Accounts discriminate against homemakers because they cannot be
jointly owned. Hence, the wife gets only as much retirement payment as her husband chooses to give her, "whereas he can take
the full amount and then name his girlfriend or a future wife as
beneficiary."[32]

The underlying fear beneath such claims rests on a distrust of
men, on the expectation that a man will pick up and leave his wife
and children if no legal ties restrict him. As Mrs. Billy Graham puts
it, the women's liberation movement is "turning into men's lib because we are freeing them from their responsibilities. I think we are
being taken for a ride."[33]

It is not just social conservative women who express skepticism
regarding men. George Gilder speaks forcefully about the inherent
unreliability of the male gender:

> This is essentially what sexual liberation is all about. It allows
> powerful men to leave their wives as they grow older and pursue
> single women, run off with their secretaries, and it allows single
> women open season on married men. That's the essential meaning
> of sexual liberation and the central meaning of the women's
> movement. It's a sort of alliance between powerful men who've
> already made it with single women on the make.

Interestingly, if married men are not to be trusted, even less trust-
worthy are single men. Gilder continues:

> What every society has to do is transform men into married men.
> This is the crucial function because every society has to face a
> continual invasion by barbarians. Barbarians are essentially single
> men. Single men commit 90 percent of all the violent crimes in
> America, for example. . . . Single men contribute much less to the

economy. Single men only earn a little more than half as much as married men of the same age and qualifications. In other words, you see the feminists walking around with that sixty-nine-cent button—oh, fifty-nine cents—well, single men can walk around with a fifty-eight-cent button.[34]

The underlying image of men is of creatures with uncontrollable passions and little sense of commitment or loyalty. Only moral *and legal* authority can restrain the savagery of male nature.

Thus, when feminists remove the safety valves that currently exist to protect women, they leave homemakers particularly vulnerable to men:

No fault divorce laws . . . have liberated many men from the obligation to support their wives and children. Women placed in these unfortunate circumstances are touted by the feminist movement as its most valiant "heroines." However, it is the feminist movement's strident insistence on eradication of all sex-related distinctions that has contributed so greatly to the present predicament of divorced women with children who must support the family unit alone.[35]

Besides the vulnerability of homemakers to men, one pro-family activist voiced distrust as well about the position career women face in regards to men:

All I can see is women with careers who then have to come home and clean their house, so all day Saturday or Sunday they are doing housework. All I see is women taking on men's roles, but not men helping. On one side of the feminist's mouth they call for universal daycare, and on the other they say, "Don't worry. Men will help." But I don't see men helping.

Again, while feminists view this double workday as evidence of women's oppression, social conservatives blame career women for bringing on these worsened conditions through their demands to enter the labor force.

Opposition to ERA expressed in such concerns speaks to the fear that homemakers will be left most vulnerable if legal bonds on men are lifted. With men free to "do their own thing," go their own way, with no obligations to support the family, the homemaker will be abandoned, with nothing left to hold on to.

Ironically, this same fear is voiced by feminists in recognizing that all women are just one man removed from welfare. Yet while feminists see this as the economic dependence of women, and therefore seek security through encouraging women to be independent, to be able to earn their own livelihood, social conservative women seek the same security through trying to ensure women's rights and entitlements within marriage, thereby binding men to a stable family unit. It is not, then, that social conservative women suffer from "false consciousness" in not recognizing their own self-interest as women, as some feminists charge. In fact, social conservative women are well aware of their interests as women and act in defense of these interests. The difference between social conservative women and feminists, rather, is rooted in the fundamentally different meanings each attaches to being female. Because social conservative women define femininity in terms of traditional roles of male breadwinner/ female caretaker, they seek to extend and secure female rights *within* the context of marriage and the family. In this way, social conservative women are women for themselves; they act for themselves as traditional women.

Feminism as Big Government

Besides viewing Feminism as anti-family, as narcissistic, and as attacking the status of homemakers, social conservatives see Feminism as a force of moral decay because it implies Big Government. Feminism represents the extension of Big Government at the expense of the traditional authority of the church, the neighborhood, and the family. As one critic of Feminism comments: "The real effect of this collective delusion of women's rights is only to reduce the once sovereign family to a support system for various governmental agencies."[36] Similarly, Phyllis Schlafly refers to ERA as a "blank check" by which federal politicians and judges take the authority out of local hands.[37]

Opposition to this transfer of authority is tied to fear of the levelling effect of Big Government. The fear is that once the feminist agenda is in federal hands, the essential differences between the sexes will be eliminated, replacing diversity with uniformity. The ultimate fear in equating Feminism with levelling is the fear of Communism. Senator Jeremiah Denton, speaking at the Over the Rainbow celebration, paints a vivid picture of the grim consequences of women's equality under Communism. In recalling his experiences as a prisoner of war in Vietnam, Denton tells this story of one woman, whom the prisoners called "Princess":

> She carried herself erect. She had the unmistakable stamp of innocence, of nobility even, on her face. She was a water girl like many of the others. . . . She obviously, although trying to get along in this unisex, equal rights society, wasn't going to last very long. Sure enough one night during TET . . . I heard this whining and moaning and crying and I was able to climb up to that window and look out and see that young woman. She was lying there in a pool of blood. She was in great agony. And she moaned and groaned for about three hours. I could not sleep all night long. She'd been gang raped.
>
> About a week later, after she got back under that yoke of the water that she carried—only the women carried the water and it was heavy. . . . She —in order to survive —took up with the leading guard in the camp who wore a wedding ring on his finger. . . . He would take her to the movies and [she had] this artificial cheerfulness about her. . . .
>
> Now that's an idea of what equality woman gets in the nature and context of that which you have been fighting against. And I've seen it and would Gloria Steinem be able to see it or Betty Friedan? Or any of the others. If they could see it in action, they'd

be joining your ranks. . . . They did have women in combat and they would chain them to the wheels of this obsolescent artillery so they couldn't retreat. . . . It is not a good deal when you deny God, when you say women and men *are* equal, and that's why I so joyously began my speech last night with "Vive La Difference." Why do women want equality when for four or five thousand years they enjoyed the superiority which we accord them as men? [38]

Yet while this story is about Vietnam, and Communist society, social conservatives envision the women's movement as calling forth a similar type of totalitarianism in America, as women seek to use state power to dictate "women's rights." As one activist, the Eagle Forum organizer, puts it:

The women's liberation movement wants to use the economic lever and, two, they want to use the military. . . . They want to achieve their goals with both methods. . . . Their goal with ERA is to create a framework for society. That's why the Army is such a perfect way to do it because the Army is compulsive. . . . You can keep assigning roles completely the opposite to what people want. You can wipe out all role stereotyping against people's will. That's what they're about.

The implication is that the women's movement wants to impose its agenda through the structure of the Army.

According to Brigadier General Andrew J. Gatsis, the women's liberation movement already *has* infiltrated the military and thus poses an immediate threat to American security. He warns:

I must tell you that the top command structure of our military forces, the Pentagon, is saturated with ERA proponents, and under the complete control of avid supporters of the women's lib movement. Members of various women's organizations such as NOW have been placed in key manpower positions of authority who formulate and direct policies concerning U.S. military readiness posture. The result and outflow is that U.S. readiness revolves more around enhancing the women's liberation movement than it does meeting the military capability of a potential Army.[39]

In short, the danger Feminism poses is real and immediate.

Feminism is, then, a threat to homemakers, a threat to the family, and ultimately a threat to the security of America. In the final analysis Feminism is linked with other groups actively working to destroy the American way of life. This belief was apparent during a talk by Brigadier General Albion Knight at the Over the Rainbow celebration:

> You have dealt with the feminist movement; you're dealing with another group in the nuclear freeze. You're dealing with a nastier group because I don't think the feminist movement really intended to destroy the U.S. of A. but the groups working on the nuclear freeze *are* attempting to destroy the U.S. of A.

To this statement, members of the audience yelled out, "They're the same groups," to which he responded: "They may be the same, I agree. Because ultimately it comes down to the destruction of society and that's the destruction of the nation." This final remark was met with much applause and cries of "Right!"[40]

The Paradox of the Social Conservative Woman

The question inevitably arises concerning the seeming paradox of the social conservative woman. Given her adherence to traditional gender roles in which men are breadwinners and protectors and women are helpmates and caretakers, how does the social conservative woman understand her own position as a political activist involved in the public arena? How does she justify her own participation, given this ideological commitment to men and women's separate spheres? Does her activism contradict her beliefs?

This conflict between the traditional female passive role and the vocal political leader is personified by Phyllis Schlafly. Educated at Harvard, a lawyer, an author of nine books, and twice a candidate for Congress, Schlafly is anything but passive or submissive. As past NOW president Karen DeCrow comments: "I admire her. . . . I just can't think of anyone who's so together and tough. I mean, everything you should raise your daughter to be. . . . She's an extremely liberated woman. She sets out to do something and she does it. To me, that's liberation."[41]

In fact, Schlafly serves as a role model of female leadership for hundreds of women every year. She holds an annual conference in order to pass on her political organizing skills to other women in the pro-family movement. One national organizer explains the importance of these efforts:

> Phyllis has done a lot to encourage and inspire and train women, give them a lot of self-confidence. I had never given a speech, written a speech, testified, never been on radio, never been on television, never *really* done a lot of political nitty-gritty campaign management until I met Phyllis.
>
> I think the reason she was so successful was because she encouraged her women to go for it, that there was nothing they couldn't do. You know, she has a meeting every fall where she really revs up the troops. She literally took women who were bright and talented but who *had* been very traditional women. They had gone to school; maybe some of them had gone to college. They had gotten married and they were in the process of raising families. Some of them were very talented and very organized. They could run five children, keep their house cool and do something at the church and school and do the carpools and all that good stuff. All they had to do was transfer all that organizational ability to campaigns and newsletters and learning the issue and getting it down pat. You know, if you can go study the Bible once a week, you can go study the issues of ERA once a week and get it straight and go on TV and debate.
>
> Our women learned. Phyllis encouraged them to debate. She'd say, "No, I can't come to Virginia. *You* debate. They want some-

body to debate, you do it." And then you start getting some self-confidence. You beat a lawyer in a debate a couple of times and you start thinking, "Well, gee, that's pretty good. I didn't know I could do that."

Clearly, Phyllis Schlafly has been an inspiration to scores of women, to raise their voices, to take control, and to step into the public arena. Yet a hint of why such a position does *not* challenge traditional roles is evidenced in another comment made by this national organizer:

I think that women generally, and especially conservative women, see a role for themselves as being the power behind the throne, you know, the people who are behind the candidates. People have said to me in past years, "Well, why don't you run for the Virginia House of Delegates?" And I'd say, "Well, I can either run and maybe get myself elected or I can work in five campaigns and maybe help get five people elected who wouldn't have gotten elected." It's not that I think I'm that great. It's just that if you spend a certain amount of money in the right places and if you really organize the precincts in a legislative race, you have a big impact. I think that women will continue to do that. I think that women have a good talent for that.

When female political activism is conceptualized as the power behind the throne, women altruistically working for the benefit of a larger cause, the seeming paradox disappears. For social conservative women recognize no tension between their political activism and the traditional female role. In fact, these "new" political roles are defined within the bounds of traditional gender ideology. Social conservative ideology expands to incorporate these "new" female roles. Schlafly, for example, includes an assertive political role in her ideal of womanhood, what she terms "The Positive Woman." Because of her positive mental attitude, the Positive Woman is not crushed by life's disappointments: "To the Positive Woman, her particular set of problems is not a conspiracy against her, but a challenge to her character and her capabilities."[42] Clearly an attack against feminists who, in Schlafly's eyes, think the world is against them, the Positive Woman looks affirmatively upon the world. She continues: "The Positive Woman accepts her responsibility to spin the fabric of civilization, to mend its tears, and to reinforce its seams. . . . God has a mission for every Positive Woman. It is up to her to find out what it is and to meet the challenge."[43]

Pro-family leader Connie Marshner has another name for this expanded female role. In a speech to the Family Forum conference, Marshner introduces the "New Traditional Woman":

> She is the mother of the citizens of the twenty-first century. It is she who will more than anyone else transmit civilization and humanity to future generations and by her response to the challenges of life, determine whether America will be a strong, virtuous nation. . . . She is new because she is of the current era, with all its pressures and fast pace and rapid change. She is traditional because, in the face of unremitting cultural change, she is oriented around the eternal truths of faith and family. Her values are timeless and true to human nature.[44]

In explaining the New Traditional Woman, Marshner distinguishes between conventions and traditional values. Conventions, she says, are mutable, changing with the times. For instance, the idea that women should not be educated was a convention derived from the days when survival and the maintenance of the home took all of a woman's time. As the burden of housework lightened, this convention changed, allowing women to obtain an education. On the other hand, traditional values are eternal. Traditional values are moral norms that must be followed without exception. For example, fidelity is a moral norm; adultery is always wrong. In short, Marshner argues, traditional values are non-consequentialist ethics.

The distinction between conventions and traditional values is the framework by which Marshner understands women's "new traditional role." Certain changes in gender roles must be seen as a mere change of conventions. For example, the fact that more women today feel that boys should be as responsible as girls for doing the laundry does *not* challenge traditional values; this merely indicates a change in convention because doing laundry is a morally neutral act. Marshner articulates the difference between conventions and values in this way:

> I think people make the mistake, if you're talking about a traditional value, you're talking about mother at home with the kids which is a fallacy. You're talking about what they believe, what they're taught and what their values are. You're not talking about who cooks the breakfast. That's a different question. . . . It's the values that they're given, it's what they think is important, the policies of the family, if you will, more than who wipes the nose. That kind of stuff is fairly neutral.[45]

While conventions may change, adapting to the times and rearranging the tasks of each sex, the underlying values must remain untouched. Marshner gives this example:

> One traditional value is that the husband is the head of the family. A number of conventions have supported that value but one of the most widely accepted has been the general practice of the husband bringing home the paycheck, or at least the larger paycheck. Perhaps one reason for the convention is that when the husband is the economic provider, it is easier to accept his headship. Due to extraordinary circumstances, however, the woman may become an equal or chief provider. Nevertheless, the husband is still the head of the family. Accepting his authority may be more of a challenge for the woman to accept in that circumstance, but if traditional values are to be preserved, it must be accepted. What is moral is the fact that the wife accepts her husband's authority. It is not immoral that she earns as much or more money than he does. Who earns what is accidental, and not intrinsically moral or immoral.[46]

It is moral values which root our experiences in the day-to-day world, acting as guideposts by which to live. Women may adopt new roles, as long as these moral values remain firmly in place. Hence, Marshner urges women whose God-given talent is to rear children not to be judgmental of women whose talents lie elsewhere. As long as the husband is still the head of the household and the greater good of the family is being served, then moral norms will be preserved.

Neither Marshner nor Schlafly sees a contradiction in the politically active social conservative woman; both interpret such involvement within the bounds of traditional gender ideology. It is, in fact, woman's role as moral gatekeeper, as protector of the moral realm, that allows her to adopt these new positions, to be a voice of righteousness in the political world. For, through such action, the social conservative woman hopes to bring moral purity to a world filled with sin. As Betsy Barber Bancroft puts it: "The concerned Christian woman who would pull on her boots and grab her mop to clean up the filth from overtaxed plumbing, can, when she has the necessary tools, rise to stem the flow of the amoral filth in which our society is awash." [47]

Through the Laissez-Faire Conservative Lens

Just as laissez-faire conservative ideology contains little commentary on the proper roles of men and women in contrast to the central place such commentary holds among social conservatives, so, too, the symbol of Feminism is noticeably absent from the laissez-faire conservative world view. Feminism is not identified along with Communism and Big Government as a foe of freedom, responsible for America's decline.

It is, in fact, because the laissez-faire conservative world is constructed around a fundamentally different conception of gender that Feminism does not loom as a threat. Where social conservatives reject Feminism as an anti-family force that encourages women to be egotistical, laissez-faire conservatives uphold individualism as an ideal, embracing the extension of self-determination to all. Where social conservatives view the emphasis on female self-fulfillment as narcissistic, laissez-faire conservatives applaud each individual's attempt to rise to the level of his or her talents, believing it adds to the wealth of the nation. Where social conservatives see Feminism as blurring the sacred differences between the sexes, disrupting the natural hierarchy of authority, and attacking the status of the homemaker, laissez-faire conservatives reject the notion of a "natural hierarchy of authority" in which homemaking is the desired female goal and instead view both men and women as autonomous actors. Rather than fearing a total masculinization of the world, laissez-faire conservative women actually uphold as ideal a world in which every person is self-interested.

As a consequence of these different outlooks, social conservatives view any positional differences between the sexes as natural and therefore deny the existence of sexual discrimination, while laissez-faire conservatives acknowledge the existence of sexual inequality. However, despite the fact that laissez-faire conservatives recognize discrimination, they share a certain hostility toward Feminism in relation to Big Government. It is really not Feminism itself that they oppose; rather, it is certain feminist solutions to sexual inequality. In fact, it is the very means to achieve women's equality that separates laissez-faire conservatives from most feminists. For example, laissez-faire conservatives oppose ERA. Yet while they share this opposition to ERA with social conservatives, they do so for fundamentally different reasons. For social conservatives, ERA symbolizes a force of decay that seduces women to place their own needs above those of their husband and children and blurs traditional sex roles, resulting in the erosion of family life. The laissez-faire conservative stance against ERA, however, must be interpreted above all in terms of opposition to Big Government. It is not the usurpation of the traditional authority of the church or family that laissez-faire conservatives oppose. Rather, ERA symbolizes the expansion of bureaucratic control, the federalization of one more area of life, resulting in encroachment on individual liberty.

In short, laissez-faire conservatives depart from social conservatives in recognizing sex discrimination; nevertheless, they share antipathy toward ERA because they view ERA as a misguided way of eliminating such prejudice. The libertarian activist involved in public education reform puts it this way: "There are two parts to the ERA. The first part regarding equality I agree with, but I don't think we need that. That's already established by the Constitution. . . . But the second part I don't agree with. The second part gives the government the right to enforce equality." When asked how, practically, she would deal with discrimination, she replies:

> Yes, that *is* a problem. I'm not sure. But you know people can always fight discrimination. First of all, if someone doesn't hire you because of sex, go somewhere else. You're free to go to other employers. Also, boycotts are effective and powerful tools to use. Women can start a boycott of a particular company to educate people about their practices. I think individual businesses will begin seeing it is against their own interests to discriminate, that they are cutting out a part of their business community. Women have a powerful tool in being a big part of the consumer community. Also women have always started their own businesses.

Another activist, a Reagan administrator who works in the Department of Health and Human Services, comments: "I support equal rights for women, but I don't think the ERA is going to give us that. I think we need equal job opportunities and equal careers open to women. But that has to be done on the state level." Typically, laissez-faire conservative activists respond to ERA by calling for individual efforts to fight discrimination or by proposing changes on a state or local level.

The schism between the two worlds of the right is further evidenced in the stance each takes toward other "women's" or "family" issues. For example, opposition to daycare, abortion, and homosexuality is at the very core of the social conservative world view, all seen as evidence of the moral decay of American society, of the erosion of traditional values. Yet many laissez-faire conservatives support these very issues. Viewing abortion or homosexuality as private, individual matters, laissez-faire conservatives argue that government legislation of such issues intrudes on individual liberty. As one woman, active in college conservative organizations, states: "Personally, I'm against abortion. But I think it's not for the government to decide. I think it's an individual woman's choice whether to have an abortion or not. I wouldn't myself, but others should be able to decide." Another national Republican activist puts it this way:

I believe life begins at conception, but I don't see how you can legislate that. I much prefer the way it is now. . . . Women are not butchered. But do I want government to pay for abortions? Well, no, because that's not morally justifiable. But then I also don't want those teenage mothers to be a drag on the system, so it's a complex issue. But I think the consequences are worse if you ban abortions. Ideally, those people should have contraception, but realistically, will that happen? Hopefully, each generation will be more liberated.

Typically, this laissez-faire activist is pro-choice but against government-sponsored abortion. The decision is totally up to the individual. The government has no right to deny a woman's choice, or to support her decision with funding.

Similarly, many laissez-faire activists support daycare as long as it remains in private hands. In one Reagan administrator's words:

I think we need to expand daycare. . . . If a woman has to work an eight-hour day to make money, she needs daycare. I just don't believe the government should pay for it. I think it should be in private hands. There's a daycare center here in the basement. I've toured it. . . . It's great, too, because women can breastfeed. They can bring their children in and either breastfeed or see their kids for lunch. I think there's got to be more daycare, but it should be in private hands.

Laissez-faire conservative support for women's rights coincides with a skepticism regarding the use of Big Government as a means to ensure equality. It is not the feminist *issues* that these women oppose; rather, it is reliance on the federal government to solve women's problems. Jeane Kirkpatrick, for instance, concludes her study of women in political office by urging the government to aid women's role in public life — by appointing women to high positions and by helping women gain equal access to the professions through refusing public support to universities that discriminate against women. But she cautions, as well, about the abuse of government involvement:

> What else could government do? Establish quotas requiring equal numbers of female and male employees at all levels and in all branches of the civil service? Require that one Senator from each state and half of each congressional delegation be female? . . . Adopt a system of compulsory voting to assure that at least half the electorate will be female? Such measures might accelerate women's participation in power but would surely involve the sacrifice of such other values as equal opportunity, intra-party democracy and self-government.[48]

Once again, liberty must not be sacrificed in the quest for equality.

To summarize, laissez-faire conservatives are in accord with feminists in their view of gender and their recognition of sexual discrimination, but they depart from most feminists in envisioning the solutions to women's problems. While most feminists call for federal support in addressing women's needs, laissez-faire conservatives oppose any further reliance on Big Government. While many feminists look toward collective solutions to change sexual inequality, laissez-faire conservatives tend to look toward individual solutions as a way to end discrimination. Hence, despite the coincidence of interest between feminists and laissez-faire conservative women, these differences in world view have inhibited any alliance between these two groups to date.

Finally, although laissez-faire conservative women do not call themselves feminists, there certainly is no paradox to their activism. Because they do not see women as bound to traditional roles, there is no seeming contradiction between their beliefs and their own role as public leaders. In fact, Jeane Kirkpatrick speaks of the need for more women to be in positions of power in order to act as role models, breaking through traditional female roles. In contrast to social conservative women, then, laissez-faire conservative women do not conceive of themselves as the moral gatekeepers, as the care-takers of society, altruistically at work for the benefit of all. Instead, they see themselves as no different from men, self-interested actors working for a political cause.

Thus, at base the activism of laissez-faire conservative women is not rooted in defense of their role as women. To borrow a phrase from Marx, social conservative women act as a class *for* itself, while laissez-faire conservative women remain a class *in* itself. That is, while social conservative women act in their collective interest as women, laissez-faire women act in defense of their interest in the marketplace and not as members of a particular gender.

Conclusion

Women of the New Right are not a monolithic group. Nor are all right-wing women anti-feminists. They do not all "fear equality and prefer preferential treatment"[49] nor are they "lackeys" of men,[50] suffering from "false consciousness." In fact, the paradox is not that social conservative women are vocal and active as they call for tradi-tional roles. Rather, the paradox is that those women who are fur-thest from feminists in their beliefs actually do act in their own interests as women, while laissez-faire women, who actually share a portion of the feminist vision, do not act in their collective gender interest. In this way, social conservative women and feminists both act as "women for themselves"; each acts in defense of the status of women. The conflict between social conservative women and femi-nists derives from their radically different understanding of male and female. Laissez-faire conservative women, meanwhile, remain women in themselves. While they share the feminist belief in the social construction of gender and also recognize the existence of sexual inequality, they do not act in the collective interest of women. It is Communism and Big Government, but not Feminism, that pose a danger to the laissez-faire conservative world. And it is individuals, and not men and women *as* men and women, that are threatened by these foes of freedom. Thus, laissez-faire women act as members of the market, not as members of their gender group, in the effort to return America to strength and freedom.

CHAPTER SIX

Portraits of Two Women

Mary Donnelly and Dora Remington are complex women who "fit" within the ideal types of social and laissez-faire conservatism.[1] Their portraits should not be viewed as composite profiles of the quintessential activist of each school. Rather, the following interviews are meant to add depth and texture to the picture presented thus far, to pencil in the details of the women's lives—their growth and development, how they became active, the meaning and motivation behind their involvement.

Portrait of a Social Conservative: Mary Donnelly *

The interview with Mary took place at her husband's office building in downtown Boston, a large, prestigious insurance company. Mary, fifty-nine, was dressed in a floral print dress and a raincoat that had a baby's feet pin on the lapel, symbol of pro-life. Her grey-streaked shoulder-length brown hair was pulled back by a gold headband. She began by pulling out some things she brought to show me, beginning with a photo of her entire family. She explained who everyone was—her husband and seven children—three daughters, four sons. Then she gave me a paper her daughter Carol had written for college about Mary's and Mary's mother's lives. She explained:

*Names and details have been changed to protect the identity of the women interviewed.

"Carol's paper will give you the background of how I was raised—my mother's philosophy—and my life. She compares me to Betty Friedan; we're about the same age. She explains how although we grew up at the same time, we are different. She says this is because we had such different mothers and upbringings. You can see for yourself." Excerpts from her daughter's paper appear below, as block quotations, as a counterpoint to Mary's comments.

Upbringing

I majored in chemistry in college. I went to an all-girl's Catholic college, St. Theresa's. We were really brought up to think there wasn't anything we couldn't do. That's why I couldn't believe these women saying we're second-class citizens. I never thought I was second class. I thought we were first-class citizens, that we could do anything. My mother raised us that way, too.

I was raised to believe life is serious. I wasn't raised frivolous. It was that life is serious and you are responsible for your actions. I read *The Feminine Mystique* and I suppose a lot of it was true. But I was never brought up to believe things were going to be easy. I knew that the Lord didn't just hand us a rose garden. It depends on your perspective, the way you were raised. I thought it would be hard for both women *and* men.

> My mother describes the Catholicism of her youth as "More hellfire and brimstone. . . . We feared God, but fear implied respect. God was not simply all-loving. He was also all-judging, all-just, and also all-rewarding. Hell and final judgment were constantly on people's minds." My grandmother was a daily churchgoer, and the only organized non-home activities she participated in were church-based; she was part of prayer groups, participated in novenas and special periods of group prayer and sacrifices. My mother, as early as seventh grade, taught religion to the young children, and often attended daily Mass with my grandmother.
>
> Religion [was] the center of family life. My grandmother re-

calls that the whole family used to pray together at home several evenings a week and they were part of several church-related organizations. . . . Acts of self-restraint at all times of the year were considered "spiritual exercises," a way to show how few earthly things one needs to survive. . . . Most of all, the emphasis on self-denial and personal, spiritual preparedness was in preparation for the Day of Judgment. My grandmother lived with a constant awareness that one day she would have to "account for" her life on earth—before God; one day she would stand alone and be judged. All her life she has been readying herself for that day. . . . In my grandmother's family, life was not centered around earthly gains and material pleasures; spiritual goals superseded tangible, material rewards.

Marriage and Family

Things were different then. For example, let me tell you about how I met my husband—what a story! My mother had arranged for me to meet this Harvard boy; she was interested in me getting married. I took a flight to Boston, the first time I had flown alone. You see, then [1945] it was scandalous for a woman to travel alone. That just shows you how much times have changed. But my mother agreed to let me go meet this boy. So on the flight I met my husband! I was sitting there and I saw this man walk down the aisle. He was dressed in his naval officer's uniform and I thought, "How handsome, how distinguished he looks." He had stripes all along his jacket. I thought he must be an admiral. He began to talk to me and at first I thought he was so interesting. But then he asked me about myself, and before I could say much, he interrupted and talked on about himself. So that was it, I thought, "Oh, he's one of those kind that goes on and on about himself." I still thought he was handsome and all, but I just forgot about him. Well, I had told him what college I was at. So one day he called me there and asked if he could see me. I was so surprised. It turned out this young man who I was going out with at the time didn't like Greek plays. There was a Greek play that night so I said, "Okay, you can come to the Greek play tonight out on the lawn." Well, it turned out he loves Greek plays. Shakespeare is his favorite. So he was in seventh heaven. . . .

In May '45 I graduated college. In July I began working as an analytic chemist at a pharmaceutical company. Let's see — we got married in May of '47. Then in November of '47 my husband decided to leave the Navy to go into insurance in Boston. So we had to move. So I ended up quitting my job. I think sometimes that if we hadn't moved, I would have kept on working. That was a great job. . . .

I was infanticipating, my first child. I had baby number one in March of '48. I had five kids in six years, so I was very busy. It was marvelous. I loved it. My husband's attitude was: "That's your area of expertise just like I have mine at work. I'll run mine and you run yours." That was a wonderful time. I'd do exactly the same again. I had a diaper service for ten consecutive years! We had this great barn with grounds for the children to play on. And this wonderful caretaker who would bring armfuls of lilacs. And he would always be there to help whenever I brought a new baby home. It was great. I couldn't write the script. . . .

Let's see. I was involved then with the Sodality, a church group. I was program chairman. We'd get speakers on current events. I was always involved in something. The next thing would be the Brownies; I was Brownie leader for my daughters. I wanted them to join, but there wasn't anyone to lead it. I planned everything but the mothers helped, too. I'm always an innovator. It was great fun. I did that for two or three years. When my mother heard that I was doing that she said, "Boy, you're going from the frying pan into the fire. Why don't you play cards or something?" But I'm not a cards type.

My husband would always be setting dates to get away. He called me every day and would say, "Let's go out tonight." And I'd have to say, "There's no need to go out. We have everything." Great reverse psychology; that was very smart because I never felt like a martyr staying at home. We went out a lot. We always went out to eat. . . .
We always had sitters. Then every afternoon we had a girl from the

high school come in and take all the young children out to the beach. . . . And every summer we had a girl who would live in and help out.

It's wonderful raising children. Every one is an individual with strong and weak points. They learned to get along. We wanted them to know that they are here to try to get along and to recognize that each one has strengths and weaknesses. But it's funny; I was talking to one of my daughters the other day . . . and she was saying that this friend of hers just had a baby—just one—and she didn't know what to do. She said to me, "We both can't understand how you did it. She only has one and you had seven!" They're both around thirty. It's different. I didn't have a whole lifestyle entrenched. I was twenty-three when I got married. And then things were different.

My mother—I wish there were more mothers like her in the world today. She waited up for me every night no matter what. Whenever I'd go out on dates, the boys would have to walk past her to say goodnight. And I lived at home most of college! So that we thought marriage was heaven. Finally, we didn't have to walk past my mother! Marriages were a different lifestyle then. Previously, you only had a smattering of privacy. Families were very careful of their daughters; they didn't want them to get abused. So they were very protective. You weren't on your own much before marriage. So marriage was heavenly. [Do you think marriage was more romantic then?] Yes, definitely. And you had real honeymoons. Which was great for the man—and the woman. Today you have the honeymoon before you're even married! It's nothing. The men come in and out so the honeymoon doesn't even mean anything. But we'll never go back to that way.

Occasions of Sin and Religious Faith

Do you know what occasions of sin are? They'd speak of occasions of sin then. Occasions of sin were an offense against God. For example, the trip to Boston could have been an occasion of sin. If you, with the full consent of your will, did something which committed an offense against God, that was a serious sin, the death of your soul. For example, if you went out with a man and he was drinking—I didn't touch the stuff much—and he drank a few and then the next drink he had he was going to be too drunk to drive home, but he did it anyway, willfully, that is an occasion of sin. And that might put a man in an uncontrollable circumstance; that is a sin. So you were not to abuse the mores, not to give a scandal. It was better if you hadn't been born or—like a millstone around your neck you walked into the water—if you give scandal. If Mary is seen in a questionable place or at a questionable time, then that could give a scandal. Because if someone might see Mary, and Mary was known to be brought up in this way, they might think it was okay to be seen this way. So that might influence others. And then those others might do the same act and if someone saw them, that might influence still others. So then I would be held responsible for that person and all the others. . . .

Now, then . . . where was I? I taught high school CCD [Confraternity of Christian Doctrine] for ten years. I quit about five years ago. I thought, "I'm getting such satisfaction out of this—let someone else get the same satisfaction." So I quit. Then the Church got into psychology and all of that—no longer taught right and wrong. So I began to think that teaching was a way that I could influence and educate. So then I went back to teaching. . . .

I know from facts that suicide increased two hundred times in the last fifteen years. Suicide increased because all the restraints have been removed from kids. I would have known, when I was growing up, that the Lord didn't promise us a rose garden. I didn't expect to be given anything. But kids today do. So then they're dissatisfied. I was told [snaps fingers] that's this life, and then there's eternity. This life is just preparing us for eternity. But kids today don't know about eternity. They're very materialistic. I have absolute faith.

[My mother told me,] "I was never allowed to sleep past eight in the morning and had to account for all of my time. . . . My father came home every night at exactly ten before six and dinner was eaten and dishes were done by seven-fifteen *every night without fail*; I *never* went anywhere in a car alone with a boy. I *always* obeyed my mother and father no matter how much I disagreed; they were my parents. . . . It was easier to control people then because nobody really thought to resist or question things. For instance, the whole 'today' emphasis on the 'rebellious teen years' was unheard of. Kids didn't control their parents the way they do now. There was so little to draw us away from the way of life our parents wanted us to live."

I lost the faith for awhile. With my daughter's death. I felt, "How could the Lord let this happen?" Here was a young person so full of life and everything. She was beautiful and so popular and had everything. I saw her go from this strong, bright girl to like a little puppy. She would lie on her bed and cower; that's what chemotherapy does. She would be startled by a car going by or a noise in the room. And I thought, "How could the Lord cut down a young life like this?" It was terrible. Then in the middle of this—right when she was so sick—my son Patrick came to me one day and said he had an assignment for school that he had to look up all these biblical quotes. He had to do it by the next day, so he asked if I would help him. I said, "Sure." So one of the quotes was: "Why are you so fearful? Oh, you of little faith." I'll tell you where that came from. It was when the Lord was out on a fishing boat with the apostles. He fell asleep and a storm came. They got very frightened and so they woke Him up. He turned to them and He said, "Why are you so fearful? Oh, you of little faith." And that spoke to me. I was in a boat in the middle of the storm, and I thought He had fallen asleep. That gave me such strength. After that everything was easy. . . . After she died, we got all kinds of messages and notes from people all over the country. . . . Many sent all kinds of biblical passages to tell us what got them through their troubles. I keep these quotes now. And I have those mosaics you hang in windows—I have a bunch of them with a boat on them to remind me. If you have faith, you can do anything. Without it, you can't.

Spreading the Word

So I was teaching at St. Matthew's. They used to bus the children one afternoon a week for religious training. My children must have been at First Communion age by then, about second grade. You know, now that I think about it, another girl from the all girls' college ended up as the head of the League of Women Voters; just to illustrate what girls can take on when they're brought up at a girls' college. Anyway, the priest asked me to take on the religious training; he knew I went to St. Theresa's. This was the period of anti-Establishment. The students decided they wanted to write their own curriculum. So I teamed up with another girl. Also the girls wanted to meet with the boys; before, they had been separated. They wanted to discuss the Vietnam war, abortion, drugs—all of these in the religion course. So we spent hours trying to become knowledgeable. I'd call her up and we'd try to plan. So we could present both sides of the Vietnam issue, for example. The one valuable thing I got out of that experience was that I read the Pope's encyclical "Humanae Vitae." The message of that was responsible parenthood. It points out the road ahead for artificial contraception —teenage pregnancies, promiscuity, et cetera. It says it all there. That renewed my faith in the infallibility of the Pope, particularly on moral issues.

Another thing my mother always said to me was, "To whom much is given, much is expected." I was given this marvelous education, and I had to help spread the word of God. I was not to keep this education for myself. . . . I'm still teaching. . . . But I've noticed over the five years I was away that the kids don't respect the teachers anymore. When I complained, the others said, "You think the kids are bad here. You should see them in public school." All I can say is they must be very casual about school these days.

During my mother's childhood, structure and discipline were emphasized at home and at school. From the very beginning grades teachers stressed things like penmanship, neatness, and orderly conduct and work; school . . . was not an extended playpen. A teacher's authority was respected and was never doubted or challenged. . . . It was this rigidness, this unchallenged structure and order that leads my mother to say that, "High school was serious. . . . People seemed more mature than they do now. We respected our school and our teachers."

[Mary gets out her resume to give me; we look at her various activities. I comment on her involvement with the League of Women Voters.] Yes, I was one of the charter members of the League of Women Voters, but I'm too busy now. I can't just sit around at meetings and make light conversation. I'm not that type; I have to be doing something. I joined again around 1976 or '77 because I thought it would be a good way to meet others of a different philosophy. I had surrounded myself with everyone with the same philosophy as me. I thought it might look scandalous to some, but then I thought that, if enough women joined like me, we could change things. Also, I was interested in doing the study of the urban crisis. They were investigating federal money being spent, HUD and all the others. The League was trying to decide which federal programs to hang on to. It was amazing to see how many federal programs there were; so many should have stayed here at the state level. We send these programs out to the federal to be laundered. All of our tax money goes down there. Each state should keep the money and use it. This is what our friend Reagan is doing, to make states stronger. After I worked on this—and I learned a lot—I bowed out. . . . But it did open up doors with those people in the community who I hadn't talked with before. I had been labelled. I think it made them see that there was more to me than one issue. There were other things I was interested in.

Political Awakening

[When did you first get involved in politics?] In 1973 I was involved with the Mass. Citizens for Life. I helped get out a newsletter. [Did you get involved through the Church?] No, it was after the Supreme

Court legalized abortion. I had been watching that, keeping track. Because when we lived in New York I had seen how Rockefeller vetoed the anti-abortion legislation. The "Humanae Vitae" foresaw all of this. Once again, "To whom much is given, much is expected." I had to get involved. We raised people's consciousness. . . .

When ERA came along we saw that it was part of the same parcel, the same people were pushing it. Bella Abzug said that the ERA would seal in abortion. We knew the amendment would legalize abortion. [How did it do this?] The Massachusetts ERA makes us have to pay for abortions for the poor women. I've heard some naive people say you can be pro-life and also pro-ERA. But that's not true; ERA ensures abortion. [How?] There are clever lawyers of ERA who wouldn't publicize that the state ERA is causing Massachusetts to pay for abortions to the poor. In very simple terms, if a man can get any medical procedure, the ERA guarantees that women have to be allowed to get any medical procedure. What is an abortion anyway? It's a medical procedure. So women would be guaranteed the right to abortion under the ERA.

I have files on everything—the ERA, abortion, Secular Humanism, sex education. I first heard the ERA debated by a college classmate of mine who was head of the ERA. A large number of NOW women got into the League to have the League study the abortion issue and take a stand. I understand that they changed the rules. . . . They used every possible means to educate about the necessity of abortion. After that, a lot of people bowed out of the League.

The Mass. Citizens asked someone to speak against ERA. . . . We never had that meeting. But the Republican Town Committee had a debate. That was the beginning for me. I could see what we were in for. There were two females. One saw it as the greatest thing ever done, and the other saw how ambiguous the ERA was, how it wouldn't do anything. . . . Then I saw in the church bulletin that the League was sponsoring a woman speaking for the ERA. I said to myself, "This is the one place that I should be." So I went and she spoke for the ERA. During the question period, I shot up my hand and I said, "I think to be fair to the citizens here we should hear the other side of the issue. There is a whole other side." And I explained some points about the ERA. Well, you would have thought that I had said something just awful! One woman finally stood up and said, "I think she's right. We should hear the other side." Afterwards I asked the woman who defended me how it was that she was supporting me. She said, "I get the Phyllis Schlafly newsletter. I believe in this." And I said, "*You do?*"

We decided—the Mass. Citizens for Life—that we had an insurmountable task ahead of us. The League refused to consider the opposition. I came up with the idea of hiring a hall and selling tickets. . . . We sold two hundred fifty tickets to hear the women speak. Then one of the women said we should organize another one. This time we sold three hundred tickets. But it was only a month before the election. It was like taking on Goliath. New York and New Jersey had defeated the ERA the year before, so we tried to figure out how to meet the women who were successful there. I saw in *Parents* magazine a letter written by one of the women against ERA from New York—Westchester, I think. So we got her on the phone and you know what she said? She said, "We were trying to reach *you.*" They had been trying to reach us because they heard there were people in Massachusetts fighting the ERA. I didn't know what we could do in that short a time, but thought we'd try.

This priest gave us a hall for free. So we talked with the woman in New York and she sent this, what she called, a "bomber" of a woman. It turned out it was Dotty Burlow, who was in my class at college! I said, "Now I know why New York was defeated, if Dotty was working on it!" We tried to get the press to cover this, but they didn't want to come.

And do you know what the missing link was in Massachusetts that New York had that made it win? Guess. [I have no idea.] Just guess. Who in New York would you suppose is so influential as to make a difference? [I don't know.] Jewish women! It was Jewish women working in a group called Operation Wake-Up who made the difference. They're still meeting; they monitor all the legislation in Albany to inform voters.

Continuing Activism

I went to the International Women's Year conference in Houston, the White House Conference on the Family. I can't tell you what I've seen. The IWY in Houston in '77—the delegates were supposed to be democratically elected. State elections were held. A group of forty-two women planned it in Washington; they were appointed by Carter. Only one of those women represented me. The rest were pro-ERA, pro-abortion. When we found out how much of our tax money, how many organizations in Washington were supporting this. . . . Do you know only two people in all of the New England states were elected who were on my side? Two pro-life people from Springfield, Massachusetts. Those forty-two women only told their friends, and their friends organized the conventions to choose delegates. We never even heard about it. It shows you how easily things can be controlled. . . . I wrote it up for the local papers.

So I went as an official observer to the IWY. Each congressman had two official observer passes to be given out. So I called up my congressman and said, "I'm now officially applying." He didn't even know he had them. They didn't pay for anything, but they got me in. I got sick when I saw all those presidents' wives in pastel suedes. And the charade of voting. There was no way they could lose on any plank. They went through all the parliamentary procedures. And then women just shrieked when they passed the Reproductive Rights —as if there was any way they could lose. I was sitting in the Astrodome watching all of these females and you know what I did? When I give you this litany, you won't believe it. . . . I thought of this National Right-to-Life man I saw who dressed up like Bella Abzug and went out to where Bill Baird and all of his paid demonstrators were marching for abortion. He started marching with them and he chanted: "Got to keep up the killing! Got to keep up the killing!" Bill Baird had to pack up and leave. So I stood up and I just started to yell in all directions, "We've got to keep up the killing!" Because that's what they want, after all, to kill. Well, people couldn't believe it. I got spit on and elbowed. I really hit them with that [excited, gleefully]. I was only one and they were all of one mind. And for the American public to think that this is the average American women, why I think that's the greatest travesty. . . .

Reagan says it best. When someone questions him on ERA he says, "I'm for the E and the R but not the A." That's me. I have three daughters so of course I want equal rights for them. I just don't want them saddled with having to be like a man. . . .

My mother was raised by a mother and father who saw the job of homemaking as a great responsibility, a vocation that tapped a woman's mental and physical faculties and demanded creativity. In that same household she came to value personal, spiritual strength and independence more than material, monetary security. Judging from the example of her own mother, my mother saw the role of wife and mother as ideal for herself; she grew up with a great respect for motherhood and home-making. My mother knew that it was a selfless occupation in which a woman made constant material and emotional sacrifices, but also reaped many spiritual rewards. My mother grew up seeing the value of a life of give and take, a life in which "nothing worthwhile comes easy . . . the future belongs to those who prepare for it . . . and, sweet are the uses of adversity."

A few years ago Joan Kennedy and Margaret Heckler had a big event for the ERA extension, to raise money. I was invited somehow so I called up two of the most attractive females I know and a priest and a couple of others and we all went. I remembered there was a back door; it was at the Copley. We snuck in so we didn't have to pay. The priest decided to just picket in front. So my friend and I were standing around talking. Some women recognized me and I'm sure they were wondering, "What is she doing here? What trouble is she going to cause?" After awhile I was tired of polite conversation. I said to my friend, "We came here for one thing, to talk to Tip O'Neill." So we went up to him. There was a circle around him and we waited politely. Finally, he turned to me. I introduced myself and then I said, "My aunt lives on Russell Road and her children are your constituents." We talked about that. He loved that because he always talks about Russell Street, where he grew up. His face lit up and then I said, "You know, we aren't a part of this organization that is running this event." And he said, "Well, I'm pro-ERA." And I said, "Do you know who is sponsoring this event?" He said, "I'm here for the ERA." And I said, "If you don't know who is sponsoring it, I'll tell you—the National Organization for Women. And they're for abortion and contraception for minors without parental consent and they're for homosexual rights." He was absolutely livid! He said—without moving his lips—"Get out of here. How dare you act so friendly and then try that. . . ." Well, he was so mad I didn't know what to do. I just stood there. Then the one person in the world who could help me was sent by the Lord. Who do you think that was? Who was the one woman of anyone who could help me in this circumstance? [I don't know.] Well, this legislature is unique in the country; it's the only one who has elected an avowed lesbian to office. Right then and there Elaine Noble came running down to say hello to Tip. It was perfect! Right after I said all of those things. He was so mad.

Then a friend noticed that the return address for this invitation was on Ethan Allen Road. She said to me, "Do you know what Ethan Allen Road is? It's the headquarters for Planned Parenthood." They had been asking for donations to be sent there, to Planned Parenthood, without telling anyone. Here was Tip O'Neill, supposedly a pillar of the Church, supporting Planned Parenthood. So this friend sent this packet of information to Tip O'Neill. . . . But he never answered, not a word. So once I was in Washington and I went to his office and left word, "Tell Tip O'Neill the woman who took him on at the Copley came to see him." I think he probably worries when he's out on the street that I'll come up to him [laughs]. But I'm thankful to the Lord that I had the courage. . . .

Reflections

I still write letters to people. But I'm weary. You're labelled. People think I'm a fanatic. And with the Moral Majority. The Moral Majority is only saying what the Catholic Church has been saying all along. Vatican II said what a Catholic is—someone who goes to church, who doesn't engage in premarital sex, et cetera. But now there's a lack of guidance. Now the Moral Majority is doing a lot of guiding where it is needed.

[Is your husband supportive of what you do?] Yes, my husband is very good. He and I think alike. [Does he do political work as well?] Well, he'll speak for me when I'm not there. Sometimes he says to me when we're going out, "Let's not get into it tonight." And then I'll hear him across the table arguing—the same things I think.

My father always told me, "Don't even go out with non-Catholics." It's so important to marry someone who is from a similar background as you. It makes a marriage so much more secure. You know, out of the two hundred girls who graduated at St. Theresa's with me, I can count on one hand the number of marriages which have broken up. That's how prepared we all were for marriage. Something is missing today. That *was* another era. . . .

But my daughter Carol said to me that she doesn't know any one of her friends at Princeton with parents who are divorced. So you know how I explain that? I figure if you're at Princeton you must be a kid with high achievement, the ability to stick it out. And that can only come from strong parents. That must be because of a strong home.

St. Theresa's was an upper crust school, but there were also blacks there. . . . The nuns were so inspiring. Every year the top ten women in every class—the most brilliant and the prettiest women—would go into the Church to become nuns. The nuns today—I laugh— they were all brought up on the whole women's lib. . . . They want to do mass and everything. It's so sad. [She picks up the program from her commencement and begins to read from the commencement speech]:

"Tomorrow, when the sun is set on this campus, you, my dear young women, leave Alma Mater, your loving Mother, and you begin to walk—alone. It is all important then that you take with you a reliable sense of values. . . . The power of a good woman in the world has been extolled by philosophers as one of the greatest forces in life, sublimating mankind to the beautiful, the true, the holy and the ideal. . . . Woman has been entrusted with human life and all that affects it in the tender and most receptive years of its growth and development. . . . For this reason God made woman instinctively holy, pure, kind, tender, sympathetic, and religious. God has endowed her with gifts necessary for the good of the human race and the salvation of souls. The preservation of these feminine gifts is woman's highest prerogative and her greatest responsibility. . . .

"[The] de-feminization of woman as we see it today, began with the crazy crusade for her emancipation. Towards the end of the last century women yelled loudly for the equality of the sexes, for the abolition of the double standard of morality. It's a man's world they said 'and we want to get into it.' With the drastic lowering of standards, women got into man's world; they got equality but at the awful price of their superiority. . . .

"Woman has unfortunately . . . been reduced to a state where she was before Mary graced this earth. . . . She has bartered her charm for what she calls emancipation. This so called emancipation has been a boomerang, because it emancipated men from old time loyalties and enforced deference. Those women who want the new equality with men can no longer enjoy their old superiority to them. . . . In the quest of something she more than possessed but did not realize, woman has cheapened herself for she can never be man's equal, she must be either greater as God intended, or less as she determines. . . ."

That's the way we were brought up. . . . It was a different world. . . . What we had to lean on!

Today's World

Our wonderful president is trying to bring voluntary prayer back to the schools. Do you know who took prayers out of the schools? Madeline Murray O'Hair. She went to Russia to try to become a citizen, but they wouldn't take her. So she came back and when she put her children in school she said, "I couldn't send my children to a school with prayers." She was an atheist. But in May of this year the

President called a National Day of Prayer. And Madeline's son was in the audience. He repudiated his mother and had embraced a Christian religion. He is giving his whole life to compensate for the harm he feels his mother did. He brought a petition signed by a million plus people. . . .

I also spend a lot of time trying to figure out what is going on. I read *Human Events, Conservative Digest, The Wanderer.* . . . I saw a survey where pollsters in New York—very recently—questioned two hundred forty people in the media. They asked twenty-five questions. When they asked, "Are you affiliated with any Church?," only five percent were affiliated! Most had never darkened the door of a church. And 90 percent were pro-abortion, 90 percent were for homosexual rights, and under 10 percent had voted for Reagan. So I remember this when I read the newspapers.

[At this point Mary's husband interrupts to tell her their daughter Carol is waiting to be picked up. He turns to me and says, "How do you like this chick? Pretty interesting, eh? And she's my first wife!" Mary laughs and says, "I adore him."]

Reverend Wildmon—have you heard of him? He started the National Federation of Decency. He brought all the national TV stations to the bargain table and threatened a boycott. So he got them to say that in six months they would clean up their shows. They began to monitor the shows. This little guy from Toobalo, Mississippi. But he should have brought on the boycott; they haven't changed. . . . I heard from a friend of mine in New York that he would be calling me. He wanted my support when he came here. . . . What one person can do! He has a newsletter and all kinds of clout.

Then I went in 1979 to the big gala event held in Washington at the expiration of the seven years for ERA. Dr. Voth from the Menninger Clinic was there. And this retired general, Gatsis. He gave so many facts. He told us that Liz Carpenter—you know, who Carter appointed—she was at the Pentagon and she was trying to get women into all echelons of the military. Well, he gave us the facts: a high percent of women in the military are pregnant, such-and-such a percent never finish.

We were so turned on after we heard him that we went right

over to Congress. And who should we see, a cadre of naval officers coming down the hall. So I took it upon myself to say to them, "We just heard that women are being railroaded into the military to make women being drafted more palatable." We knew this would mean that women would have to enter combat, because once women are in, some smart guy will say, "I'm not going to combat unless she goes." They didn't know what hit them! A few of them walked on. But some said that they were totally with me and that their wives were with me. They gave us the names of people to talk to at the Armed Forces. So we went right over. . . . We found out that what that general had been saying was true. The Commander-in-Chief, the President, was giving orders and he's for the ERA. What does a good officer do? He doesn't question. . . . So this was what was happening. . . . This was being done by a group of women. The military was being used by the women pushing for ERA. . . .

On Women's Roles

It's not that I don't want things to change. . . . I don't expect them to stay the same. I just don't want them forced. I want it to be evolution. . . . Women's liberation is a small group of women who have forced themselves on us. . . . I think: "Why them and not me? What have I been doing?" I'll tell you. I was raising seven children. What were they doing? Hardly any of them are in an ongoing marriage. Kate Millett, Shulamith Firestone — they are blaming society for their own failure. I don't think society has failed me. They had time and a strong motivation. It became so obvious at the IWY that women with children who were at home don't have the time to do this. . . .

My mother is going on eighty-nine. . . . She has three kids and felt totally fulfilled. I have a brother with six kids—all of whom have their master's [degrees]. Five of them are married with kids. . . . All of them pay taxes, all of them are well balanced, all of them are contributors. Then I have a sister—she was named outstanding Catholic woman of the year in Tennessee. All her children are contributors, all well balanced. So you look at the results of a fulfilled woman in the home . . . and how society profits. . . . And you look at how society fails with women half in the home and half out. . . . Kids don't feel they have to honor their mother and father. Did I vandalize the schools? Did I talk back to my parents?

My grandmother saw her role, her domestic responsibilities, as God-given; she would someday be held accountable for the way she ran her household and raised her children. As the financial organizer of the family, she meticulously kept records of all expenses and kept all expenditures to a bare minimum. . . . For my grandmother, staying at home and raising a family was anything but a submissive, passive existence. While some women might see their home-oriented life as stifling and unfulfilling, my grandmother saw her role in the home as a responsibility before God. Her home was her domain to control and shape, the "stage" where she would "perform" for God.

My mother earned it. My mother had to develop everything on her own. It was the Depression. Mother had to stretch everything. She even made my father's pajamas. She canned everything, too. She was an authority on good food; we never had a piece of white bread in the house. She made a real career out of her home. . . . You owe an awful lot to a home like that. . . . Now we have labor-saving devices. My mother used to do all of her own wash. She'd take a whole day to do ironing. And she only had three children. Sometimes I think I could have three children and take care of them with my hands tied behind my back. . . . I don't think women should stay inside. . . . It's natural evolution that they don't—especially with only three children.

My mother told me, "The way people say 'just a housewife' is new since the feminist philosophy became popular. It somehow implies that a woman in the home is taking it easy and shirking responsibility by not earning money at the same time that she raises a family. The feminist movement is not improving the status of women by making motherhood look like the easy way out."

In addition, my mother sees the "Wages for Housework" campaign as an example of the excessively materialistic nature of the feminist movement. Her family experience taught her that the sacrifices and hard work that motherhood demands reaped rewards that money cannot buy: personal satisfaction, security, and the approval of God. "Putting a price tag on the work of a mother would make home-making seem just like any other job, which it definitely is not," says my mother. She goes on to say: "It is a career, however. It is a career and it is a great responsibility. Mothering has rewards all its own. To pay a mother for raising children would be degrading, for it would take motherhood out of the 'unique responsibility' category and turn it into a job; the sacred title of 'mother' would have to be changed to 'worker.' Women would gain money, but they would also lose a source of pride and identity."

Do you know what the father at St. Theresa's said to us all the time? He said, "Beware that you are not perfect. No human is perfect. And beware of the guy who likes to hang curtains. Look for the masculine guy. And you be as feminine as you can. Longevity depends on a happy marriage." And every week he repeated to us, "Get married, get pregnant. Get married, get pregnant. Then your husband will mature and be doing the most masculine of acts— supporting you. And you will be doing the most feminine of acts —nurturing. And you will mature. And you will be secure."

Portrait of a Laissez-Faire Conservative: Dora Remington

I interviewed Dora at the building where she works in Washington, D.C. She is currently "on loan" from the state of Massachusetts to advise a national government organization on energy policy. Single, aged thirty-four, Dora has short straight hair and was dressed in a tailored jacket and matching skirt. During the interview I noticed a pin on her lapel, a tiny golden rifle. I asked her about it. "Ann

Oakley gave it to my grandmother," she said proudly. "She taught her to shoot and my father to shoot. He taught me to shoot."

Politics at an Early Age

It's not issues that orient me towards policies and never has. I was wearing an Eisenhower button before I realized he had an opponent [laughs]. [Were your parents active?] No, they weren't. They'd get Nixon jewelry and that sort of thing and I always ended up with it. My brother liked to collect buttons. They gave me his button collection and I decided, "Well, the only way to keep this button collection going is to go out and to meet politicians." So I'd get on the subway and go down to Coolidge Corner and hang around and meet all the politicians and collect all the buttons. I decided that—I don't know why but—well, I suppose my family being Republicans. . . . They'd have discussions maybe, but I don't even recall. They didn't seem too concerned that I was hopping on a subway with friends of mine and tearing off to Coolidge Corner, which was the hotbed of political activism at that time, going to all the headquarters. I don't know whether the buttons were better in the Republican camp or what [laughs].

The first campaign I worked on I was eleven years old. I went door to door in Quincy of all places. [You mean you just did that because you were interested?] No, actually my mother was working on that campaign so there was some activism there. But she was only doing it because she was a friend of these people and they were all old family friends. So I went door to door. These people used to burst out laughing when they'd come to the door. Not just because I was so young. That was one reason, but because I was supporting a Republican. It just didn't exist. It was a joke. So they'd invite me in. They'd give me a little spaghetti and send me away again. That was my first campaign. Then after that I became active in debating societies and that sort of thing. I guess I just identified the family thing with Republicans.

The first campaign that I *really* dealt with the issues of the candidates was Goldwater in '64. For some reason I was more attracted to the presidential and federal level politics than local. I just didn't get excited about local at all; I never have really. But the 1960 campaign with Kennedy and Nixon I started out kind of lukewarmly toward Nixon because of the Eisenhower-Nixon connection. This one woman used to nag me about Kennedy. She used to lecture every night on Kennedy. So I thought, "Well, maybe Kennedy's the guy." Then I watched the debate. I didn't know what he was talking about but Nixon didn't look too hot. And I'll never forget it—the day before the election I switched back to Nixon. I don't know why. I just said, "You know, there's something about this Kennedy I just don't like." That was probably when I was beginning to think issues. For the first time I really started to think about the issues. [How old were you then?] When was that, 1960? I was born in 1948 so — [Oh, I thought you were voting.] No, no, no—this was in school. In school we voted. [And you were already starting to think in terms of issues at twelve years old?] Well, I think I was just starting to. I was just starting to identify with issues at that point. I was pretty progressive on this whole political—really was getting the fever. It's pretty obvious I was taken with the whole process. [Do you remember what issues you thought about?] No, I just remember all of a sudden thinking Kennedy's not the right guy. . . .

The Goldwater Campaign

In '64 I was a junior; that was an interesting year. I had been active in the gubernatorial race because it was there, more or less. When Goldwater came along, that was my candidate. All of a sudden, I was really into issues. I thought he walked on water. . . . I still think he walks on water. Every time I see him I could go up and hug him. [Were you going to rallies then?] Oh, yes. The only time I've been in Fenway Park until recently was to see Goldwater. I have friends of mine all over the country who are just disgusted that I live in Boston and don't go to Fenway Park except to see Barry Goldwater. Yes, I had my candidate in Goldwater.

Oh, God, I got so active on the issues it was terrible. I used to clean up things on the school newspaper, the mimeograph machine or whatever it was—these civil rights papers, Goldwater's position, Johnson's position. Goldwater always had a really positive civil rights position. He did a lot. He just didn't like this constitutional amendment. He had *good* reason not to like it; it was terrible. I had it all printed up and I distributed it in school. I was told to go home for two weeks to think about it. Well, my parents didn't want me at home. They told me I couldn't even mention the word "Goldwater" in the house because I was such a fanatic. I wouldn't stop. They just thought I was a complete fanatic on the subject. So when I got thrown out I thought, "This is great. I have two weeks off to campaign. I'm just going to solid campaign for Goldwater." So I stood outside the school gates passing out literature and pamphlets. Well, one day they decided to yank me back into school. They had better control of me in the school than out. So they put me back and they told me I couldn't use any more of the school machinery to campaign. That didn't stop me.

[Did you have other friends helping you or were you by yourself?] I campaigned by myself. . . . This was for real. This was eleventh grade. We had mock elections every year, usually a couple days before the real elections. I converted my entire class to Barry Goldwater, the *entire class.* No one voted against Barry Goldwater. I mean if they voted against him, we took them outside and explained to them why they couldn't and that they had to change their mind after a few black eyes [laughs]. I had my own little gang that was really doing the—sweeping things. . . . We were really spreading out. We were doing as thorough a job as we possibly could.

The faculty was pretty Republican but they were all Republicans for Johnson. They would have signs "Republicans for Johnson." It used to make me so angry. I used to go around and tear them off. I used to say, "You can't be a Republican and be for Johnson. Don't insult our intelligence." They just couldn't stand it. A friend of mine who was the president of the student body, running for the head— we had a headmaster. She was sort of the head dean, or I don't know what they call it. She was the second in command. She was called in for something. . . . She came up to me and I said, "What's wrong?" She said, "I've got to get out of here. I've got to get out of here. I've got to get out of this school and go home quickly before you get to me." Because they were scared to death I was going to change all the votes [laughs]. I would argue with anybody. I would just take them all on. I was placing bets all over the place. I lost more money that year than I've ever lost in my life [laughs]. I agree with Barry. I think we should have a recount. This country wouldn't be in the mess it's in today, if we had him for president.

Continuing Activist

[So what did you do when the election was over? Did you turn to something else?] I cried a lot [laughs]. . . . I was very upset by the whole thing. [Did it make you want to do more political work?] Yes, so after that I decided, "Well, I better get really involved." I still couldn't vote, but I decided to go to the next national convention. So I managed to get myself some money. . . . But Rockefeller won the state, so all the Nixon people got thrown off the plane and, of course, I was with Nixon. So off the plane I got thrown. At the last minute. At this point I figure —I was fifteen, no, twenty —yes, it was right before I could vote. Well, I said, "This is terrible." I didn't have a hotel room or anything else. We'd really been axed out at the last moment. So I said, "I'm going anyway." So I made my own arrangements and everything.

Meanwhile, I had designed this whole organizational chart for Nixon for the whole state of Massachusetts. It could have been used as a national model for how to set up the voting network. . . . And I came to find out that this woman that had me thrown off the plane had taken my organizational chart down and put *her* name on it and was telling everybody that this was her project. I wouldn't even have minded if she had put her name on it and had said that somebody else had done it for her. But no, she was telling everybody that it was hers. So I went to the national headquarters. I said, "I'm sorry, but I designed that and, if her name's on it, it's not going to be used. And that's that." So I don't know what happened because I never saw it again. That was more than I could take. My ego was beginning to develop at this point. We've gone from candidates to issues to ego [laughs]. Those were the good old days, though, when politics was fun.

[Did you then decide to have your whole life be politics or what?] No, I don't know. I don't know if I've ever gone *that* far. Maybe when Goldwater was running I thought my whole life should be politics. It's hard to say. I liked Reagan then. I remember I had buttons, "I'm still mad about Barry." We had a few fights between the Rockefeller people and the Goldwater people. I had a good time. I got around, met a lot of people, did a lot of my own bullying, . . . part of the process. I came back with my Reagan poster. I made a friend of mine carry the poster back on the plane. She carried it all the way back and then delivered it to me at the dinner that Reagan was speaking at. He was so impressed that I had this poster that I'd picked up at the convention floor. I still have that thing somewhere.

[So you moved right along to the next campaign?] Well, not exactly. I'll never have the same feelings that I had for Goldwater. I just found Goldwater to be so incredibly honest and straightforward and I don't find that in any of them now. I think personally probably Reagan is. [You stayed active?] Yes. It was like a comedy this last time though. I'd preferred him to all of them. I thought he was the smartest one.

Current Activities

[Have you been active in every campaign?] Yes. A friend of mine once asked me — we were working on the Nixon campaign together in 1972 — and she said, "What do you do when there isn't a campaign?" And I said, "I wait for the next one." [You don't do things in between?] Oh, no, I do, because I have to make a living. So I went into the brokerage business thinking: "Well, this will be good. I'll build up some business, some clientele, and then I'll be able to play with my politics." I found that I was playing with my politics too much. And it really didn't work that way, particularly in the new market environment where you can't get as much directed business as you used to. You used to be able to sort of have business directed to you from major accounts from banks and things like that. It's real hard to get that kind of business now. [So now your full-time job is political?] Well, this is more governmental. There's a difference between governmental—being a bureaucrat—it's terrible. . . . I like the overall big picture, but I don't want to get into the nitty-gritty little details. I like to see something of substance produced, but I don't particularly want to be the one that's in there getting that and forgetting everything else on the big scale.

I was working on a program in Massachusetts. We were the first in the nation—fuel oil conservation market program and it's the best. . . . I'm pretty proud of the accomplishments made there but so what [laughs]? A hundred years from now they dig up the time capsule. We're not going to be here whether we have the best fuel oil conservation marketing program. They'll wonder who was president then, right?

I'm also still the president of a local Republican women's group. The thing about that is that I have such a fantastic board that I really do very little, very little. I sort of come up with the big ideas and then I say, "Okay, go get them." And they do all the—I just really have a very good board. I can lean on them. They're committed enough to do the job. [What is the purpose of the organization?] For educational purposes, educational meetings, that kind of thing. . . . It was dying when I became president. The last person just tried to keep it alive. Then she orchestrated the little coup and got me in. I said I wouldn't come in without bringing my own board. I brought only part of what I wanted to bring because they said, "Forget it. You can't just come in here and turn it upside down." That's what we tried to do. I'd like to see it turned into something that has a bigger scope. Women's clubs are a bore. They really are. Who the hell wants to go to a meeting with a bunch of women? So I think my whole feeling is to use that as kind of an umbrella for more major activities like establishing PAC groups, targetting, doing some polling, and doing some really significant things under that.

[What other activities are you involved in?] I do a lot of fundraising. But I'm getting a little rusty at that. I haven't done that in a couple of years. Did some for Reagan but not much. I got angry with the Reagan committee because they tried to buy me and they were lying [laughs]. If you're going to buy somebody, honestly buy them. Don't lie to them. They told me that if my organization would give them a certain size loan—it was rather large—that they hoped we would look the other way when it came time to repay. Actually, what they were asking for was an illegal gift. And they told me if I could arrange this—they didn't say it that way—they *did* say point blank that if I could arrange this, I would be made an elector. Well, I said I would think about it. . . . I considered our finances to be privileged information. So I decided to do a little work on that. I started investigating the whole thing and found out that they'd already submitted the list of the electors; it was already established who the electors were going to be and my name wasn't on it. So they came back the next day asking for the loan and I said, "Forget it. You already gave away the elector position. . . . Let *her* get [the money] for you" [laughs]. They were sort of embarrassed.

[What are your future plans politically?] A friend of mine wants to run for Congress, asked me to manage his campaign. That might be interesting. [Do you ever think about running yourself?] Yes, I have. Right now it's not possible, not through the congressional level. I really think there are probably more important things to do in terms of party politics right now than running. I think that part of the mistake that the Republican Party has made is that they're running around with their candidates all the time instead of building any kind of base from which these candidates can launch themselves. You can't just take somebody who doesn't have any kind of name recognition and throw him into the pile and say: "Okay, spend some of your own money and win. See you later." That's why I hope that my group can do some of the—not as a membership organization. We're not looking for members. . . .

Schlafly and the Social Issues

It can be done. Phyllis Schlafly did it. She's a real example of someone who's built something, a base or something. She could probably run for anything anywhere and do a really incredible job. She'll bring out the haters [laughs]. I think she would like to be appointed to something. There's a woman that she wanted appointed secretary of defense. . . . Well, that's a case where the issue doesn't really matter—it's who wins. Who really cares about the ERA? Do you think it would really make one bit of difference one way or the other? It might screw up everything but that's about all it would do [laughs]. So I mean that's a perfect kind of an issue to build a fantastic base on. Like Phyllis did there.

[Why do you think it's a perfect issue?] Because it really doesn't matter. I just don't think it's an important issue. It's not like it's the economy. There are so many more important issues. But it's the perfect issue for somebody to launch themselves on because not that many people are going to get all hot and bothered about it on that side of it. But she *got* them hot and bothered. She clobbered her opposition. I mean she *clobbered* them. In five years not a state passed that thing! It's the kind of issue that I don't think people would have gotten heated up about on their own. It's something where she realized she could rally some leadership for herself out of it and really take off. That's *my* opinion for whatever it's worth.

[What *do* you think are the important issues? You said the economy—] Certainly not the ERA and certainly not all these stupid social issues. I can't see that they're important issues. I think they're smokescreens. [For what?] Well, right now I think the whole idea that Reagan's going to introduce a constitutional amendment against abortion—well, if that isn't to cover up the mess that the economy is in, then I don't know what it's for. I mean people vote their pocketbooks. They don't vote these other issues. They get *polarized* on these other issues and they get heated and all excited about them, but they don't vote them. When it comes down to the bottom line, it's whether or not they've got spending money. The problem with those other issues, though, is they can hurt a candidate. They can't help a candidate as far as I can see, but they can hurt him. If they come out on either side, you're on the wrong side. That's the problem with those issues.

Role of Government

[Do you think those issues are important at all or are they secondary?] I guess they're important to somebody. They're not important to me. Well, they *are*—I shouldn't say that—they're important to me in that I don't think they should be federally stated at all. I just don't think so. Because I don't want Big Brother in my house. I think we're headed towards "1984" fast enough without having him come in and say, "Hey, you can't determine what you're doing with your own body." Or "Hey, lady, get back there and do the dishes" or whatever. I don't want him in my home. That's what's important to me. I just don't want government involvement in my personal life. That's why I don't like any of these issues. I don't think the federal government belongs— I don't rush right out and get an abortion but then I don't want the federal government telling me whether or not I can. I'm absolutely opposed to funding them. I don't think that the federal government should be funding anything now in terms of that. Just missiles.

[Do you agree more with the libertarian position on the role of government?] Some of it. I think some of those libertarians go a little too far overboard though. Legalizing drugs and stuff like that. I don't think we should legalize drugs at all. Because I've seen too many people who've gone overboard. They use too much and then they're vegetables. You know, if you could sweep up all those vegetables and put them somewhere where you didn't have to look at them and put up with them every day, that would be different. We don't have camps for vegetables [laughs], LSD camps or whatever it was— What was that movie where the rock star got elected president?

Views of Gender and Family

[What *is* the relationship between the economic and social issues? It sounds like from what you said that you don't think there is much connection.] Well, I've read part of [George] Gilder's book. He makes some pretty strong arguments. It would be almost like saying I don't belong in the workplace to believe that stuff, wouldn't it? There's sort of an overemphasis on family, that every woman's got to have children and to be fulfilled kind of thing, and you've got to give your twenty years in the kitchen or whatever. I mean, hell, how can you spend twenty years in the kitchen today? I mean everybody's got a Cuisinart or something else. It takes fifteen minutes to prepare a gourmet meal today. How can you spend your whole entire life in the kitchen? You can only vacuum a house so many times before you start sucking up the carpet! I don't like floors and windows [laughs].

[Do you think it's hard to maintain the kinds of activities you do and also bring up a family?] No, I don't think— I think it's an individual personal decision. The idea that you should just get married for the whole sake of getting married *really repulses me*. I mean that's going back to a day and age that I don't think we need to go back to, that kind of thinking. I hate to sound like somebody who's a sentimental sap, but I think there ought to be a little love in the relationship [laughs].

[Do you think there's been more involvement by women in the past few years?] I don't think that any candidate could be elected to anything without the involvement of women. I really don't. They'd never get elected. There's a real tendency—and I think it's a growing tendency which bothers me —in that there's a tendency to pay a young man for his time and expect a woman to volunteer. I thought for a while that that tendency was tapering off, but I don't know. I'm getting more concerned about that cropping up again. It gets back to the whole "send 'em home" philosophy. I don't like the idea that a young fellow needs a paycheck because he's got to give up a job on the job market and some woman maybe doesn't have to. Although I feel very strongly that volunteers are something very important to politics. . . . The Republican National Committee contends that they've let more women into positions than the Democratic National Committee. I don't know how they define —they said executive positions. They should have said professional positions. I don't call the positions that they were talking about executive positions. Head of the Speaker's Bureau is not an executive position [laughs] as far as I'm concerned. You can call it a professional position. . . .

[Let me ask you this; there have been some reports in the media that women tend to be more peace-minded—] I think that's true. I really do. I would never have thought it was true except that I belong to a thing called the National Executive Defense Reserve. We had a first meeting, and I really wouldn't have come to this conclusion, except that after hearing about the megaton blasts and all the rest of it—and basically we're the group that's going to take charge of sorting out the mess of trying to get people to move when it's time to move and that sort of stuff— And it was clear that the women in the room had really seriously—aren't we almost having a wish fulfillment here because there was so much talk about a wartime economy and all this kind of stuff? It was the women who were really turned off by the whole thing. And these were conservative women, *very* conservative women. They were just sort of turned off by the sort of casual chat about a megaton here and a megaton there [laughs].

[Why do you think that is that women are more peace-minded?] I'm not too sure that it's *peace*-minded; I think it's that they're not macho. They don't have to prove themselves by blowing something up. There's a little tendency in men to play wooden soldier and all of them love the idea of being a soldier. I'm convinced that if you want to end a war, you send a troop of women in [laughs]. You think they'd stay in Vietnam that long? They'd figure out a way to end it. I just think that it's a little bit of macho, you know, proving that they're males. I'm not too sure that we're necessarily more *peace*—like the dove and the hawk kind of bit.

Importance of Defense

[But you yourself think that defense is one of the most important things we have to face?] Well, see, it's probably the whole orientation I have. I happen to believe that the federal government defends the United States, its job. They shouldn't be screwing around in all those other things. They should be defending the United States. The reason that we've got a country that's going to bust right now is because they've got their mob in every little town project that they can find to get involved in. Because these silly congressmen get up there and say, "I got a letter from my mother-in-law, who says her apartment house is falling down. Let's get her a grant" [laughs].

[So you think that the main purpose of government is to defend rather than do any of these other things?] Yes, right. So it's not a matter of should you increase the amount of spending on defense. You should get rid of all this other garbage, in my mind anyway.

I *don't* find a Communist under every bed. I suppose at one time I really felt that they wanted Cuba. I think that we've got bigger problems than the Soviet Union. I mean the Soviet Union's *definitely* a *major* problem. But these little countries want these nuclear warheads right now; that's what scares me. And the terrorism—things like that. I'm sure that the hands of the Soviets are in there, but I worry about those guys pushing the wrong button. . . .

I love Maggie putting down the Argentines [laughs]. I really rooted for her. That's the third time Argentina's been put down by a woman—Queen Elizabeth was one, Evita, and now Maggie. I mean, think about what *that* does to machismo. They're always blessing their mothers. The women have beat them three times. I love it. . . .

I'm probably the only one you've interviewed so far who says women are peace-oriented. See, but I don't think Communists are going to go to war with us, because we can blow them away faster than they can blow us away. . . . There's so much we can do to them. I *just can't see*—they don't want to inherit the cinder blocks. The threat of the Soviets is the slow erosion of our own public, the infiltration of them into—the leftists you've got in every newspaper and that sort of thing, convincing us that we're all wrong in everything we're doing. . . . No, I think if we want to blow them away, we can. I think that the problem is that they're snooping around out there. They're not under my bed this week, but they're sneaking around out there [chuckles]. They're in our press. That's why I don't like them. They're in our government department and all this. I mean, I don't know if they're actually *agents* or dupes or if people are just stupid and they play to that mentality.

Our educational process in the schools stinks, too. When did a teacher ever give a good government course that taught the meaning of the Constitution and what the federal government's purpose is? Has there ever been one? They want to talk current events and get kids to go out and picket on the Common. They were picketing [Proposition] 2½ or something. They give them a day off to go picket. Probably their parents don't even know that they're out there. I see it all the time in Boston.

Reflections on Politics

[Let me ask you another question. Do you have any idea why some people are driven to politics?] It's a disease —slow erosion of every-thing in you or something [laughs]. It's like having cancer or some-thing. You can't shake it. You know, every election you lose you say, "That's the last one I'll work on." Even if you win, sometimes you go away disgusted. I've been on winning campaigns where I've left disgusted or burned out. But it's just such an incredible —I mean where do you get that kind of excitement? [Is that the main thing that keeps you going or are there other things?] I guess at this point it's habit. . . . I have friends who can't stand politics; they just can't *stand* to do that. They don't want to talk about it. They just don't want to hear or do anything. I envy them [laughs]. It would be nice to just relax, go live somewhere on an island and not worry about the world. I mean why do you want to worry so much about the world? Some people manage to isolate themselves.

But in Washington the bureaucracy's so big. . . . It's a Disneyland of the East. Every one of these congressmen ought to go home and live—every one of them. Pay Social Security taxes for a change. See what it's like not to have a seventy-five-dollar a day allowance. The argument that they need pay raises all the time and all that stuff—you get what you paid for— What difference does a pay-check mean? You'd still have people running. For a dollar a year, you'd still have people running. We had *better* representation when it *was* a dollar a year [laughs]. They all get fed by lobbyists anyway. What is the big deal? To get paid so much and then not have to pay taxes, not come under the same laws we come under—to me it doesn't make sense. It's so incredible. Send them all home [laughs].

[As we get up to leave, I thank Dora and tell her, "If there's anything I can do for you in Massachusetts, please let me know." Smiling, she replies, "How about the floors and windows?"]

Conclusion

World views are symbolic constructions of reality. People learn the import and meaning of symbols during the early years of childhood —through their family, school, church, and peers. To a large extent, this symbolic universe is acquired non-consciously and becomes part of a taken-for-granted reality.[2] Mary and Dora are both women of the right, but they come from separate worlds, worlds rooted in different beliefs and values.

The symbolic construction of Mary's world is strongly influenced by her religious upbringing, by the devout belief inculcated by her parents, her schooling, and the Church. The social mores of the time, the Church doctrines, and the strict discipline of her family, all provided a sense of stability and security for Mary. "What we had to lean on," she says wistfully of those days from her past.

As a homemaker and mother of seven children, Mary has formed her world around the family. Further, religious belief and absolute faith remain the mortar cementing together her world. Yet now, as a mother, Mary has witnessed the crumbling of that mortar, the decay of parental authority. The carefully ordered ·world of her youth, in which one knew right from wrong, is now in disarray. Mary looks longingly upon the days of her youth, mourning the loss of romance and the loss of certainty in today's world.

In particular, women's liberation—and accompanying Feminism, abortion, and ERA—pose a fundamental challenge to the traditions in which Mary was raised. In her eyes, there is a sharp division between the feminine role as nurturer and the masculine role as breadwinner. Each is to be respected, for society prospers through women's role within the home. Women's liberation has caused the collapse of respect for these traditional gender roles, the erosion of the old ways. The career of homemaking is no longer valued. Mary is disdainful, for example, of the feminist call for "Wages for Housework," which she sees as a degradation of women's sacred responsibilities, representing the imposition of materialism onto the spiritual realm.

In striking contrast to Mary, Dora never mentions religious belief or spiritual faith. She has a secular orientation. A spunky and independent child, she began her political involvement at an early age. Her symbolic world was affected more by her Republican upbringing than by devout religious belief.

Further, as a single woman of thirty-four with a professional career, Dora's lifestyle falls outside the bounds of traditional gender roles. In fact, Dora is critical of social conservatives' overemphasis on family. She is firmly against the "send 'em home" philosophy that calls for women to get married and raise a family. She is disdainful, too, of the macho attitude of "playing wooden soldier."

While Dora would not define herself as a feminist, she clearly is closer to a feminist view of gender than she is to Mary's vision of male and female roles. While Mary dismisses any notion of sex discrimination, declaring, "I never thought I was a second-class citizen," Dora is upset by the double standard by which women are expected to volunteer while men are paid for their political work. Hence, while ERA poses a fundamental threat to the very construction of Mary's world, Dora thinks ERA won't make much difference, except "to screw things up."

Also unlike Mary, Dora places economic and defense issues firmly at the center of the political agenda, dismissing the social issues as a smokescreen for these more central concerns. The pocketbook is the main thing in her eyes, not absolute faith. America's problems have to do with the government being too big and with the infiltration of Communism into domestic life. Dora fears government will become Big Brother, intruding into her personal life, instead of simply acting in defense of the country.

Typically, while both women share a distrust of the media, Mary criticizes the media for its secular viewpoints, blaming those in the media for "never darkening the door of a church," while Dora is skeptical of the Communist viewpoints creeping into the media, continually slanting the news.

At base, Mary and Dora's political involvement derives from two separate sources. Mary's entrance into the political arena springs from her distress over the turmoil she sees around her. Originally induced to action over the abortion issue, Mary came to activism above all as a result of her deep religious commitment and as an extension of her female caretaker role; thus, she acts out of a moral obligation to return the decaying world to decency.

Dora, on the other hand, has been active much longer, having "caught the fever" for politics at an early age. Her activism does not stem from her religious faith; the symbols she names in explaining "the mess this country's in" are not forces of moral decay. Nor does Dora act out of the selflessness of the traditional female role, as a moral guardian of society. Rather, Dora has a burning desire to "play with politics." She finds politics rewarding in itself, a form of self-fulfillment. "Where else do you get that kind of excitement?," she asks.

It may be that for Dora politics provides the kind of meaning and orientation that Mary finds through religion. In her comment on time capsules, Dora notes that what survives the years is politics— people want to know who was president. Thus, for her the sense of higher purpose, the eternal, derives from her political activism itself, not from her contribution to cleaning up the moral order.

In fact, looking at the activists overall, we see that women in each group respond differently to discussion of their future activism. While both groups of women affirm their intent to remain politically active, laissez-faire women discuss their involvement in terms of the personal satisfaction they derive from their work. In contrast, social conservative women typically respond, as one activist did, by saying, "[I will remain active] as long as the Lord wants me to."

What is essential about the stories of Mary and Dora is that they are not simply individual constructions of the social world; rather, they are grounded in *group* life. While the particular experiences and details of every individual's life varies, in Max Weber's terms there is an "elective affinity" between world views and particular social groups.[3] That is, it is not random or coincidental which individuals look at the world in similar ways. Class, religion, ethnicity, and gender all influence the meaning, the degree, and the intensity with which people respond to particular political symbols. Specific groups become the "carriers of meaning" for political symbols that, grouped together, form a world view.

While no conclusive statements can be made from the small sample in this study to conservative activists as a whole, the distinct sociological pools that form the base for social and laissez-faire conservatism parallel the findings on the Old Right discussed in Chapter One.[4] In brief, social conservative women are older and less educated than laissez-faire women and are predominantly from fundamentalist and Catholic backgrounds. Laissez-faire women are typically from non-fundamentalist backgrounds, with a larger percentage having professional degrees and positions. In addition, laissez-faire conservative activists are more likely to be single, divorced, or living with men outside of marriage, while all the women who are full-time homemakers fall within the social conservative group.

Clearly, not only demographic differences but also differences in lifestyle separate the two groups. For example, the aspirations expressed by the women regarding the question of family versus career distinguish the two groups. Not surprisingly, the laissez-faire conservative activist tends to be more "career-oriented" than her social conservative counterpart, expressing much more ambivalence about the prospect of family and children. A common refrain heard among both single and married laissez-faire conservative activists concerns the recognition that marriage and/or children may not be part of their future. For example, one single woman interviewed, aged thirty-three, reports that the past several years have been devoted to building her career. Perhaps she won't marry until she's forty, she says, nor is she sure she will have children; however, she adds, amniocentesis makes it possible for her to have children at a later age.

Similarly, a married laissez-faire activist, considering the prospect of children, said:

> I'm thirty-one and my biological clock is running out. I don't want to have children and then be too old to enjoy them. My husband would like me to be a full-time housewife. But there's no way! Can you imagine "ring around the collar" fulltime? I'm not going to join a country club and do shopping and soap operas— that just *not* my thing.

Another woman, who is divorced and living with her boyfriend, reflected on the tension between home and career by saying: "I would never have a job and be a housewife so I've solved that problem by not doing any housework. My son vacuums and fixes dinner."

In contrast, social conservative activists—even if they have careers —express much more commitment to family and children. Typically, one single social conservative activist said:

> I would much prefer staying home with my children. But I'm kind of lucky; my job in politics, all you really need is a phone line. So it's something you can do at home. Phyllis [Schlafly] does not seem to impair her career. . . . Really children grow up very quickly and before you know it they're in high school and college. Once they're in college, they're out of the house. . . . I would consider [being at home] a more enriching life. I consider that a luxury. . . . Very few people have a job that is more pleasant to them than taking care of their own children.

Another social conservative activist had this to say about balancing a career and family:

> I guess I'm a traditionalist. I see my sister-in-law raise five kids. She's at home and it's tough to find enough hours in a day to do everything for those five children. If she were working full time, it couldn't be done. I'm really interested to see fifteen years from

now what happens to all these kids who are being raised in day-care centers who are turnkey kids. I know that when I was teaching school, I had problems with kids who weren't properly supervised in the afternoons in far greater number than I did with children who had a parent at home when they got home from school taking care of them. If I were to have a family, I would want to be home with them.

These differences in "traditional" versus "non-traditional" attitudes toward family and career are also evidenced in the women's reflections on their own political involvement. Each group discusses their accomplishments in different terms. For instance, contrast the following two statements:

If it wasn't for my husband, I could have never done it. He was very supportive and took care of the girls at night. I was always home for supper. But then I'd go out and wouldn't get home 'til late. But he believed in what I was doing. He really helped.

[My husband is] very supportive. He's come a long way; he was in the military. Every once in a while he gets insecure. He needs to know that I need him. I don't really. I could get along fine without him. . . . But I need to let my husband think I really need him. So I let him take care of the checkbook. I deposit my check in his account every month. He takes care of finances. . . . Every now and then he has to be reassured.

The first statement was made by a social conservative woman, a full-time homemaker. The second statement was made by a laissez-faire conservative activist who, because of the political office she holds, lives in a different city from her husband, only seeing him on weekends. Clearly, the differences in background and aspirations of the activists also extend to the degree of autonomy and independence the women feel toward their lives and accomplishments.

We have seen that the two worlds of the New Right are divided not only by beliefs and values but also in background and lifestyle.

Clearly, different life situations influence the symbolic construction of reality. There is a relationship between a woman's social location and her values and beliefs. It is not coincidental that a woman with a devout religious upbringing who is a full-time homemaker is more likely to see the family at the center of the world and to adhere to a traditional ideology regarding gender. Nor is it a coincidence that a single professional woman in her mid-thirties who is devoted to her career does *not* see the family as central and holds non-traditional attitudes about men and women's roles. As Kristin Luker puts it, commenting on women on either side of the abortion debate, "We might say that for pro-life women the traditional division of life into separate male and female roles still works, but for pro-choice women it does not."[5] As applied to women of the New Right, traditional gender roles "work" for social conservative women not simply due to faith but because they themselves are more likely to be in life situations that correspond to traditional roles. Laissez-faire women, on the other hand, who are more likely to be single, divorced, or living with men outside of marriage, and who have higher levels of education and hold more professional positions than do social conservative women, are in life situations and have social resources outside of the traditional female sphere.

Interestingly, the differences in background and lifestyle of the women in this study parallel the findings regarding the social bases of anti-feminist and feminist women. Thus, the composite portrait finds anti-feminist women to be overwhelmingly white middle-aged housewives, married or widowed, new to politics and oriented toward single issues. Protestant fundamentalism plays a primary role in motivating these women to political action, while Catholicism is an important source of activism to women in the Northeast. Feminists, on the other hand, are typically somewhat younger than anti-feminist women, are employed outside the home, with a higher percentage of them single, divorced, or separated. Feminists tend not to be new to politics, have more years of education, and have a more secular orientation than anti-feminist women. Finally, anti-feminist women tend to be much less oriented toward careers than feminists, with their life goals being directed toward taking care of others, in contrast to feminists' life goals' being directed toward personal growth and achievement.[6]

While it is not surprising that social conservative women have the same profile as anti-feminists, the similarity in backgrounds between feminists and laissez-faire conservative women is striking. What needs to be explained is, given the similarities in background, why do some women adopt a feminist ideology while others do not? A fascinating area for future inquiry would be an analysis of the particular factors that differentiate laissez-faire women from feminists in terms of upbringing and social background.

Given the distinct backgrounds and separate realities of the two worlds of the right, the New Right's ability to form a unified movement seems amazing. It is only through shared symbolism and wise political leadership that these separate realities appear as one. We must, finally, ask: What is the future of the New Right? Can the New Right sustain the coalition between these two worlds?

CHAPTER SEVEN

The Future of the New Right

Symbols are markers of meaning. They order social reality, providing orientation and understanding to the individual amidst the complexity of social life. They capture images of people's innermost dreams and most protected fears. Because symbols are endowed with such meaning, they bring individuals together, solidifying them into a community, a group, or a social movement. It is the power of political symbols that creates social solidarity, a power socially constructed through human belief. And yet part of the potency of symbols rests in the fact that symbols harbor different meanings. Beneath the seeming unity of shared symbols rest disparate beliefs, a multiplicity of meanings.

There are two worlds among women of the New Right, two worlds rooted in different realities. While social conservatives peer out at the world through a religious lens, laissez-faire conservatives look at the world through the lens of liberty. The fundamental values, the basic assumptions regarding human nature, the hopes and fears at the heart of each world are distinct. And yet despite all of the differences the two worlds converge in naming the forces responsible for America's decline. Hence, any discussion of the New Right must not only acknowledge the existence of these two worlds but must also look beneath the political symbols that appear to unite the right to uncover the meanings underlying these symbols. For while it may appear that the right shares a common ideology, beneath these shared symbols rest essentially different constructions of social reality. Thus, the New Right speaks a common language devoid of any common meaning.

To understand the multiplicity of meanings of political symbols is to recognize the danger of relying solely on survey results to understand a political ideology. By labelling individuals "conservative" based on their responses to a set of questions, we may overlook important differences in the meaning of such response. For example, while both social and laissez-faire conservatives might respond to a questionnaire with "strong approval" of law and order to address the rise in youth crime, there are critical differences in the perceived roots and proposed solutions to such an issue. Social conservatives view youth crime as a sign of America's moral decay, as the result of a decline in authority, and as a failure to instill traditional values of honesty, hard work, and respect for others. Laissez-faire conservatives interpret youth crime as a result of restrictions on the free market; minimum-wage legislation, they argue, restricts jobs for the young, leading to teenage unemployment and consequently to crime. Further, government handouts inculcate youth with the ethic that "you can get something for nothing," which destroys individual initiative and sanctions criminal activities. Consequently, while social conservatives look to the moral realm to address crime by youth, laissez-faire conservatives seek economic solutions to cure America of this ill.

Understanding these sub-universes of meaning among those who are grouped together under the common label of "conservative" or "right-wing" is as important as understanding how conservatives are distinct from liberals. Such knowledge not only reveals a fuller spectrum of the variations of political belief but also points to areas of potential conflict between the two worlds, raising questions about the future of the conservative movement.

As we have seen, the two worlds of the New Right are not simply dissimilar; they are fundamentally incompatible. There are three basic areas of tension between social and laissez-faire conservatism. Yet a "myth of common meaning" sustains the unity of the two worlds.[1] Until the underlying content meaning of these shared symbols is exposed, revealing the chasm within the right, common meaning will be assumed. Thus far, the political leaders of the New Right have been successful in wedding together the coalition of groups that elected and re-elected Ronald Reagan. Yet, given the deep division of ideology and interest beneath this seeming unity, what is the possibility of divorce? What is the future of the New Right?

Human Nature and Society

The first area of tension between the two worlds centers on different beliefs regarding the individual and society. For social conservatives, Man is fallen, sinful, a creature of unlimited passions and desires. There is a deterministic strain to the social conservative view of human nature; skeptical of Man's ability to "pull himself up by the bootstraps," social conservatives believe that human perfectibility will only be achieved in the next world. In *this* world it is society's role to leash Man's appetites, to tame human nature. Acting as a force of integration, society brings the individual under the moral authority of God, the church, and the family, thereby restraining Man's instincts and curbing individual self-interest. Only through such integration does Man attain his civilized state as a moral being. If a world of balance and integration is the ideal, what social conservatives fear, above all, is anomie, social chaos. Without binding moral values and obedience to God's laws, individual passions are unleashed, the foundation of social cohesion disintegrates, and anarchy reigns.

While social conservatives view the religious realm as primary and focus on Man as a moral being, laissez-faire conservatives place primary importance on the marketplace, with humans as self-interested actors. This is not to say that laissez-faire conservatives are irreligious; rather, religious belief does not play the central role for laissez-faire conservatives that it does for social conservatives.

In stark contrast to the social conservative view of human nature, laissez-faire conservatives praise human potential, believing that humans are best left on their own, unrestricted by imposing constraints.

By placing ultimate faith in individual initiative and free will, laissez-faire conservatives adhere to a voluntaristic view of human nature, taking pride in the human capacity for self-improvement. Rather than viewing humans as beings of unlimited appetites that require moral restraint, laissez-faire conservatives view humans as autonomous beings, capable of critical thought and independent action. Consequently, society is viewed as the aggregate of individual action in which the marketplace—rather than God or moral authority—creates social harmony out of individual interest. The ideal society preserves liberty, allowing the individual unrestrained pursuit of self-interest, which thereby yields the greatest productivity and the maximum freedom. What laissez-faire conservatives fear, above all, is the loss of individual freedoms, the imposition of collectivism, and ultimately the slavery of the totalitarian state.

While the laissez-faire conservative, then, dreams of a world in which the individual is freed from the external constraints of authority and thereby attains total autonomy, such a vision is anarchic to the social conservative. The free individual of the laissez-faire conservative world is the masterless man feared by social conservatives.

By placing the individual on center stage, and by stressing autonomy and free will, the laissez-faire conservative perspective comes perilously close to the Secular Humanist model abhorred by social conservatives. In fact, the libertarian dictum of total freedom of action, barring the use of force or fraud, parallels the very slogan of the 1960s that social conservatives condemn: "Do your own thing as long as it doesn't hurt anyone else." Social conservatives view such "pure liberty" as defiance of divine law, which results in social disintegration. Humanists are accused of being selfish and narcissistic, of viewing life merely in terms of gratification of the ego. Yet this charge of "Me-Firstism" could just as well be made about laissez-faire conservatives. New Right leader Howard Phillips alludes to this in his remark: "The liberals believe that the state is God. The libertarians believe that Man is God. And the conservatives, at least those to whose doctrines I subscribe, believe that God is God."[2]

Another New Right spokesman, commenting on the difference

between what he terms "true conservatives and false conservatives," condemns the "Natural Rights craze of false conservatives," according to which "I am entitled to everything I can lay my hands on"; he renounces John Locke's doctrine of individual rights, "inasmuch as society is composed not of individuals, but families." Further, this author's criticism of "false conservatives" erupts into overt hostility against the basic tenets of laissez-faire conservative belief:

> The typical Northern capitalist . . . is a strong defender of what he likes to call Free Enterprise, by which he too often means a government-encouraged monopoly or oligopoly of business interests. He stands up for America against the menace of Soviet Communism . . . although he is not averse to turning a profit from trading with countries "behind the Iron Curtain." . . . Religion, he is heard to argue, is a very good thing, so long as it is not contaminated by fanaticism. . . .
>
> It is obvious to anyone that many capitalist "Conservatives" are nothing better than nineteenth century liberals with a hangover. Their libertarian ideas of freedom, expressed almost always in economic terms, are tempered only by the recognition that it takes force to keep the discontented masses in their place. However, when a Southerner calls himself a conservative, he is usually thinking of a way of life, of a social and moral order for which the people of the 1860s went to war. He is more disturbed by the disintegration of the family than by rising interest rates. . . . He is not so delighted with the mobility and tawdriness of modern life, with the fast food and fast buck artists who seem intent on turning the New South into a suburb of Chicago. . . .
>
> Our capitalist friends have made an idol of freedom and have invoked its aid to solve every social ill that man is heir to. But freedom is not a god; it is not even something precious like gold, an entity like the church, or a condition like goodness. It is just an abstraction.[3]

The disparity between the two world views is striking: posed as North versus South, as free enterprise versus traditionalism, as turning a profit versus loyalty to a style of life, and, ultimately, as worshipping freedom versus true faith in God. As critics of modern culture, social conservatives are concerned, above all, with the restoration of values. Hence, the self-interested individuals of the laissez-faire world are viewed as beings "obsessed with economics," morally deficient in their preoccupation with individual freedom and material well-being.[4]

Yet while signs of strain between the two worlds are evident in such comments by leaders of the New Right, it is improbable that this area of tension will lead to outright divorce. Because assumptions regarding human nature and the ideal society are philosophical at base, and therefore are remote from the everyday world of most people's lives, it is unlikely that the demise of the New Right will result from this tension alone.

Role of the State

The second area of tension is potentially explosive. The two worlds hold diametrically opposed positions regarding the role of the state. While both social and laissez-faire conservatives criticize the existing state, essentially they call for its replacement by different kinds of state. Social conservatives attack the present state—government institutions, the schools, and so on—as representative of a competing belief system, that is, Secular Humanism. They wish to replace the values and interests now embodied in public institutions with their own set of beliefs and values. Laissez-faire conservatives, however, do not want to replace the values embedded in public institutions with some other set of values; rather, they wish to cut back or eliminate the public sector altogether.

Further, the two worlds are in fundamental disagreement over the role of the state in the private realm. Social conservatives reject any notion of moral neutrality. They are willing to use the state to achieve righteous ends, calling for the insertion of traditional values based on biblical principles. In particular, social conservatives rely on the state to legislate moral issues, for example, abortion and homosexuality. Laissez-faire conservatives, on the other hand, reject any effort to introduce public authority into the private realm, vehemently opposing government as "morals police," as Big Brother watching over the individual. Extension of the state into the private realm violates the sacred tenets of laissez-faire conservative belief— limited government in *both* the public and private spheres. For laissez-faire conservatives, then, the state itself is inherently evil, a threat to individual rights.

As a consequence of this difference, each side rebukes the other's position. For instance, a reporter for the *Moral Majority Report* asserts:

> Libertarianism in a free society ultimately brings on bondage. . . . It is impossible to legislate morality altogether, but law does go a long way in being a persuader of doing better things. When there are no teeth in the law, no one fears it, and many will live as if there is no law. That is not freedom; it is bondage —the bondage of anarchy.[5]

On the other side, a libertarian writer warns that "emphasis on prayer-in-the school, anti-sex education, anti-gay rights, anti-pornography, anti-ERA, anti-abortion amendments and anti-evolution is a one-way ticket to the Swamp of No Return."[6] He argues that there is a deepening conflict between libertarianism and traditionalism, and uses a quote from William Safire to sum up the conflict:

> The traditionalists want government to uphold society's values— to bolster the family unit, to censor the pornographic, to discourage divorce, to encourage prayer, to curb abortion, to lend government sanction to their cultural propensities. . . . The libertarian conservatives are quite different: they may believe fiercely in some or all of the above "family values," but they are even more fierce in the belief that government is wrong to legislate morality. Moral matters are for individuals to decide, provided they do not brutalize others.[7]

Because the role of the state is tied to so many political issues, it is here that the myth of common meaning is most likely to be exposed. In fact, signs of strain are already evident. Since the early days of the Reagan administration, social conservatives have expressed dismay over Reagan's neglect to use state power to endorse traditional values. Social conservative critics charge Reagan with being preoccupied with economic and defense issues, ignoring the social issues that helped get him elected. In July of 1982 the *Conservative Digest* ran an entire issue entitled, "Has Reagan Deserted the Conservatives?" Connie Marshner's answer was an emphatic "Yes":

> Since taking office the White House has expressed precious little
> concern about anything but economic problems. . . . By ignoring
> the social agenda or relegating it to a place at the bottom of the
> heap the people who run the Reagan administration are losing the
> 1982 election *and* their own chances to achieve economic reform,
> as well as the country's best chance for moral and social
> reclamation.[8]

Social conservatives criticize Reagan for only giving rhetorical support to such issues as abortion, busing, and school prayer. They claim, for instance, that while Reagan made an all-out effort to muster support for the MX missiles or for sale of the AWACs to Saudi Arabia, no major lobbying effort was undertaken in support of a constitutional amendment banning abortion.[9]

Should this strain lead to conflict, what is the likely outcome? Which side is likely to be victorious? Thus far, laissez-faire conservatives seem to be in the stronger position. Reagan's emphases should not be surprising because, contrary to the claims of social conservatives, analyses of the 1980 election show that Reagan's election did *not* represent a triumph of social conservatives.[10] Abortion and ERA, for example, were not very important issues during the election; in fact, people supporting abortion actually voted for Reagan nearly as frequently as those who opposed abortion.[11] While the media played up the social issues, they were not stressed in Reagan's campaign nor were they mentioned prominently in exit polls of voters during the election.[12] Further, Gallup polls indicate that the social issues have declined in general import among the mass public since the early 1970s.[13]

Additionally, while there seems to be a conservative trend among the college-age generation, with 58 percent of young voters (18–29) supporting Reagan in 1984,[14] it is not the social issues that they support. One Reagan campaign official, for instance, acknowledged that in October of 1984, when television ads castigated Republicans as the party of the Moral Majority, Reagan support among eighteen-to-twenty-four-year-old voters plummeted twenty points in five days.[15] Similarly, Edward Rollins, the director of Reagan's 1984 re-election campaign, reported that most of the young voters Republicans had success with in 1984 were libertarian in orientation.[16] As Martin Franks, executive director of the Democratic Congressional Campaign Committee, put it: "If there is anything that puts a shudder into young voters, it's the right wing's social agenda."[17] The baby boom generation also rejects social conservatism. Predicted to be the single biggest bloc of voters in 1988 by election forecaster Patrick Caddell, the baby boomers tend to be economically conservative but liberal on the social issues.[18]

These factors indicate that should conflict erupt within the New Right, laissez-faire conservatives, who have a greater degree of support among the mass population, are likely to be the victors. However, there are two factors that could militate against a laissez-faire victory. First, if the Moral Majority, Christian Voice, and other religious organizations led by social conservatives are successful in their efforts to register millions of fundamentalist voters, this could have a significant impact in the promotion of their cause. Pat Robertson's recent success in the delegate selection process for the Republican primaries in Michigan took contenders Jack Kemp and George Bush by surprise, indicating the possibility that social conservatives may be successful in mobilizing the religious right. Continued gains by social conservatives are particularly dependent on the amount of resources available to mount such efforts. Matthew Smythe, director of the Christian Voice Moral Government Fund, reports that his organization increased the funds spent from $500,000 in 1980 to $1 million in 1984 in order to support candidates.[19]

A second factor that must be considered in assessing the future of the New Right is the role of the judiciary. While social conservatives have been relatively unsuccessful in promoting their social agenda through legislative means,[20] the judiciary offers another avenue for social conservative victory. In fact, because judicial appointments are made for life and are only removable for "treason, bribery, or other high crimes and misdemeanors," judges have more long-term impact than elected officials. In fact, President Reagan has made more lower court appointments than any of his recent predecessors. By October of 1985 30 percent of all U.S. district court judges and 27 percent of all U.S. court of appeals judges were Reagan appointees. Predictions are that by the end of his term Reagan will have appointed over half of the 743 federal judges.[21] In terms of the Supreme Court, while social conservatives were angered by the appointment of Sandra Day O'Connor, due to her mixed voting record on abortion, the recent appointment of Judge Antonin Scalia and the promotion of Justice William H. Rehnquist to Chief Justice show more promise for social conservatives.[22]

In terms of issues, while the Supreme Court recently upheld the *Roe v. Wade* decision, preserving a woman's right to abortion, the vote shifted from the original 7–2 vote in support of the decision to a 5–4 vote. Although disappointed by the decision, social conservatives were encouraged by the possibility of overturning abortion during the Rehnquist court. Further, the recent decision upholding Georgia's law that outlaws homosexual sodomy signifies a triumph for the social conservative view of the state's role in legislating morality.

In short, while the two worlds of the New Right will continue to share a mutual hostility toward federal power and continue to favor dismantling the welfare state, tax cutbacks, rearming America, and a foreign policy based on anti-Communism, disputes over the *priorities* of the political agenda are bound to escalate in the coming years. Certainly, the selection of the 1988 Republican presidential candidate will raise the issue of the relative import of the social issues versus economic and defense issues. Predictably, candidates on either side will attempt to speak to both camps. Jack Kemp and George Bush have already appealed to the anti-abortion constituency just as Pat Robertson is downplaying his references to Christianity and the moral issues. Despite the use of common language, the issue of state involvement in the private realm could become the battleground of the New Right. Because the debate over morality raises issues concerning the family, sexual freedom, and reproductive rights, women will continue to have a central stake in this battle.

Gender and Feminism

The third area of tension between the two worlds specifically concerns women. As we have seen, women of the New Right are not a monolithic group. A further line of differentiation concerns each group's perception of Feminism. Consistent with the varying position each group takes regarding the role of the state, social conservative women want to use state power to validate a traditional view of the division of labor between men and women. They do not really want *less* state, as laissez-faire women do. Rather they want a different kind of state. Opposition to daycare, abortion, and gay rights are at the top of the social conservative political agenda, all viewed as detrimental to the family and to the preservation of traditional values. Laissez-faire women, on the other hand, are pro-choice and support daycare, as long as it remains in private hands; they firmly reject any government role in legislating sexuality or moral matters as an intrusion on individual liberty. Given these differences, what is the future of women's activism?

We have seen how the motivation behind the activism of the social conservative woman resides in her role as a traditional woman. Amidst the moral chaos of the 1960s, when the "do your own thing" cult of the New Left and the feminist movement fomented an attack on the family and on traditional gender roles, the social conservative woman was provoked to action. Feminism symbolized a threat to traditional ways, the devaluation of motherhood, scorn for home-making. Feminism was perceived as encouraging women to abandon their husbands and children, to pursue their own self-interest, to become more like men. Whether instigated to guard her youth from the dangers of Secular Humanism, to ensure her parental rights against Big Government, or to protect her own status as a home-maker, the social conservative woman joined in the effort "to clean up America." She was drawn into the political arena, then, to defend traditional values, to retain her sense of self-worth, and to protect against the total masculinization of the world.

Like feminists, the social conservative woman protests male values, but she does so on totally different grounds. The social conservative woman fears that a gender-free society will mean a world enveloped in self-interest, devoid of qualities such as nurturance, altruism, and self-sacrifice associated with the female role. If women become more like men, she reasons, there will be no one left to instill moral values in the young, to ensure that passions are controlled, to guard against a world besieged by self-interest. Social conservative women, then, act as an extension of their role as women—as mothers, as nurturers, as caretakers, as the upholders of moral values.

Put in different terms, the social conservative response can be interpreted as a reaction to an increasingly technological society, an organized effort to preserve traditional authority in an ever more bureaucratized world. Against the trend toward specialization and professionalization, the traditional female role represents the last pocket of common humanity, of the private and personal in an impersonal, mechanized world.[23] Connected to this is the specific distaste with which the social conservative woman views the encroachment of the economic sphere onto all other realms of society, and particularly the monetarization of the final pocket of privacy, the romantic realm. The social conservative woman reacts vehemently against the proposition that marriage is, after all, only an economic partnership. She holds out against this final disenchantment and acts to preserve the last remnant of mystery, the final haven remaining in the modern world.

Acting out of her role as woman, as mother, as protector of

her children, as moral gatekeeper, the social conservative woman finds an affinity between the traditional female role and the adoption of an ideology that rejects narcissism and self-interest for the "higher" values of self-sacrifice, faith, devotion, and compliance with authority. Yet because of this affinity between the traditional female role and social conservative belief, the future activism of social conservative women is uncertain. For, despite ideological commitment, the possibility of women's living a traditional lifestyle as full-time homemakers is diminishing. Each year more and more women enter the labor force due to economic necessity.[24] Moreover, research shows that employed women are more likely to believe in equality between the sexes than are full-time homemakers.[25] Thus, as women become paid laborers and face the realities of the job market, there may be a consequent shift of women away from social conservatism.[26]

Another possibility is that the very act of being politically involved may transform the social conservative woman. The "rough and tumble" political world, which involves competition, aggression, power, independence, and rational decision-making, may pose contradictions for the traditional female ideals of docility, passivity, dependence, and irrationality.[27] While we have seen how social conservative ideology expands to incorporate new roles for traditional women, there may be a point at which the social conservative woman crosses over the boundaries of traditional gender roles to enter the "non-traditional" domain. Indicative of the changes political activism can bring, one anti-ERA activist mentioned several friends of hers who had gotten divorced after becoming involved in politics. Unfortunately, it was not possible to interview these women. Another social conservative activist commented: "Well, it would be a little difficult to go and organize Brownie parties after this [political involvement]. I mean it doesn't make sense. Can you imagine Howard Phillips picking up his job and deciding he was going to run a PTA?"

Anita Bryant stands as an example of a woman transformed. In 1977 she became a national leader of the social conservative cause, heading the Florida crusade against homosexual rights. Three years later she announced she was divorcing her husband of twenty years, saying, "Everything may be gone, but now I can stand up and be counted for what I am—not for what someone else wants me to be."[28] She also remarked, "There are some valid reasons why militant feminists are doing what they're doing. Having experienced a form of male chauvinism among Christians that was devastating, I can see how women are controlled in a very ungodly, un-Christ-like way." Renouncing her former campaign, she now professes people should "live and let live."[29] In short, there may be latent effects to the social conservative woman's activism that undermine her own beliefs. However, given the deep-rooted nature of world views and the resiliency of ideology to incorporate new behavior, a mass exodus among social conservative women is unlikely.

And what will happen to the daughters of these activist mothers? As we saw in Chapter Six, Mary Donnelly's daughter grew up with an outspoken and self-confident mother, a mother who was a leader in the community. At the time she was interviewed, Mary's daughter was a student at Princeton. With her mother's support, she had spent the previous summer working on a feminist newspaper, just "to learn about the other side." Whether such daughters of social conservative women will follow in traditional ways or whether their mother's vocal and active roles in the political world will provoke their own departure from tradition remains to be seen.

What about the future activism of the laissez-faire conservative woman? Unlike her social conservative counterpart, the laissez-faire conservative woman is not motivated by religious belief. The laissez-faire woman acts out of a secular desire to return America to supremacy as the land of liberty. For example, some laissez-faire conservatives are propelled into politics in reaction to the ever-expanding growth of the welfare state and the subsequent increase in taxation. Other laissez-faire conservatives act to defend American status in the wake of Soviet ascendancy. The perceived Soviet gains in Vietnam, Afghanistan, Angola, Poland, and so on over the past decade, combined with reported Soviet superiority in the military realm, compel action to protect American status and American interests.

Nor does the laissez-faire woman act as an extension of the female role. She does not act from an altruistic need to protect her children or to be the moral guardian of society. Nor is she motivated to action to protect the interests of her gender. While gender identity is central to the activism of both social conservative women and feminists, laissez-faire women do not recognize their collective interests *as women*. While social conservative women act to protect women's interests within traditional bounds, and feminists act to advance non-traditional roles for women, laissez-faire women remain women in themselves, acting as self-interested members of the market rather than as members of the female sex.

Yet given the similar background of laissez-faire women and feminists, and their mutual views of gender and "women's issues," can laissez-faire women be transformed from women in themselves to women for themselves, acting specifically to promote their interests as women? What are the possibilities of an alliance between laissez-faire women and feminists? While feminist groups to date have not appealed to a constituency of conservative women, the coincidence of interest between the two groups indicates the possibility for coalition. Given the current direction of the Supreme Court, in the event of simply protecting a constitutional right to abortion, laissez-faire women may be an untapped constituency of support. However, while an alliance may be possible around single issues, any hope for an enduring coalition would be on shaky grounds. First of all, the laissez-faire opposition to government involvement restricts the possibility of any broad agreement. Laissez-faire women, for example, might be persuaded to rally in support of abortion or to appeal to a company to set up daycare facilities, but they would not support government aid to poor women to ensure the right to abortion nor would they endorse public support for daycare.

A second limitation to an alliance between laissez-faire women and feminists concerns priorities. Again, any long-term alliance is unlikely. The laissez-faire woman's support for issues related to the economy and defense supersede her concern about women's issues. Indicative of this, in a May 1984 meeting of the Republican National

Committee's National Women's Coalition, a group of seventy business and professional women conceded that, while they disagreed with Reagan on a number of women's issues, they agreed that the state of the economy overrode these concerns. In their view, only when inflation and interest rates were down, and employment was on the rise, would both men and women prosper.[30]

Alternative Visions

The future of the New Right does not simply depend on the continued activism of women or on whether or not internal dissension results in divorce between the two worlds. The future of the New Right also depends on the response by those who fall outside its borders. For those who are concerned about America's shift to the right, it is essential to understand that the New Right speaks to real social problems. Too often those on the left have dismissed the right as being fanatics or pathological.[31] Only to the extent that the issues raised by the right are recognized and addressed is it likely that the rightward tide will be turned.

Social conservatism speaks to problems and fears created by the enormous social upheaval of the past few decades, which witnessed changes in blacks' relations to whites, women's relations to men, and children's relations to parents. In her study of the right-to-life movement, Rosalind Petchesky warns that the pro-family movement should not be written off as religious fanaticism or as mere opportunism. The pro-family movement expresses fears resulting from teenagers' cultural independence from parents; it expresses parents' concerns about their children's getting pregnant, having abortions, abusing drugs, or being sexual without a context of responsibility. Petchesky argues that neither the left nor the women's movement has offered a model for a better way for teenagers to live and urges the development of alternative visions that provide a sense of orientation in dealing with this disruption and insecurity.[32] Added to this, the pro-family movement speaks to fears regarding women's precarious position in society. During a time of increased divorce and the feminization of poverty, women seek to assuage their anxiety, to secure their place in the social structure.[33] Social conservatives also react against the vision of a society steeped in self-interest. They criticize the hedonism and obsession with self of a society that has taken individualism to an extreme, in which self-fulfillment takes priority over responsibility to others.

These concerns over excessive materialism, over the instilling of values beyond self-interest, over the need for a larger community, are shared with those of other political persuasions. Christopher Lasch, for example, is also troubled by cultural anomie. He argues that the moral climate of the country is defined by the narcissistic personality, witnessed in the demand for immediate gratification, the concern with living for the moment, and the obsession with self. He, too, attacks the helping professions for invading the family, replacing parental authority with the need for outside experts.[34]

In *Habits of the Heart: Individualism and Commitment in American Life*, Bellah et al. report that while individualism remains a deeply held and precious tradition in America, excessive individualism has led to isolation and to a preoccupation with self and with private interests. Whereas in the past people derived meaning from their connection to others, to parents and to children, to a religious community, and to participation in public life, today freedom is largely defined negatively; people define themselves through breaking from past connections. Like Lasch, Bellah et al. are critical of the therapeutic attitude that encourages self-development and self-actualization at the cost of denying all forms of obligations and commitment.[35]

Lasch distinguishes himself from conservative critics by rooting the "non-morality of modern America" in monopoly capitalism, in a culture of competitive individualism that has carried the war of all against all to an extreme. He argues that those institutions of cultural transmission that might have countered narcissism—the school, church, and family—have instead become the very promoters of the cult of self. Yet Lasch's only antidote is an all-out struggle against bureaucracy, which, he argues, requires a struggle against capitalism. Bellah et al., on the other hand, point out that, during a time in which neither work nor public participation provides meaning, people look for meaning through "expressive individualism" of shared lifestyles. "Freed" from all social ties, people choose others like themselves, forming lifestyle enclaves centered on a private life of consumption and leisure. Echoing Tocqueville, Bellah et al. conclude that the antidote to excessive individualism is participation in public life and a reconnection of individuals to true communities, which, unlike lifestyle enclaves, are inclusive, celebrate the differences among individuals, and reconnect people to their past and to their future.

In contrast, the social conservative answer to cultural narcissism is moral absolutism—the firm and unquestioning assertion of biblical principles and traditional values. There is a certain irony to this moral absolutism. On the one hand, social conservatives have faith in divinely ordained laws, solid and eternal truths that form the moral code by which to live. On the other hand, they continually fear that, with even the smallest of questioning, the entire foundation of morality is likely to crumble.[36] This fear of collapse results in antagonism toward critical thought.

Further, the moral absolutism that divides the world into two camps of right and wrong, Good and Evil, reduces society to irreconcilable conflict. There are no shades of grey. For, if moral absolutism leaves little room for different interpretations of the Bible, it leaves even less room for the existence of a plurality of cultural and moral codes. In American society, historically rooted in heterogeneous cultures of diverse traditions, such a stance is suicidal.

If the urge toward community is a central concern underlying social conservatism, the urge toward freedom is one of the central concerns of laissez-faire conservatism. Laissez-faire conservatives speak to the reality of living in a world that is increasingly so huge and technological that the individual is lost, submerged in the structure. The laissez-faire conservative response expresses fear that, as bureaucracies grow bigger and bigger, the individual will be abandoned by the wayside. Horrified by the curtailment of civil liberties, appalled by Big Brother's intrusion into the private realm, ultimately the laissez-faire conservative fears the imposition of the totalitarian state.

Again, the very real issues voiced by laissez-faire conservatives are shared by those outside its borders. Bellah et al. find that nostalgia for the small town was common in discussions with Americans across the country regardless of political ideology. They interpret this longing, as well as the opposition to Big Government, as the desire to replace large-scale organizations with face-to-face interaction.[37]

The concern, as well, over protection of civil liberties and opposition to government involvement in the private realm are issues laissez-faire conservatives share with those of other political persuasions. In their study of American's attitudes toward civil liberties, Alida Brill and Herbert McClosky find that, whether ideology is measured by membership in particular groups, by self-identification, or by use of a scale, the strongest support for civil liberties is found among liberals rather than among conservatives.[38] But there are critical differences between laissez-faire conservatives and liberals, in response to the curtailment of liberty. While all concerned might agree with the laissez-faire call to protect individual rights and to uphold freedom of action, for laissez-faire conservatives this translates into opposition to Big Government and support for a foreign policy based on anti-Communism and military strength. Consequently, while laissez-faire conservatives advocate less government intervention and uphold individual self-determination, many of them also support paternalistic foreign policies that rely on Big Government and deny self-determination to people in other lands. They fear state expansion and cherish individual liberties in America, yet support authoritarian dictatorships abroad in which the state reigns through terror, curtailing even the most basic liberties. Support for such policies is couched in terms of protecting America's interests and making the world safe for democracy.

A consistent state policy, however, would come closer to the isolationist position promoted by a faction of the libertarians. Yet even the libertarian notion of liberty defines liberty negatively as the absence of coercion. As Stephen Newman points out, the sensitivity to external power and control embedded in this notion of liberty disappears at the entrance to the marketplace. There is no recognition, for instance, of the private power wielded by large corporations. Telling a woman living in a company town that she can fight discrimination by finding another job is certainly a limited concept of economic liberty. Arguing that autonomy is limited to the extent that the alternatives among which we may choose are conceived by others, Newman calls for a return to classical citizenship in which individuals participate in the decisions that determine their lives.[39]

Bellah et al. also conclude that prevention of public despotism must entail a strengthening of citizen influence rather than a knee-jerk reaction to "get government off our back" or to "decentralize our economy." Recognizing that in a large and complex society some degree of centralization is necessary, they recommend individual participation through associations and social movements aimed at humanizing rather than abolishing government. They, too, urge a renewal of citizenship, by which individuals make the state more responsive and responsible to the community.

Ironically, the fears expressed by each of the worlds of the New Right are actually being realized through the actions of the other. The social conservative fear of a world enveloped in self-interest is, in fact, the world promoted by laissez-faire conservatism. The laissez-faire world of autonomous actors is a world of anomic individualism. Driven by self-interest, it is a world without altruism, void of any notion of responsibility and care for others. A world of social atomism is a world without community. In the extreme, the libertarian ideal reduces the entire world to private interest. It rejects the world of public citizens for a world of individuals, each pursuing his or her own ends.

On the other hand, the laissez-faire conservative fear of a world in which the individual is constrained by external authority is the very world promoted by moral absolutism. In a world in which there is one true interpretation of the Bible, one cultural tradition, one correct way to live, the individual cannot act autonomously. There is no freedom in a world reduced to black and white.

Epilogue

It is possible, of course, that under modern conditions the avenues of choice are being closed, and that the culture of the future will be dominated by single-minded men of one persuasion or another. It is possible; but in so far as the weight of one's will is thrown onto the scales of history, one lives in the belief that it is not to be so.[1]

Some say humans are social beings; others say humans are political beings. What is clear, above all, is that humans are meaning-making beings. The need to make sense of the world around us, the drive to fit reality into categories and to communicate that reality through symbols, cuts across cultures, reaches across time. Symbols serve as signs of collective consciousness, as rallying cries that represent shared beliefs, common values. Yet symbols by nature are fluid, resilient, open to interpretation. As we have seen, while symbols may coincide, they also may represent different universes.

In America such words as "liberty," "democracy," "freedom," and "justice" are national symbols, assumed to be part of a common culture. Yet while a plurality of groups may refer to these national symbols, they do so from different vantage points. Use of such symbols entails a multiple set of meanings representing very different world views. There is the inherent probability within *any* society that multiple meaning systems exist, competing definitions of reality. But in heterogeneous societies, rooted in a plurality of cultures, this problem is particularly acute. As Berger and Luckmann put it, "This multiplication of perspectives greatly increases the problem of establishing a stable symbolic canopy for the *entire* society."[2]

The problem is that different symbols do not simply represent the presence of different groups in a society but, as we have seen, these symbols are components of belief systems rooted in different assumptions about human nature, different visions of the ideal society, and different values about how we are to live. Given this multiplicity of value systems, then, who is to determine the public consensus?

Which group's morals shall take precedence? Whose values shall prevail?

There is a consensus in every society about certain fundamental mores. Murder, for example, is considered abhorrent and therefore prohibited by law. Yet even what gets interpreted as murder, how mores are evaluated, raises the whole issue of these multiple meaning systems. To some people abortion is murder. Others consider the leaking of nuclear wastes, the cancerous materials in our air, as slow and silent murder. In short, there is no "public consensus," no "sacred canopy," that defines one social reality and makes clear what is right and what is wrong. Part of what is involved in the struggle for power is a struggle over whose symbolic definition of a situation will prevail.

Thus, the problem of multiplicity at times seems insuperable, the conflict between competing world views appears resolvable only through sheer force. As one pro-choice leader commented about abortion activists: "You could put both sides in one room for fifty years and no one would change positions. We operate from totally different views of the world, views that are more complex than abortion itself, involving a philosophy of life, one's approach to God and religion."[3]

But if there is any hope for surmounting such conflict, if discovering common meaning can ever be more than a pipe dream, then it must be based on public debate, on reasoned critique. And if the political arena can ever be a forum for true dialogue, we must begin by making clear those differences, by understanding that complexity. The very existence of multiple meanings, the fact that our world views do *not* coincide, makes it all the more imperative that we listen to the voice of the other, that we begin by respecting those who are different from ourselves. For only by realizing that difference is *not* a sign of weakness, that pluralism is *not* the same as relativism, that there is *not* simply one way to live, to act, or to think, does hope remain for common symbols that truly unite us ever to be forged.

Notes

CHAPTER ONE

1. Robert E. Lane, *Political Ideology: Why the American Common Man Believes What He Does* (New York: Free Press, 1962), p. 462.

2. During the 1970s the number of women elected to state and local government positions doubled. The most dramatic rise was at the state legislative level. While in 1969 there were 295 women in state legislatures, by 1982 the number had more than tripled to 903. At the local level, the number of women holding positions as county commissioners, mayors, and council members doubled between 1976 and 1980. See Martin Gruberg, "From Nowhere to Where?: Women in State and Local Politics," *Social Science Journal* 21 (January 1984): 5–11.

3. The 1980 election was a landmark for women's political participation in two ways. First, the proportion of women voting equalled that of men for the first time during peacetime. Second, the gender gap was clearly evidenced in the 1980 presidential election, with women preferring Reagan to Carter by only 47 percent to 45 percent and men supporting Reagan by a margin of 55 percent to 36 percent. See Adam Clymer, "Women's Political Habits Show Sharp Change," *New York Times*, June 30, 1982, p. A1.

4. This distinction between the emotional and substantive meaning of political symbols relies on the work of Charles Elder and Roger Cobb. See *The Political Uses of Symbols* (New York: Longman, 1983).

5. Seymour Martin Lipset and Earl Raab, *The Politics of Unreason: Right-Wing Extremism in America, 1790–1970* (New York: Harper and Row, 1970).

6. Raymond E. Wolfinger et al., "America's Radical Right: Politics and Ideology," in *The American Right Wing: Readings in Political Behavior*, ed. Robert A. Schoenberger (New York: Holt, Rinehart and Winston, 1969), pp. 9–47.

7. Grace A. Pheneger, "The Correlation Between Religious Fundamentalism and Political Ultra-Conservatism," M.A. thesis, Bowling Green State University, 1966.

8. Richard Hofstadter, *The Paranoid Style in American Politics* (Chicago: University of Chicago Press, 1952).

9. Immanuel Wallerstein, "McCarthyism and the Conservative," M.S. thesis, Columbia University, 1954.

10. Lipset and Raab, *The Politics of Unreason.*

11. Wolfinger et al., "America's Radical Right."

12. Ibid.

13. Wallerstein, "McCarthyism and the Conservative."

14. Pheneger, "The Correlation Between Religious Fundamentalism and Political Ultra-Conservatism."

15. George Nash, *The Conservative Intellectual Movement in America Since 1945* (New York: Basic Books, 1976).

16. For discussion of the ideology of neoconservatism and how neoconservatives differ from the New Right, see Gillian Peele, *Revival and Reaction: The Right in Contemporary America* (Oxford: Clarendon Press, 1984); also see Peter Steinfels, *The Neoconservatives: The Men Who Are Changing America's Politics* (New York: Simon and Schuster, 1979).

17. Nash, *The Conservative Intellectual Movement*, pp. 128, 179.

18. According to Richard Viguerie (*The New Right: We're Ready to Lead* [Falls Church, Va.: Viguerie Co., 1981], p. 53), the term "The New Right" was first used by Lee Edwards in 1962 in proposing a conservative platform for Young Americans for Freedom. The use of the term did not become popular, however, until 1975, when conservative writer Kevin Phillips associated the New Right with the efforts of Paul Weyrich, Howard Phillips, Richard Viguerie, and Terry Dolan, and linked the term specifically to social conservatism. This association of the New Right with the increased importance of the social issues has been noted by others as well; see, for example, Allen Hunter, "In the Wings: New Right Ideology and Organization," *Radical America* 15 (Spring 1981): 112–128, and William A. Rusher, "The New Right: Past and Prospects," in *The New Right Papers*, ed. Robert W. Whitaker (New York: St. Martin's Press, 1982), pp. 2–24.

Other commentators distinguish the New Right from the Old Right by the dominance of particular social issues. For linkage specifically to the issue of abortion, see Bill Peterson, "How the Honeymoon Ended: Leaders of the New Right Decide Reagan Is a Bridegroom No Longer," in Data Center, *The New Right: Issues and Analyses* (Oakland, Calif.: Data Center, 1982), pp. 27–29. For the prominence of issues related to the family and sexuality in the New Right, see Rosalind Pollack Petchesky, "Antiabortion, Antifeminism, and the Rise of the New Right," *Feminist Studies* 7 (Summer 1981): 206–246; and Barbara Ehrenreich, "The Social Issues Game: Family Feud on the Left," *The Nation* 234 (March 13, 1982): 289. For a more general association between the New Right and anti-feminism, see Linda Gordon and Allen Hunter, "Sex, Family and the New Right: Anti-Feminism as a Political Force," *Radical America* 11–12 (November 1977–February 1978): 9–25.

19. In the literature on the Old Right, Adorno's study is one of the few to detail traits associated with *female* authoritarianism. While Adorno found that those high in authoritarianism had similar family backgrounds with domineering, rigid parents, he documents some of the different defenses that develop in the male and female authoritarian personality. For example, he finds that authoritarian women cling to a self-image of conventional femininity defined by subservience to men at the same time that they are hostile toward men due to the unsatisfactory female role; see Theodor W. Adorno et al., *The Authoritarian Personality* (New York: Harper and Brothers, 1950).

Other than Adorno's study, the vast majority of research on the Old Right makes no mention of female activists. In a footnote to "The Sources of the Radical Right," Lipset makes reference to women's greater intolerance —for example, women are more likely to support repressive measures against Communists and other "deviant" groups than are men. Lipset relates this to women's greater concern with family status in the community than men, suggesting that women are generally more prone to status anxiety and frustration. He also notes women's greater concern with morality in politics, which he relates to women's greater religiosity. See Seymour Martin Lipset, "The Sources of the Radical Right," in *The Radical Right*, ed. Daniel Bell (Garden City, N.Y.: Doubleday and Co., 1963; reprint ed., Garden City, N.Y.: Anchor Books, 1964). Also see Robert E. Lane, *Political Life: Why People Get Involved in Politics* (Glencoe, Ill.: Free Press, 1959).

In his study of support for McCarthyism in a New England community, Martin A. Trow justifies the elimination of women from his study on the grounds that women would bias his sample with the uninformed and the apathetic; see "Right-Wing Radicalism and Political Intolerance: A Study of Support of McCarthy in a New England Town," Ph.D. dissertation, Columbia University, 1957.

20. See, for example, Theodore S. Arrington and Patricia A. Kyle, "Equal Rights Amendment Activists in North Carolina," *Signs* 3 (Spring 1978): 666–680; David W. Brady and Kent L. Tedin, "Ladies in Pink: Religion and Political Ideology in the Anti-ERA Movement," *Social Science Quarterly* 56 (March 1976): 564–575; Pamela Johnston Conover and Virginia Gray, *Feminism and the New Right: Conflict Over the American Family* (New York: Praeger, 1983); Andrea Dworkin, *Right-Wing Women* (New York: Perigee Books, 1983); Zillah Eisenstein, *Feminism and Sexual Equality: Crisis in Liberal America* (New York: Monthly Review Press, 1984); Kristin Luker, *Abortion and the Politics of Motherhood* (Berkeley: University of California Press, 1984); Andrew H. Merton, *Enemies of Choice: The Right-to-Life Move-*

ment and Its Threat to Abortion (Boston: Beacon Press, 1981); Carol Mueller, "Rancorous Conflict and Opposition to the ERA," paper presented at the American Sociological Association meetings, New York, August 1976; Carol Mueller, "Women's Issues and the Search for a New Religious Right: A Belief Systems Analysis, 1972–1980," paper presented at the American Political Science Association meetings, New York, September 3–6, 1981; and Rosalind Pollack Petchesky, *Abortion and Woman's Choice: The State, Sexuality, and Reproductive Freedom* (Boston: Northeastern University Press, 1984).

21. Shirley Rogers Radl, *The Invisible Woman: Target of the Religious New Right* (New York: Delacorte Press, 1983), p. 117.

22. Dworkin, *Right-Wing Women*, p. 17.

23. A notable exception to this assumption of the "false consciousness" of the anti-feminist woman is Kristin Luker's *Abortion and the Politics of Motherhood.* Luker carefully and sensitively portrays both sides of the abortion debate, revealing how the pro-life and pro-choice positions are rooted in different sets of interests and values.

24. I am indebted to Kristin Luker for making use of this distinction drawn from Marx. Marx discusses a class in itself and a class for itself in discussing how capital creates a mass of people in a common situation who share common interests. For example, in "The Poverty of Philosophy" Marx states: "The combination of capital has created for this mass a common situation, common interests. This mass is thus already a class as against capital, but not yet for itself. In the struggle, of which we have noted only a few phases, this mass becomes united, and constitutes itself as a class for itself. The interests it defends become class interests. But the struggle of class against class is a political struggle." See Karl Marx, in *The Marx-Engels Reader*, ed. Robert C. Tucker (2nd ed.; New York: W. W. Norton and Co., 1978), p. 218.

25. While I argue here that social conservative women are motivated out of gender interests and laissez-faire conservative women out of their self-interest as actors in the marketplace, I believe both act to protect both status and class interests. Contrary to much previous research on right-wing movements, heavily influenced by status politics arguments, I think it is a mistake to separate the motivation for political activism into these two separate types. The social conservative woman's defense of traditional gender roles protects a particular economic arrangement in which the male is the breadwinner of the family. Thus, while participation in an anti-ERA demonstration might be interpreted as expressive action, support for Social Security payments for homemakers or tax benefits for one-earner families is not purely symbolic in nature. Similarly, while social conservatives act to

defend their status against the perceived decline in parental authority, advocacy for tuition tax credits to restore parental control over children's education has a concrete effect on the distribution of material resources.

So, too, the activism of the laissez-faire conservative woman is motivated by a mixture of both expressive and instrumental elements. Clearly, anti-tax legislation and support for right-to-work laws speak to the interest of a particular economic group. In fact, laissez-faire conservative belief is premised on support for small business. Yet the laissez-faire conservative world view encompasses more than action that protects material interest. Belief in individual liberty and anti-Communism are deeply held values that translate into more "symbolic" behavior as well—for example, petitions condemning Polish repression of Solidarity or participation in counter-demonstrations to the nuclear freeze movement.

Reducing political action into this dichotomy of either instrumental action based on economic interests or expressive behavior based on status or values does not do justice to individual action. Political behavior of both the right and left involves elements of *both* class and status, of material interests *and* values, of instrumental *and* symbolic action.

26. Herbert Blumer, *Symbolic Interactionism: Perspective and Method* (Englewood Cliffs, N.J.: Prentice-Hall, 1969), p. 51.

27. See, for example, Adorno et al., *The Authoritarian Personality*; Bell, ed., *The Radical Right*; Allen Broyles, *The John Birch Society: Anatomy of a Protest* (Boston: Beacon Press, 1964); Erich Fromm, *The Fear of Freedom* (London: Kegan Paul, Trench, Trubner and Co., 1942); William Kornhauser, *The Politics of Mass Society* (Glencoe, Ill.: Free Press, 1959); Harold D. Lasswell, *Psychopathology and Politics* (Chicago: University of Chicago Press, 1930).

28. Max Weber formulated ideal types as a generalized construct that abstracts the "pure type of subjective meaning attributed to the hypothetical actor." Thus, the ideal type is a methodological device used to tease apart differences in motivation and meaning of the subjective actor. See Max Weber, "The Fundamental Concepts of Sociology," in Weber, *The Theory of Social and Economic Organization*, trans. A. M. Henderson and Talcott Parsons (New York: Oxford University Press, 1947; reprinted, New York: Free Press, 1964), p. 89.

29. George Nash defines conservatism as "identifiable as resistance to certain forces perceived to be leftist, revolutionary, and profoundly subversive of what conservatives at the time deemed worth cherishing, defending, and perhaps dying for." See Nash, *The Conservative Intellectual Movement*, p. xv. Clearly, exactly what is identified as the forces to resist goes to the very heart of the issue. As the findings of this study unmistakably indicate, there

is much variation within the conservative camp as to exactly what is worth cherishing, defending, and dying for.

30. For analysis of the right-to-life movement, see, for example, Michael A. Cavanaugh, "Secularization and the Politics of Traditionalism: The Case of the Right-to-Life Movement," *Sociological Forum* 1 (Spring 1986): 251–283; Donald E. Granberg, "The Abortion Activists," *Family Planning Perspectives* 14 (July 1981): 157–163; Luker, *Abortion and the Politics of Motherhood*; Merton, *Enemies of Choice*; and Petchesky, *Abortion and Woman's Choice*.

31. Several points of entry were used to acquire names of conservative female activists. In the fall of 1981, Howard Phillips, a leading figure of the New Right and founder of the Conservative Caucus, offered a study group on the New Right at Harvard University. Through him, and through other guest speakers of the New Right, I gathered names of right-wing female leaders. These became part of a sub-sample of national leaders of the right. In all, national leaders comprised approximately one quarter of the total sample. Interviews with leaders were conducted in Washington, D.C.

In addition, local activists were located through a variety of sources including: inquiries to national organizations requesting names of local activists; contact with the American Opinion bookstore and headquarters of the John Birch Society in Belmont, Massachusetts; use of newspaper articles to locate names of local activists in the conservative movement; an inquiry to the producer of a local radio program on right-wing women in Massachusetts. Once initial contact was made, I used the snowball technique of asking activists for other contacts. However, because one of my aims was to gather a diverse sample, references from any one person were limited so as not to bias the sample.

32. The interview guide consisted of questions that fell into three main topic areas. First, I asked about current involvement in the conservative movement and the history of the activist's political participation. This included questions regarding what originally instigated the women's activism, the types of political activities and level of commitment involved, how and why their present activities were chosen, the purpose of their work, as well as their visions of future political work.

Second, I asked a group of questions aimed at understanding how the activist views America's problems. Questions focussed on the roots of current political and social ills and how the activist views her own work as helping to solve these problems. Of interest, too, was the activist's perceptions of the relative importance of social versus economic issues, what connection she sees between these two areas, and whether the women view themselves as similar or different from those working in other areas of the conservative movement.

The third set of questions concerned attitudes toward sex roles, including questions regarding views on the proper role of men and women, feminism, the importance of a family/career to the activist's own life, and how the activist's own lifestyle fits into the traditional female role.

33. The textual analysis of printed organizational materials includes regular and miscellaneous publications (for example, pamphlets, newsletters, journals) from the following groups: Alabama Christian Educational Association, American Conservative Union, Center for Family Studies, Christian Voice, Citizens for Educational Freedom, Coalition for Decency, College Republican National Committee, Conservative Caucus, Eagle Forum (including *The Phyllis Schlafly Report*), the Free Congress Research and Education Foundation (including *The Family Protection Report*), the Freemen Institute, Free the Eagle, Home Education Resource Center, Intercessors for America, the John Birch Society, the Libertarian Party, the Moral Majority (including *The Moral Majority Report*), National Federation of Parents for Drug Free Youth, Pro-Family Forum, the Republican National Committee (including *First Monday*), United Families of America (including *National Family Reporter*), Utah Association of Women, and the Young Americans for Freedom.

34. Regarding the issue of class, the measurement of class as applied to women is problematic. Recent feminist scholarship has pointed out the difficulty of delineating women's class position. While clearly women cannot simply be reduced to the class position of their husband or father, on the other hand all women do not occupy the same class position. Most studies of anti-feminist women measure class by father's background or husband's employment. Even so, the findings are discrepant, varying between finding anti-ERA women to be from lower-middle-class backgrounds and with fathers and/or husbands employed in lower-prestige occupations (see Janet K. Boles, *The Politics of the Equal Rights Amendment: Conflict and the Decision Process* [New York: Longman, 1979], and Arrington and Kyle, "Equal Rights Amendment Activists") and finding them to be from upper-middle-class backgrounds and married to men in high-income and high-prestige occupations (see Brady and Tedin, "Ladies in Pink").

While the present study did not systematically analyze the variations in class, the tentative findings based on this sample did not indicate significant differences overall in the class backgrounds of the two groups of women. Any conclusive statements regarding class must be based on a national sample that measures class more extensively. In fact, given the different class bases of the division within the Old Right, discussed earlier in this chapter, one would expect a national sample to find class differences between women of the two types.

35. See, for example, Hunter, "In the Wings," pp. 112–128; also Jerome L. Himmelstein, "The New Right," in *The New Christian Right*, ed. Robert C. Liebman and Robert Wuthnow (New York: Aldine Publishing Co., 1983), pp. 15–31.

36. Weber, "The Fundamental Concepts," p. 88.

CHAPTER TWO

1. Pat Robertson started the Christian Broadcasting Network in 1960 and is currently host to one of the most successful evangelical talk shows, "The 700 Club."

2. M. G. Pat Robertson, "The Family and the Law," speech presented at the Family Forum II conference, Washington, D.C., July 27, 1982.

3. Phyllis Schlafly, "America's Great Religious Document," *Phyllis Schlafly Report* 15 (July 1982): 4.

4. See Jerry Falwell, *Listen, America!* (New York: Bantam Books, 1980), p. 12.

5. Samuel S. Hill and Dennis E. Owen, *The New Religious Political Right in America* (Nashville: Abingdon Press, 1982), p. 111.

6. Phyllis Schlafly, quoted in Carol Felsenthal, *Phyllis Schlafly: The Sweetheart of the Silent Majority* (Chicago: Regnery Gateway, 1981), p. 50. While Phyllis Schlafly clearly is linked in the public mind with the issue of ERA, she has actually had a long history of activism on the right. In fact, besides being the leading anti-feminist figure, she has written several books on defense, foreign policy, and economics.

7. See Rosemary Thomson, *Withstanding Humanism's Challenge to Families: Anatomy of a White House Conference* (Morton, Ill.: Traditional Publications, 1981), p. 40.

8. The "pro-family" movement, according to Rosemary Thomson, is "a person or group supporting legislation protecting traditional moral values, generally opposed to a range of issues, including ERA, abortion, gay rights, federal child care, forced busing, etc." See Thomson, *Withstanding Humanism's Challenge*, p. iii. I use this term as the self-descriptive label chosen by social conservative women. Those outside the movement often label this same constituency "the anti-feminist" movement. See Chapter Five for discussion of the origins of the pro-family movement.

9. Onalee McGraw, *The Family, Feminism and the Therapeutic State*, (Washington, D.C.: Heritage Foundation, 1980), pp. 17, 27.

10. Robert Reilly, "The Vital Role of the Family," quoted in McGraw, *Family, Feminism and the Therapeutic State*, p. 69.

11. John LeBoutillier, *Harvard Hates America: The Odyssey of a Born-Again American* (South Bend, Ind.: Gateway Editions, 1978), p. 115.

12. For further discussion of the family as a primary symbol of the new Christian right, see Donald Heinz, "The Struggle to Define America," in *The New Christian Right*, ed. Robert C. Liebman and Robert Wuthnow (New York: Aldine Publishing Co., 1983), pp. 133–148. Heinz argues that the family is a symbolic means by which the religious right seeks to recover a lost past.

13. Edward E. Hindson, "Christians Are Waking Up to Protect Freedom of Religion, Sanctity of Marriage, Traditional Family Values," *Moral Majority Report* 1, no. 9 (July 14, 1980): 11.

14. Virginia Bessey, "What Is the Pro-Family Agenda?," speech presented at the Family Forum II conference, Washington, D.C., July 27, 1982. Virginia Bessey has served as legislative assistant to Senator Roger W. Jepsen of Iowa and was one of the key people responsible for the Family Protection Act, a comprehensive bill introduced to the 97th Congress by Senator Paul Laxalt of Nevada, with the stated aim "to strengthen the American family and to promote the virtues of family life through education, tax assistance and related measures."

15. Morality in the Media was organized in 1962 by three clergymen. Self-described as a watchdog organization, its primary purpose is to educate and alert parents and members of the community to obscene materials. In the past few years the organization has been particularly concerned with monitoring cable television.

16. Richard Vignuelle, "On the Moral Majority," sermon preached at Shades Mountain Independence Church, Shades Mountain, Ala., April 30, 1980.

17. The primacy of moral issues is also evidenced in a John Birch Society publication that reads: "Morality is the key in this struggle. Strong moral convictions are the only opposition. . . . If you asked Robert Welch [founder of the John Birch Society] today what is the most important, significant problem we face in this country, many would expect that he would select the U.N., or the War on Poverty, or aid to the Communists. But his answer to that question has always been 'moral decline.' As morality goes down, fewer people are left to oppose evil." See John F. McManus, *An Overview of Our World* (Belmont, Mass.: John Birch Society, 1971), p. 55.

While the John Birch Society epitomizes the radical right of the 1950s, data from this study suggest that the Society is a crucial link between the Old Right and the social conservatism of the New Right. John Birch Society literature foreshadows much of the symbolism at the heart of social conservatism. While the thrust of the Society's ideology rests on the belief that a Communist conspiracy is infiltrating American society in order to impose an international world order, the John Birch Society is one of the first organizations to identify secular humanism as a particular threat. Warnings against the dangers of secular humanism, situational ethics, and values clarification programs reveal the common symbols shared with social conservatives of the New Right. Further, the John Birch Society has consistently viewed itself as a Christian organization engaged in a moral struggle to defeat Evil. More documentation is needed to detail the exact organizational links and leadership networks connecting the John Birch Society with social conservatives of the New Right.

18. Ed McAteer, quoted in John Lofton, "Roundtable's President Ed McAteer Is Music Man of Religious Right," in Data Center, *The New Right: Fundamentalists and Financiers* (Oakland, Calif.: Data Center, 1981), p. 79. Ed McAteer founded the Religious Roundtable in 1979 after serving as national field director for the Conservative Caucus. The purpose of the Roundtable is to bring together religious leaders from the Jewish, Catholic, Baptist, Presbyterian, and Pentecostal communities to affect public policy concerning moral issues.

19. George Gilder, speech presented at the Over the Rainbow Celebration, Washington, D.C., July 1, 1982.

20. Richard A. Viguerie, *The New Right: We're Ready to Lead* (Falls Church, Va.: Viguerie Co., 1981), p. 127.

21. Edward King, keynote address presented at the South Shore Pro-Family Forum, Marshfield, Mass., May 17, 1982. This is not Ed King, former governor of Massachusetts.

22. In Thomson, *Withstanding Humanism's Challenge*, p. 124. Connie Marshner is chair of the National Pro-Family Coalition and formerly was chair of the Family Policy Advisory Board of the Reagan-Bush campaign as well as education director for the Heritage Foundation. Additionally, she advises members of Congress on pro-family issues and is an author and editor of the *Family Protection Report* for the Free Congress Foundation.

23. The population of women attending both Phyllis Schlafly's anti-ERA celebration and the Moral Majority conference was substantially higher than at the Conservative Political Action Conference. Additionally, while sixteen out of the seventy-three invited speakers at the Moral Majority conference were female (22%), only three out of the seventy-seven speakers at the CPAC were female (4%). While the statistics on membership of the various organizations is unavailable, clearly the subject matter of ERA and "Traditional Values Work," with workshops focussed on the issue of the family, speaks more to the traditional interests of women, while the CPAC conference focussed on traditionally "male" concerns—the economy, defense, foreign policy.

24. While I have included Jack Kemp within the laissez-faire conserva-

tive camp, as the 1988 elections draw closer, he is making a concerted effort to appeal to social conservatives, particularly through his anti-abortion stance. The difficulty in placing national leaders within these two types is twofold: as elites, their political ideology is likely to be more fully articulated and coherent than that of non-elites; see, for example, Philip E. Converse, "The Nature of Belief Systems in Mass Publics," in *Ideology and Discontent*, ed. David Apter (Glencoe, Ill.: Free Press, 1964). Second, as political leaders it is often in their interest to speak "across boundaries," to make appeals to the broadest audience. This is where political symbols play their greatest role, drawing in people from divergent groups.

25. Whether the founders of classical liberalism would associate themselves with laissez-faire conservatism is another question. In fact, while Adam Smith advocated free trade and extolled the self-regulating market, he also expressed much skepticism about the morals of businessmen. His view of the self-interested nature of individuals was also accompanied by belief in a natural sympathy toward others. See, for example, Adam Smith, *The Theory of Moral Sentiments* (New York: Kelley, 1966).

26. Max Lerner has examined the historical bases for an American embrace of laissez faire, pointing to such factors as the Calvinist ethic, with its emphasis on economic virtues and moral individualism, and to the tradition of a weak state and fear of government tyranny, factors congruent with the doctrine of laissez faire. See Max Lerner, "The Triumph of Laissez-Faire," in *Paths of American Thought*, ed. Arthur M. Schlesinger Jr. and Morton White (Boston: Houghton Mifflin Co., 1963).

27. Jeane J. Kirkpatrick, *The Reagan Phenomenon and Other Speeches on Foreign Policy* (Washington, D.C.: American Enterprise Institute for Public Policy Research, 1983), pp. 6–7. While I use the writings of Jeane Kirkpatrick in reference to laissez-faire conservatism, in fact, as an academic and ex-Democrat, Jeane Kirkpatrick is often viewed as a neoconservative. Again, political elites are the most difficult to "type" into categories. See note 24, above.

28. See Benjamin Ward, *The Conservative Economic World View* (New York: Basic Books, 1979), p. 4.

29. Richard T. Schulze and John H. Rousselot, "Introduction," in *View from the Capital Dome: Looking Right*, ed. Richard T. Schulze and John H. Rousselot (Ossining, N.Y.: Caroline House, 1980), pp. 1–2.

30. Young Americans for Freedom, "Statement of Principles," *Guardian Eagle* (New York Young Americans for Freedom) 8, no. 1 (February 17, 1983): 12.

31. See Jay L. Young, "The Price of Liberty," *Guardian Eagle* (New York Young Americans for Freedom) 8, no. 1 (February 17, 1983): 3.

32. Kirkpatrick, *The Reagan Phenomenon*, p. 24.

33. "Some Questions Frequently Asked About the Freemen Institute," pamphlet of the Freemen Institute, n.d. The Freemen Institute was launched on July 4, 1971, "to develop and produce programs which teach constitutional principles in the tradition of America's Founding Fathers." The Institute holds seminars across the nation to make people aware of the importance of America's charter of liberty.

34. Libertarian Party, *1982 Platform* (Washington, D.C.: Libertarian Party, 1982). The 1980 Libertarian Party presidential candidate, Ed Clark, received over one million votes, making the Libertarian Party the third largest party in the United States. See Stephen L. Newman, *Liberalism at Wits' End: The Libertarian Revolt Against the Modern State* (Ithaca, N.Y.: Cornell University Press, 1984).

35. Newman, *Liberalism at Wit's End*, pp. 79–86.

36. Representative Jack Kemp, "The New Populist Consensus," speech presented at the Conservative Political Action Conference, Washington, D.C., February 19, 1983.

37. Falwell, *Listen, America!*, pp. 130, 110.

38. Connie Marshner, quoted in Leslie Bennetts, "Conservatives Join on Social Concerns," *New York Times*, July 29, 1981, p. B6.

39. See Betsy Barber Bancroft, "A Prudent Woman's Guide to the Dangers of Secular Humanism," unpublished manuscript, 1981, lesson 2, p. 2.

40. Connaught C. Marshner, *The New Traditional Woman* (Washington, D.C.: Free Congress Research and Education Foundation, 1982), p. 12. This publication is a revised version of the speech Marshner gave at the Family Forum II conference.

41. Jaynann M. Payne, "Teach a Child to Be a Winner!," in Utah Association of Women, *The Child: Who Cares?* (Salt Lake City: Utah Association of Women, 1978), pp. 33–34.

42. Jerry Falwell, quoted in Frances Fitzgerald, "A Reporter at Large: A Disciplined, Charging Army," *New Yorker*, May 18, 1981, p. 110.

43. Marshner, "Who Is the New Traditional Woman?"

44. Phyllis Schlafly, *The Power of the Positive Woman* (New York: Jove Publications, 1977), pp. 45–46.

45. Phyllis Schlafly, quoted in Felsenthal, *Phyllis Schlafly*, p. 55.

46. Phyllis Schlafly, quoted in ibid., p. 27.

47. Jeane J. Kirkpatrick, *Political Woman* (New York: Basic Books, 1974), p. 127. During her term as United Nations ambassador, Kirkpatrick claimed that "sexism is alive in the U.N., . . . in the U.S. Government, . . . in American politics," and called foreign policy "a particularly male bastion . . . [in which] there are lots of resistances still to young women in our diplomatic service." See *Time*, December 31, 1984, p. 14.

48. Kirkpatrick, *Political Woman*, p. 245.

CHAPTER THREE

1. John Spann, "The Family: How It Fares in Europe and Latin America," speech presented at the Family Forum II conference, Washington, D.C., July 28, 1982.

2. Albion Knight, "Building a Militarily Strong America," speech presented at the Over the Rainbow Celebration, Washington, D.C., July 1, 1982. Brigadier General Albion Knight was a member of the Reagan transition team in 1980.

3. "Roundtable's President Ed McAteer Is Music Man of Religious Right," in Data Center, *The New Right: Fundamentalists and Financiers* (Oakland, Calif.: Data Center, 1981), p. 75.

4. I use the word "Man" here and throughout the text in accord with social conservative usage to capture the world in their image and language.

5. American Humanist Association, *Humanist Manifesto I and II*, (Amherst, N.Y.: American Humanist Association, n.d.).

6. Jerry Falwell, *Listen, America!* (New York: Bantam Books, 1980), p. 56.

7. Phyllis Schlafly, "What Is Humanism?," *Phyllis Schlafly Report* 14 (February 1981): 4.

8. Onalee McGraw, *Secular Humanism and the Schools: The Issue Whose Time Has Come* (Washington, D.C.: Heritage Foundation, 1976), pp. 11, 12, 14.

9. Paul Weyrich, "Debate with Michael Lerner," speech presented at the Family Forum II conference, Washington, D.C., July 28, 1982.

10. Elmer Rumminger, "Secular Humanism in Christian Schools?," *Alabama Alert News*, January–February 1980, p. 5.

11. Falwell, *Listen, America!*, p. 56.

12. Robert McCurry, "The Fatal Delusion of Trusting Political and Military Salvation," *Alabama Alert News*, September 1980, p. 3.

13. Onalee McGraw, *Family Choice in Education: The New Imperative* (Washington, D.C.: Heritage Foundation, 1976), pp. 10, 12.

14. Robert McCurry, "The Fatal Delusion," p. 3.

15. Betsy Barber Bancroft, "A Prudent Woman's Guide to the Dangers of Secular Humanism," unpublished manuscript, 1981, lesson 4, p. 7.

16. Falwell, *Listen, America!*, p. 179.

17. Bancroft, "A Prudent Woman's Guide," lesson 6, p. 3.

18. Rebecca Myer, "Coalition for Better Television," *Coalition for Decency Bulletin*, April–May 1981, p. 1. The Coalition for Decency was founded by Senator Jeremiah Denton as an educational organization "whose purpose is to strengthen and support the family as the basic unit of society and to promote good citizenship." In its national headquarters in Mobile, Alabama,

the Coalition maintains extensive files on abortion, pornography, Secular Humanism, child abuse, drug abuse, and homosexuality.

19. Tim LaHaye, quoted in Russell Chandler, "Humanists: Target of the Moral Right," in Data Center, *The New Right: Issues and Analyses* (Oakland, Calif.: Data Center, 1981), pp. 51–52. Dr. Tim LaHaye is a pro-family leader affiliated with the Moral Majority and founder of Family Life Seminars. In 1979 he and his wife, Beverly, were honorary co-chairmen for the National Pro-Family Coalition on the White House Conference on Families. Beverly LaHaye is also the founder of Concerned Women for America, a pro-family group who oppose feminism, ERA, comparable worth, abortion, and homosexual rights.

The social conservative vision of the battle against Secular Humanism as being a spiritual one is again paralleled in the literature of the John Birch Society. In a tape produced in November of 1980 entitled "An Overview of Our World," John McManus explains the battle against Communism as a battle between Good and Evil: "We talked a great deal of time tonight about political systems and economic systems and history and it's all down here at the secular level. . . . But when you boil it down to its essence it's not really the secular level we're talking about, is it? It's right vs. wrong, light vs. darkness, good vs. evil. That puts us up in the moral, spiritual realm. We'd like to impress that upon you that that's what it really is and then suggest to you, remind you, that you have a moral obligation to oppose Evil."

20. JoAnn Gaspar, quoted in Johnny Greene, "The Astonishing Wrongs of the New Moral Right," in Data Center: *The New Right: Issues and Analysis*, p. 82. JoAnn Gaspar is a pro-family leader and New Right spokeswoman. She founded the newsletter *The Right Woman: Congressional News on Women and the Family* and currently is part of the Reagan administration, serving as the deputy assistant secretary for social services policy in the Department of Health and Human Services.

21. Virginia Bessey, "What Is the Pro-Family Agenda?," speech presented at the Family Forum II Conference, Washington, D.C., July 27, 1982.

22. M. G. Pat Robertson, "The Family and the Law," speech presented at the Family Forum II Conference, Washington, D.C., July 27, 1982.

23. Falwell, *Listen, America!*, p. 101.

24. Bancroft, "A Prudent Woman's Guide," lesson 2, p. 4, lesson 4, p. 5.

25. See Christian Voice, Statement of Purpose, in Greene, "The Astonishing Wrongs of the New Moral Right," p. 81.

26. Jesse Helms, "Building a Constitutionally Strong America," speech presented at the Over the Rainbow Celebration, Washington, D.C., July 1, 1982.

27. Franky Shaeffer V, "The Myth of Neutrality," in *How You Can Help Clean Up America*, ed. Jerry Falwell (Washington, D.C.: Moral Majority, 1981), p. 87.

28. Rosemary Thomson, *Withstanding Humanism's Challenge to Families: Anatomy of a White House Conference* (Morton, Ill.: Traditional Publications, 1981), p. i.

29. Bancroft, "A Prudent Woman's Guide," lesson 2, p. 7.

30. Protect America's Children, *What in the World Is Wrong?* (Selma, Ala.: Protect America's Children, 1980).

31. Rumminger, "Secular Humanism in Christian Schools?"

32. Tim LaHaye, quoted in Russell Chandler, "Humanists: Target of the Moral Right," p. 51.

33. Falwell, *Listen, America!*, p. 178.

34. George Shultz, address presented at the Conservative Political Action Conference, Washington, D.C., February 18, 1983.

35. Jeane J. Kirkpatrick, *Dictatorships and Double Standards: Rationalism and Reason in Politics* (New York: American Enterprise Institute, Simon and Schuster, 1982), pp. 15–16.

36. Ibid., p. 101.

37. *Principles and Program of the Council for the Defense of Freedom* (Washington, D.C.: Council for the Defense of Freedom, n.d.). The Council for the Defense of Freedom originated as the Council Against Communist Aggression, an organization formed in the midst of the Korean War to disseminate information "in aid of national security and world freedom." The Council for the Defense of Freedom is a national, non-profit organization that seeks to contribute to public awareness of the dangers confronting the nation, to preserve national security, and to advance human freedom at home and abroad. The platform for the 1980s identifies the main challenge to freedom as a "militarily-formidable enemy whose avowed goal is world conquest for communism" and whose ultimate aim "is the weakening of the United States, currently the chief obstacle to the attainment of their global ambitions."

38. Walter H. Judd, "A Communist Is a Communist," in American Conservative Union, *The China Issue: Truth and Consequences* (Washington, D.C.: American Conservative Union, 1982), p. 2.

39. Jeane J. Kirkpatrick, *The Reagan Phenomenon and Other Speeches on Foreign Policy* (Washington: American Enterprise Institute for Public Policy Research, 1983), p. 24.

40. Ray Cline, "In Search of an Ally," in American Conservative Union, *The China Issue*, pp. 26–27.

41. Kirkpatrick, *Dictatorships and Double Standards*.

42. Neil Bright, "The Reagan Revolution: Why We Should Be Staying the Course," *New Guard*, Winter 1982–83, p. 12.

43. George C. Wortley, letter enclosed with the program of Conservative Political Action Conference participants, printed by Young Americans for Freedom.

44. Mike Boos, "Communist Front Groups Behind the Peace Movement: The Nuclear Freeze Fairy Tale," *New Guard*, Winter 1982–83, p. 2.

45. Stefan Possony, "Nuclear Freeze: A War Called Peace," speech presented at the Conservative Political Action Conference, Washington D.C., February 17, 1983.

46. Mickey Edwards, "A Blueprint for Peace," *Battleline* 17, no. 1 (Winter 1983): 2.

47. Libertarian Party, *1982 Platform* (Washington, D.C.: Libertarian Party, 1982).

48. See "Reagan: One Year Later," *Inquiry*, January 11 and 25, 1982, p. 5. Given the recent findings regarding the gender gap, one interesting question to examine is whether, within the ranks of libertarians, proportionally more women are isolationists/pacifists than interventionists.

49. Michael J. Dunn, "Libertarians and National Defense," *Up Against the Wall* 11, no. 5 (n.d.).

50. See, for example, Neil Bright, "The Reagan Revolution," p. 12.

51. Phyllis Schlafly, "Selling the Rope to the Soviets," *Phyllis Schlafly Report* 13, no. 11 (June, 1980): 2.

CHAPTER FOUR

1. The social conservative belief that the United States is a republic and not a democracy is also a slogan associated with the John Birch Society. In a personal interview, John McManus, public relations director for the John Birch Society, explained:

"The U.S. is not a democracy; it's a republic. This country was never meant to be a democracy. If you look at the Founding Fathers, Federalist Paper Number 47 says quite clearly that this country was set up *against* democracy. The Founding Fathers feared majority rule. That means that the government should not be run by majority vote.

"It all started in Rome. They used to have everyone called into the arena to vote on everything. Mob Psychology—you sociologists would have loved to study it. Then a republic was set up. What it means is that even if 100 percent of the people wanted something in this country, it still shouldn't get passed if it goes against the Constitution. You first have to change the Constitution."

Again, it is apparent that social conservative ideology is congruent with that of the John Birch Society.

2. Jeremiah Denton, "Building a Morally Strong America," speech presented at the Over the Rainbow Celebration, Washington, D.C., July 1, 1982.

3. James Robison, "The Family and the Law," speech presented at the Family Forum II conference Washington, D.C., July 27, 1982. Rev. Robison is an evangelist and prime-time preacher from Fort Worth, Texas.

4. See, for example, Onalee McGraw, *Secular Humanism and the Schools: The Issue Whose Time Has Come* (Washington, D.C.: Heritage Foundation, 1976), pp. 7–9.

5. Mel Gabler and Norma Gabler, "Appendix X from *Textbooks on Trial*," n.d. (mimeographed), p. 1.

6. Rod Davis, "Deep in the Heart of Textbooks," *Boston Globe Magazine*, October 30, 1983, p. 31.

7. Dudley Clendinen, "Conservative Christians Again Take Issue of Religion in Schools to Court," *New York Times*, February 28, 1986, p. 11.

8. Aubrey Garrison, Shades Mountain Independence Church, personal interview with Michael Mills.

9. George Gilder, speech presented at the Over the Rainbow celebration, Washington, D.C., July 1, 1982.

10. Tim LaHaye, "The Questions?," *Moral Majority Report* 1, no. 7 (June 6, 1980): 10.

11. See, for example, Onalee McGraw, *The Family, Feminism and the Therapeutic State* (Washington, D.C.: Heritage Foundation, 1980).

12. For discussion of the school as symbolic of the neighborhood, of the grass roots, and of the family, see Donald Heinz, "The Struggle to Define America," in *The New Christian Right*, ed. Robert C. Liebman and Robert Wuthnow (New York: Aldine Publishing Co., 1983). Heinz argues that the new Christian right is currently waging a battle in the public schools over the mythology of American history.

13. Alice Moore, quoted in Alan Crawford, *Thunder on the Right: The "New Right" and the Politics of Resentment* (New York: Pantheon Books, 1980), p. 151.

14. Connaught C. Marshner, *The New Traditional Woman* (Washington, D.C.: Free Congress Research and Education Foundation, 1982), p. 4.

15. McGraw, *The Family, Feminism and the Therapeutic State*, p. 15.

16. Frank M. Barker Jr., "Christian Perspective on Education," in Bar-

ker, "The Christian Perspective," unpublished paper, Briarwood Continuing Presbyterian Church, 1980, p. 8.

17. Mel Gabler, "How Today's Education Will Destroy the Family," speech presented at the Family Forum II conference, Washington, D.C., July 29, 1982.

18. *Moral Majority Report* 1, no. 3 (March 14, 1980): 9.

19. Onalee McGraw, "The Family and Education," speech presented at the Family Forum II conference, Washington, D.C., July 29, 1982.

20. Onalee McGraw, *Family Choice in Education: The New Imperative* (Washington, D.C.: Heritage Foundation, 1976), p. 22.

21. Phyllis Schlafly, "Prayer in Public Schools," *Phyllis Schlafly Report* 15 (July 1982): 2–3.

22. Onalee McGraw, "The Family Protection Act: Symbol and Substance," *Moral Majority Report* 2, no. 11 (November 23, 1981): 5. For further analysis of the fundamentalist right as a defensive reaction to liberal advances, see Nathan Glazer, "Towards a New Concordat?," *This World* 2 (Summer 1982): 109–118.

23. Jeane J. Kirkpatrick, *The Reagan Phenomenon and Other Speeches on Foreign Policy* (Washington, D.C.: American Enterprise Institute for Public Policy Research, 1983), p. 46.

24. Young Americans for Freedom, "Statement of Principles," *Guardian Eagle* (New York Young Americans for Freedom) 8, no. 1 (February 17, 1983): 12.

25. See Benjamin Ward, *The Conservative Economic World View* (New York: Basic Books, 1979), p. 33.

26. Neil Bright, "The Reagan Revolution: Why We Should Be Staying the Course," *New Guard*, Winter 1982–83, p. 9.

27. Norman Shumway, "In Defense of Capitalism," in *View from the Capital Dome: Looking Right*, ed. Richard T. Schulze and John H. Rousselot (Ossining, N.Y.: Caroline House, 1980), p. 98.

28. "Reagan: One Year Later," *Inquiry*, January 11 and 25, 1982, p. 5.

29. Jeane J. Kirkpatrick, *Dictatorships and Double Standards: Rationalism and Reason in Politics* (New York: American Enterprise Institute, Simon and Schuster, 1982), p. 205.

30. Bright, "The Reagan Revolution," p. 10.

31. Young Americans for Freedom, "Statement of Principles," p. 12.

32. James Wootton, "The Social Security Dilemma," speech presented at the Conservative Political Action Conference, Washington, D.C., February 17, 1983.

33. "Where We're At: Listen, CPAC," *Up Against the Wall* II, no. 5 (n.d.).

34. James M. Collins, "Too Much Government," in *View from the Capital*

Dome: Looking Right, ed. Richard T. Schulze and John H. Rousselot (Ossining, N.Y.: Caroline House, 1980), p. 107.

35. James Watt, address presented at the Conservative Political Action Conference, Washington, D.C., February 19, 1983.

36. Ron Paul, "The Same Deal or a New Direction," in *Up Against the Wall* II, no. 5 (n.d.).

CHAPTER FIVE

1. Again, the John Birch Society foreshadowed the social conservative response. In "The John Birch Society Resolutions," printed in 1970, one resolution declares: "I believe that at least 90% of all the hippies, young criminals, and heart-breaking misfits, who are now ruining the wonderful minds and bodies and opportunities for permanent happiness which nature gave them, would never have fallen for the cleverly deceptive and cruelly destructive Communist line if parental authority had seen that they were given pats on the back often enough, hard enough, and low enough while they were still at the right age for such discipline" (p. 16). Here, the social conservative emphasis on parental authority and the need for discipline is combined with the Old Right fear of Communist infiltration.

2. Allan C. Carlson, "Families, Sex, and the Liberal Agenda," *Public Interest* 58 (Winter 1980): 73–74.

3. M. G. Pat Robertson, "The Family and the Law," speech presented at the Family Forum II conference, Washington, D.C., July 27, 1982.

4. Jerry Falwell, *Listen, America!* (New York: Bantam Books, 1980), p. 52.

5. Sam Francis, lecture presented at the Institute for Politics, Harvard University, February 22, 1983.

6. See, for example, Onalee McGraw, *The Family, Feminism and the Therapeutic State* (Washington, D.C.: Heritage Foundation, 1980).

7. Rosemary Thomson, *Withstanding Humanism's Challenge to Families: Anatomy of a White House Conference* (Morton, Ill.: Traditional Publications, 1981), p. iii.

8. Ibid., p. 22.

9. Ibid., p. iv.

10. Paul Weyrich, "Debate with Michael Lerner," speech presented at the Family Forum II conference, Washington, D.C., July 28, 1982.

11. Ronald Godwin, "The Family and the Law," speech presented at the Family Forum II conference, Washington, D.C., July 27, 1982.

12. Thomson, *Withstanding Humanism's Challenge*, pp. 1–3.

13. McGraw, *The Family, Feminism and the Therapeutic State*, p. 19.

14. Phyllis Schlafly, *The Power of the Positive Woman* (New York: Jove Publications, 1977), pp. 72, 76.

15. Albert Martin, *One Man, Hurt*, quoted in Schlafly, *The Power of the Positive Woman*, p. 77.

16. Connaught C. Marshner, *The New Traditional Woman* (Washington, D.C.: Free Congress Research and Education Foundation, 1982), pp. 1, 3–4, 12.

17. Cal Thomas, "It's Do-It-Yourself Abortion Kits," *Moral Majority Report* 2, no. 5 (May 18, 1981): 4.

18. "Militant Feminists Demand Restructuring of Family Values," *Conservative Digest* 8 (May 1982): 17.

19. Godwin, "The Family and the Law."

20. Rosalind Pollack Petchesky, in her book *Abortion and Woman's Choice: The State, Sexuality, and Reproductive Freedom* (Boston: Northeastern University Press, 1984), argues that anti-feminists oppose abortion not only because it represents an image of "the emancipated woman" but also because it symbolizes a free ride for illicit sex, that is, women getting away without paying for their sins.

21. Phyllis Schlafly, in Foreword to Thomson, *Withstanding Humanism's Challenge*, p. iv.

22. Thomson, *Withstanding Humanism's Challenge*, p. 69.

23. Betsy Barber Bancroft, "A Prudent Woman's Guide to the Dangers of Secular Humanism," unpublished manuscript, 1981, lesson 2, pp. 5–6.

24. Phyllis Schlafly, "Eagle Forum Defends Wives and Mothers," *Phyllis Schlafly Report* 14, no. 9 (April 1981): 1.

25. Schlafly, *The Power of the Positive Woman*, p. 86.

26. Ibid., p. 75.

27. Schlafly, "Eagle Forum Defends Wives and Mothers," pp. 2–3.

28. Schlafly, *The Power of the Positive Woman*, p. 63.

29. Robertson, "The Family and the Law."

30. In her book *The Hearts of Men: American Dreams and the Flight from Commitment* (New York: Anchor Press, 1983), Barbara Ehrenreich states: "In the ideology of American antifeminism it is almost impossible to separate distrust of men from the hatred of feminists, or to determine with certainty which is the prior impulse" (p. 147). Ehrenreich roots the antifeminism of the 1970s in the 1950s, a reaction to the male revolt that occurred in the fifties in which the traditional male breadwinner role was replaced by the *Playboy* cult of the promiscuous bachelor.

31. Schlafly, *The Power of the Positive Woman*, p. 100.

32. Phyllis Schlafly, "Defending the Economic Life of the Family," *Phyllis Schlafly Report* 15, no. 9 (April 1982): 2.

33. Mrs. Billy Graham, quoted in Schlafly, *The Power of the Positive Woman*, pp. 72–73.

34. George Gilder, speech presented at the Over the Rainbow celebration, Washington, D.C., July 1, 1982.

35. McGraw, *The Family, Feminism and the Therapeutic State*, p. 12.

36. Thomas Fleming, "Old Rights and the New Right," in *The New Right Papers*, ed. Robert W. Whitaker (New York: St. Martin's Press, 1982), p. 197.

37. *The Blank Check Called "ERA"* (Alton, Ill.: Eagle Forum, n.d.).

38. Jeremiah Denton, "Building a Morally Strong America," speech presented at the Over the Rainbow celebration, Washington, D.C., July 1, 1982.

39. Andrew J. Gatsis, quoted in Falwell, *Listen, America!*, p. 137.

40. Albion Knight, "Building a Militarily Strong America," speech presented at the Over the Rainbow celebration, Washington, D.C., July 1, 1982.

41. Karen DeCrow, quoted in Carol Felsenthal, *Phyllis Schlafly: The Sweetheart of the Silent Majority* (Chicago: Regnery Gateway, 1981), p. 55.

42. Schlafly, *The Power of the Positive Woman*, p. 8.

43. Ibid., p. 177.

44. Marshner, *The New Traditional Woman*, p. 1.

45. Connie Marshner, "Who Is the New Traditional Woman?," speech presented at the Family Forum II conference, Washington, D.C., July 29, 1982. This particular quote does not appear in the revised form of the speech.

46. Marshner, *The New Traditional Woman*, p. 6.

47. Bancroft, "A Prudent Woman's Guide," introduction, p. 3.

48. Jeane J. Kirkpatrick, *Political Woman* (New York: Basic Books, 1974), p. 251.

49. Zillah Eisenstein, *Feminism and Sexual Equality: Crisis in Liberal America* (New York: Monthly Review Press, 1984), p. 30.

50. Andrea Dworkin, *Right-Wing Women* (New York: Perigee Books, 1983), p. 17.

CHAPTER SIX

1. For discussion of ideal types, see Chapter One, note 28.

2. For discussion of the influences on the symbolic construction of reality, see Peter Berger and Thomas Luckmann, *The Social Construction of Reality: A Treatise in the Sociology of Knowledge* (New York: Anchor Books, 1967).

3. See Max Weber, "The Social Psychology of the World Religions," in Weber, *From Max Weber: Essays in Sociology*, trans. Hans H. Gerth and C. Wright Mills (New York: Oxford University Press, 1946), pp. 284–285.

4. See Chapter One, above, for discussions of the social bases of the Old Right and of the varying social bases of the women in this study.

5. Kristin Luker, *Abortion and the Politics of Motherhood* (Berkeley: University of California Press, 1984), p. 200. For an illuminating discussion of the relationship between interests and passions for women on either side of the abortion debate, see pp. 197–214.

6. See Catherine Arnott, "Feminists and Anti-Feminists as True Believers," *Sociology and Social Research* 57 (April 1973): 300–306; Theodore S. Arrington and Patricia A. Kyle, "Equal Rights Amendment Activists in North Carolina," *Signs* 3 (Spring 1978): 666–680; Janet K. Boles, *The Politics of the Equal Rights Amendment: Conflict and the Decision Process* (New York: Longman, 1979); David W. Brady and Kent L. Tedin, "Ladies in Pink: Religion and Political Ideology in the Anti-ERA Movement," *Social Science Quarterly* 56 (March 1976): 564–575; Carol Mueller, "Oppositional Consciousness and ERA Activists in Three States," paper presented at the American Sociological Association meetings, San Francisco, September 1980; and Carol Mueller and Thomas Dimieri, "Feminism vs. Anti-Feminism: The Structure of Belief Systems Among Contending ERA Activists," Working Paper no. 47, Wellesley Center for Research on Women, 1980.

CHAPTER SEVEN

1. Charles Elder and Roger Cobb label the disparity between the commonality of sentiment felt toward a symbol and the variability in substantive meaning "the myth of common meaning." See Charles Elder and Roger Cobb, *The Political Uses of Symbols* (New York: Longman, 1983), p. 35.

2. Howard Phillips, quoted in Andrew H. Merton, *Enemies of Choice: The Right-to-Life Movement and Its Threat to Abortion* (Boston: Beacon Press, 1981), p. 148.

3. Thomas Fleming, "Old Rights and the New Right," in *The New Right Papers*, ed. Robert W. Whitaker (New York: St. Martin's Press, 1982), pp. 183–184, 199.

4. See, for example, Russell Kirk, "The Conservative Movement Then and Now," in Heritage Foundation, *The Heritage Lectures #3: Objections to Conservatism* (Washington: Heritage Foundation, 1981), p. 8.

5. William Willoughby, "Do We Need Moral Majority?," *Moral Majority Report* 2, no. 11 (November 23, 1981): 7.

6. Roy A. Childs Jr., "The Landslide Before the Storm," *Libertarian Review*, January 1981, p. 17.

7. William Safire, quoted in ibid., p. 17.

8. Connie Marshner, "Conservatives Speak Out," *Conservative Digest* 8 (July 1982): 18.

9. See, for example, Morton Kondracke, "Hard Times for the Hard Right," *New Republic*, December 20, 1982, pp. 20–23, "President Warned by Conservatives," *New York Times*, January 22, 1981, p. A20, Charles Austin, "Religious Right Growing Impatient With Reagan," *New York Times*, August 16, 1982, p. A13, and Curtis Wilkie, "Reagan's Inaction on Busing, Abortion Frustrates Far Right," *Boston Globe*, August 21, 1983, p. 1.

10. See Seymour Martin Lipset and Earl Raab, "The Election and the Evangelicals," in *Speakout Against the New Right*, ed. Herbert F. Vetter (Boston: Beacon Press, 1982), pp. 60–71. Lipset and Raab conclude that the strength of the religious right was seriously overrated. Also see Jerome L. Himmelstein and James A. McRae Jr., "Social Conservatism, New Republicans, and the 1980 Election," *Public Opinion Quarterly* 48 (1984): 592–605.

11. Pamela Johnston Conover and Virginia Gray, *Feminism and the New Right: Conflict Over the American Family* (New York: Praeger, 1983), p. 165.

12. See Himmelstein and McRae, "Social Conservatism, New Republicans, and the 1980 Election." Further, Conover and Gray report that a New York Times/CBS poll conducted after the Reagan/Anderson debate found that over 40 percent of people surveyed mentioned government spending, military strength, or oil as one of the top three issues of concern. See Conover and Gray, *Feminism and the New Right*, p. 161.

13. See Himmelstein and McRae, "Social Conservatism, New Republicans, and the 1980 Election." Conover and Gray find little evidence that the heated debate over abortion and the ERA have spread to the mass public. See Conover and Gray, *Feminism and the New Right*, chap. 6.

14. New York Times/CBS Poll in the *New York Times*, November 8, 1984, p. 19. The gender gap was evident in the 1984 election among eighteen-to-twenty-nine-year-olds, with men supporting Reagan 61 percent to 37 percent for Mondale, as compared to women supporting Reagan 55 percent to 45 percent for Mondale. In fact, only among men and women sixty years and older was there greater support by women for Reagan.

Regarding the increased conservatism of the younger generation, see Neil Miller, "Is There a New Generation Gap?," *St. Louis Post-Dispatch*, October 28, 1984, p. 3D, and "The Conservative Student," *Newsweek on Campus*, March 1985, pp. 6–14.

15. From Kevin Phillips, "Hubris on the Right," *New York Times Magazine*, May 12, 1985, pp. 48, 50, 56, 57, 58, 59, 60, 61. Also see Himmelstein and McRae, "Social Conservatism, New Republicans, and the 1980 Election."

16. Phil Gailey, "Evangelism and a Fight with Peril to Both Sides," *New York Times*, March 17, 1986, p. A16.

17. Ibid.

18. Sara Rimer, "Experts Study the Habits of Genus Baby Boomer," *New York Times*, April 21, 1986, p. 6. Also see Steven Roberts, "Making Mark on Politics, 'Baby Boomers' Appear to Rally Around Reagan," *New York Times*, November 5, 1984, p. 18, and David Boaz, "In '88, Who'll Win the Baby Boomers?," in *New York Times*, November 7, 1985, p. A35.

19. John Herbers, "Church Issues Spread to State Races," *New York Times*, September 19, 1984, p. B9.

20. See "New Right Flop," *The Nation*, January 15, 1983, pp. 36–37, and Gillian Peele, *Revival and Reaction: The Right in Contemporary America* (Oxford: Clarendon Press, 1984).

21. "Reagan Justice," *Newsweek*, June 30, 1986, pp. 14–19, and *Facts on File: World News Digest* 45, no. 2344 (October 25, 1985): 803.

22. According to the *New York Times*, June 15, 1986, students of Justice Rehnquist's and Judge Scalia's records report they are both more consistent, more energetic, and more intellectually formidable advocates of conservative views than Chief Justice Warren Burger has been. Judge Scalia, for example, has questioned the basis for the Supreme Court's recognition of a constitutional right to sexual privacy, including abortion rights, and joined in a ruling that the Constitution does not protect private homosexual acts between consenting adults. See Stuart Taylor Jr., "More Vigor for the Right." Also see "Reagan Justice," *Newsweek*, June 30, 1986, pp. 14–19.

23. Similarly, Susan Marshall argues that the anti-suffrage movement was a reaction to industrialization, an attempt to give ideological justification for the growing separation of work and home. Like social conservative women, the anti-suffragists viewed the home as an oasis of non-commercial values in the midst of an acquisitive society and sought to defend the profession of homemaking and women's role as noble and self-sacrificing, while portraying suffragists as selfish and demanding. See Susan Marshall, "In Defense of Separate Spheres: Class and Status Politics in the Anti-Suffrage Movement," paper presented at the 79th Annual Meeting of the American Sociological Association, San Antonio, August 27–31, 1984.

24. See U.S. Department of Labor, *Employment in Perspective: Working Women* (Washington, D.C.: The Department, 1981).

25. See Virginia Sapiro, *The Political Integration of Women: Roles, Socialization, and Politics* (Urbana: University of Illinois Press, 1983), p. 182.

26. After completing a study of evangelical women, Carol Pohli urges feminists not to dismiss the possibility of alliance with women of the Moral Majority. Arguing that it is a mistake to assume that the evangelical right is a united constituency, Pohli found a minority of evangelical women rethinking their opinion about "women's place." See Carol Pohli, "Church Closets and Back Doors: A Feminist View of Moral Majority Women," *Feminist Studies* 9 (Fall 1983): 529–558.

27. Sapiro, *The Political Integration of Women*, pp. 30, 87.

28. Anita Bryant, quoted in Joyce Brothers, "The Surprising Breakup of Anita Bryant's Twenty-Year Marriage to Bob Green," *Good Housekeeping* 191 (September 1980): 106–111.

29. Anita Bryant, quoted in Cliff Jahr, "Anita Bryant's Startling Reversal," *Ladies' Home Journal* 97 (December 1980): 68.

30. Sandra Salmans, "Women's Panel Using Economy to Back Reagan," *New York Times*, May 22, 1984, p. 22.

31. See Chapter One, note 27.

32. Rosalind Pollack Petchesky, *Abortion and Woman's Choice: The State, Sexuality, and Reproductive Freedom* (Boston: Northeastern University Press, 1984).

33. See Barbara Ehrenreich, "The Women's Movements: Feminist and Anti-Feminist," *Radical America* 15 (Spring 1981): 98–104.

34. Christopher Lasch, *The Culture of Narcissism: American Life in an Age of Diminishing Expectations* (New York: W. W. Norton and Co., 1979).

35. Robert Bellah et al., *Habits of the Heart: Individualism and Commitment in American Life* (Berkeley: University of California Press, 1985). Unlike Christopher Lasch, Bellah and his collaborators recognize the potential benefits of therapy in helping the individual reconnect to family and community.

36. Zillah Eisenstein points out a similar tension regarding Phyllis Schlafly's view of gender. On the one hand, men and women's roles are assumed to be God-given and biologically based. On the other hand, there is a continual need to reassert the differences between the sexes. See Zillah Eisenstein, *Feminism and Sexual Equality: Crisis in Liberal America* (New York: Monthly Review Press, 1984).

37. Bellah et al., *Habits of the Heart*, pp. 204–205.

38. Alida Brill and Herbert McClosky, *Dimensions of Tolerance: What Americans Believe About Civil Liberties* (New York: Russell Sage Foundation, 1983). Brill and McClosky find that within mass and elite samples political ideology affects support for civil liberties; see especially pp. 259–260 and chap. 7.

39. Stephen L. Newman, *Liberalism at Wits' End: The Libertarian Revolt Against the Modern State* (Ithaca, N.Y.: Cornell University Press, 1984).

EPILOGUE

1. Richard Hofstadter, *Anti-Intellectualism in American Life* (New York: Vintage Books, 1962), p. 432.

2. Peter L. Berger and Thomas Luckmann, *The Social Construction of Reality: A Treatise in the Sociology of Knowledge* (New York: Anchor Books, 1967), p. 86.

3. Jeannie I. Rosoff, quoted in "Abortion Ruling: Ten Years of Bitter Conflict," *New York Times*, January 15, 1983, p. 17.

Index

Abortion, 13–14, 113–114, 129–130, 149–150, 201–205, 209
Abzug, Bella, 163
Affirmative action, 107, 151
America: laissez-faire conservative vision of, 32–44; social conservative vision of, 22–31
Anomie, 63, 197, 211, 214
Anti-Communism. *See* Communism
Anti-feminism, 9, 10, 223 n, 236 n. *See also* Pro-family movement
Anti-suffragist movement, 240 n
Authoritarian personality, 219 n

Baby boom generation, 203
Bancroft, Betsy Barber, 69, 130, 147
Bellah, Robert, 211, 213–214
Bentham, Jeremy, 33
Berger, Peter, 215
Big Brother, 115, 201, 212
Big Government. *See* Government
Blumer, Herbert, 12
Brill, Alida, 213
Bryant, Anita, 207–208
Bureaucracy, and government, 104–105
Bush, George, 203, 205
Busing, opposition to, 90–91, 117

Captive nations, 72
China, 74–76
Civil liberties, 212–213
Class in and for itself, 152, 220 n
Communism: laissez-faire view of, 71–83; Old Right view of, 5, 7;

social conservative view of, 55–59. *See also* Secular Humanism
Consequentialist ethics. *See* Situation ethics
Conservatism: definition of, 221 n; intellectual movement of, 7–8. *See also* Laissez-faire conservatism; Social conservatism
Conspiracy theory, 68–71, 226 n
Constitution, 22, 35, 104, 149
Creationism, 87, 93
Culture of narcissism, 64, 121, 211–212

Day care, 72, 149–150, 205, 209
Declaration of Independence, 23, 35
DeCrow, Karen, 143
Defense, laissez-faire conservative view of, 77–82
Denton, Jeremiah, 21, 84, 140
Dewey, John, 60, 67
Discrimination, sexual, 49–53, 148–149
Divorce, 25, 121, 128, 136, 138, 210

Economic conservatism. *See* Laissez-faire conservatism
Edwards, Mickey, 79
Ehrenreich, Barbara, 236 n
ERA, 48, 68, 122, 132, 136–141, 148–149

False consciousness of anti-feminists, 10, 152
Falwell, Jerry, 23, 44, 47, 60, 70
Family, social conservative view of, 23–26, 56, 90–102, 120–127

Farris, Michael, 87
Feminism: and conflict between
    social and laissez-faire conserva-
    tism, 205–210; laissez-faire
    conservative view of, 53,
    147–153; social bases of,
    193–194; social conservative
    view of, 9, 122–142
Feminization of poverty, 211
Foreign policy, and anti-
    Communism, 75–77
Founding Fathers: laissez-faire
    conservative view of, 37, 76,
    102–103, 110, 116; social conser-
    vative view of, 22, 26, 68, 84–85,
    97
Freedom. See Liberty
Freedom fighters, 76
Free enterprise, 34, 43, 71, 75–76,
    103, 112, 199
Free market, 33, 35, 81, 103, 105
Friedan, Betty, 140, 155
Fundamentalist right. See Social
    conservatism

Gabler, Mel and Norma, 86, 96
Gaspar, JoAnn, 65
Gender: laissez-faire conservative
    view of, 9, 48–49; social conser-
    vative view of, 9, 44–47
Gender gap, 3–4, 239 n
Gilder, George, 28, 89, 137–138
Godwin, Ronald, 126, 130
Goldwater, Barry, 13, 79; 1964
    campaign, 174–178
Government: and conflict over role
    of, 6, 200–205; laissez-faire
    conservative view of, 40–42,
    102–116, 148–152; opposition to,
    as impetus to activism, 116–118;
    social conservative view of,
    84–102

Hatch, Orrin, 13, 59
Helms, Jesse, 13, 68
Homemakers, social conservative
    view of, 131–139
Homosexuality: and campaign by
    Anita Bryant, 207–208; and
    laissez-faire conservative view
    of, 112–113, 149–150, 201, 205;
    and social conservative view of,
    47, 69, 99, 126, 201, 204
Humanist Manifestoes, 60
Human nature: and conflict
    between social and laissez-faire
    conservatism, 197–200; laissez-
    faire conservative view of,
    33–36; social conservative view
    of, 24–25, 61–63

Ideal types, 12, 221 n
Individual rights, and laissez-faire
    conservatism, 33–34, 41, 102–103
International Women's Year
    conference, 122–124, 127,
    165–166, 171
Invisible Hand, 105, 112
Isolationism, 42, 79–80, 213

John Birch Society, 14–15, 225 n,
    230 n, 232 n, 235 n
Judiciary, and future of New Right,
    204

Kemp, Jack, 13, 31, 43, 203, 205
Kirkpatrick, Jeane, 34, 36, 51,
    72–76, 102, 106, 151–152, 228 n
Kohlberg, Lawrence, 63

LaHaye, Tim, 70, 89
Laissez-faire conservatism: and
    conflict with social conserva-
    tism, 63–64, 67, 114–115, 149–
    152, 197–214; future of, 197–214;

historical roots of, 6, 7, 32–34, 227 n; social bases of, 16–17, 190–194; and view of Communism, 71–83; and view of defense, 39–40, 77–82; and view of Feminism, 9, 53, 147–153, 209–210; and view of gender, 9, 48–49, 51–53, 147–148; and view of government, 40–42, 102–116, 149–150, 213; and view of human nature, 33–36, 197–200; and vision of America, 33–44

Lasch, Christopher, 211

League of Women Voters, 162–164

Liberalism, classical, 32–44, 227 n

Libertarianism, 7, 40–42, 79–82, 112–113, 213

Libertarian Party, 13–15, 40–41, 79

Liberty: laissez-faire conservative view of, 32–38, 103, 105–116; social conservative view of, 85

Lipset, Seymour Martin, 6

Locke, John, 33, 199

Luckmann, Thomas, 215

Luker, Kristin, 193, 220 n, 238 n

McAteer, Ed, 28, 58

McCarthyism, 59, 70, 219 n

McClosky, Herbert, 213

McGraw, Onalee, 23, 61, 96, 101, 127

Macho feminism, 128–129

Marshner, Connie, 30, 45, 49, 94, 202; and macho feminism, 128–129; and the new traditional woman, 145–147

Marx, Karl, 10, 220 n

Masculinization, 129, 206

Maslow, Abraham, 63

Massachusetts Citizens for Life, 29, 162–164

Me generation, 26, 64, 95, 121–122, 127–130

Men, distrust of, 136–139

Men's roles. *See* Gender

Methodology, 12–19

Mill, James, 33

Mill, John Stuart, 33

Moral absolutism, 7, 66–67, 212, 214

Moral decay, social conservative view of, 25–31, 119–122

Morality, legislation of, 97–102, 112–115, 200–205

Moral Majority, 18, 29, 96, 203

Moral neutrality, myth of, 65–67, 97–98, 200

Myth of common meaning, 196, 202, 238 n

Nash, George, 7–8, 221 n

National Organization for Women, 88, 141, 167

Neoconservatism, 8

New Deal, 33, 104

New Left, 120–121, 205

Newman, Stephen, 213–214

New Right, 4, 6, 8, 10–11, 19; definition of, 4, 13, 218 n; future of, 6, 197–214. *See also* Laissez-faire conservatism; Social conservatism

New traditional women, 45, 145–147

1960s, and impact on social conservatism, 119–122

Nuclear freeze movement, 57, 78, 82–83, 142

Occasions of sin, 158–159

O'Connor, Sandra Day, 204

Old Right, 5–8, 55, 59, 219 n. *See also* John Birch Society

O'Neill, Tip, 166–167
One-world government, 57, 60–61
Orange juice, 207–208

Parental rights, 90–99
Petchesky, Rosalind, 210
Phillips, Howard, 198
Political symbolism. See Symbolism
Pornography, 100–101, 114, 201
Positive Woman, 144–145
Possony, Stefan, 78
Private realm, 101, 112–114,
    149–150, 200–205
Pro-family movement, 23,
    123–125, 210, 224 n
Property, rights of, 33, 36
Public education, and promotion
    of Secular Humanism, 86–97

Raab, Earl, 6
Rand, Ayn, 40
Reagan, Ronald, 13, 29, 202–204
Rehnquist, William H., 204, 240 n
Relativism, 66–67, 94–96
Religious right. See Social
    conservatism
Right-to-life movement. See
    Abortion
Robertson, Pat, 22, 66, 120, 135,
    203, 205
Robison, Rev. James, 85
Roe v. Wade, 130. See also Abortion
Rothbard, Murray, 42

Safire, William, 201
Scalia, Antonin, 204, 240 n
Schlafly, Phyllis, 22–23, 50, 60, 81,
    98, 125; the paradox of, 143–144;
    and Positive Woman, 144–145;
    and view of Feminism, 128, 130,
    134–137, 140
School prayer, 92, 114

Secular Humanism: definition of,
    59–61; and Feminism, 130–131;
    and government, 69–70, 86–88,
    200; and link to Old Right,
    226 n; and parallels to laissez-
    faire conservatism, 63–64, 67,
    198–200; and public education,
    86–97; social conservative
    opposition to, 60–71. See also
    Communism
Sexual inequality. See
    Discrimination
Shultz, George, 31, 71
Situation ethics, 94–96, 121
Smith, Adam, 33, 105, 227 n
Social conservatism: and conflict
    with laissez-faire conservatism,
    63–64, 67, 114–115, 149–152,
    197–214; future of, 197–214;
    historical roots of, 6–7, 225 n,
    230 n, 232 n, 235 n; and the
    paradox of female activism,
    142–147; social bases of, 16–17,
    190–194; and view of Commu-
    nism, 55–59; and view of
    Feminism, 9, 122–142, 205–208;
    and view of gender, 9, 44–47,
    49–51, 144–147; and view of
    government, 84–102, 149–150,
    200–205; and view of human
    nature, 24–25, 61–64, 197–200;
    and view of Secular Humanism,
    59–71; and vision of America,
    22–31
Socialism. See Communism
Social Security, benefits for
    homemakers, 134
Soviet Union, 57–59, 72, 74–83
Star Wars, 79
Status politics, 219 n, 220 n
Steinem, Gloria, 122, 125, 140
Supreme Court, 204, 209

Symbolism, political, 5, 55, 187–190, 195, 215, 238 n

Taxes, opposition to, 108–112
Textbook censorship, 87, 92–94, 133
Thomson, Rosemary, 69, 123, 126–127
Totalitarianism, fear of, 41, 73, 75–76, 141, 198, 212

United States. *See* America
Utilitarianism, 33

Value clarification, 94–96

Watt, James, 32, 115

Weber, Max, 19, 190, 221 n
Weinberger, Caspar, 31
Welfare, opposition to, 88–89, 106–112
Weyrich, Paul, 125
White House Conference on Families, 123–127
Women: in and for themselves, 10, 139, 152–153, 209, 220 n; and labor force participation, 207; and political participation, 3, 217 n
Women's liberation. *See* Feminism
Women's roles. *See* Gender

Young Americans for Freedom, 35, 78, 103